SOCIOMETRIC RESEARCH
Volume 1 Data Collection and Scaling

By the same editors

SOCIOMETRIC RESEARCH
Volume 2   Data Analysis

Sociometric Research

Volume 1   Data Collection and Scaling

Edited by

Willem E. Saris
Professor of Social Science Methods and Techniques
University of Amsterdam

and

Irmtraud N. Gallhofer
Managing Director, Sociometric Research Foundation
Amsterdam

for the International Sociological Association

St. Martin's Press   New York

© Willem E. Saris and Irmtraud N. Gallhofer, 1988

All rights reserved. For information, write:
Scholarly & Reference Division,
St. Martin's Press, Inc., 175 Fifth Avenue, New York, NY 10010

First published in the United States of America in 1988

Printed in Hong Kong

ISBN 0-312-00419-2 (vol. 1)

Library of Congress Cataloging-in-Publication Data
Sociometric research.
Papers presented at the first international
methodology conference of the International
Sociological Association, Oct. 3-6, 1984, in
Amsterdam.
Includes bibliographies.
Contents: v. 1. Data collection and scaling—
v. 2. Data analysis.
1. Sociometry—Congresses. I. Saris, Willem E.
II. Gallhofer, I. N. (Irmtraud N.) III. International
Sociological Association.
HM253.S63   1988   302'.072   86-29834
ISBN 0-312-00419-2 (v. 1)
ISBN 0-312-00418-4 (v. 2)

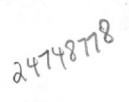

Contents

Preface vii

Notes on the Contributors ix

Part I Data Collection by Survey Research

1 The Noises from the Spiral of Silence: Measurement Errors in Variables, Related to the Assessment of Other People's Opinions
   H. 't Hart and *T. Vorst*   3

2 Types of Inadequate Interviewer Behaviour in Survey-interviews
   W. Dijkstra and *J. van der Zouwen*   24

3 Surveying Ethnic Minorities
   A. E. Bronner   36

Part II Data Collection by Content Analysis

4 A Coding Procedure for Empirical Research of Political Decision-making
   I. N. Gallhofer and *W. E. Saris*   51

5 Ideology in International Propaganda
   S. Splichal and *A. Ferligoj*   69

6 On Agreement Indices for Nominal Data
   R. Popping   90

Part III Scaling Categorical Data

7 The Use of Models for Paired Comparison with Ties
   T. J. H. M. Eggen and *W. van der Linden*   109

8 Unidimensional Unfolding Complemented by Feigin and Cohen's Error Model
   A. W. van Blokland-Vogelesang   123

9 Stochastic Unfolding
   W. H. van Schuur   137

10	Reliability Estimation in Mokken's Nonparametric Item Response Model K. Sijtsma	159

Part IV Scaling Continuous Data

11	Some Empirical Tests of the Predictive Strength of Three Multi-attribute Preference Models K. J. Veldhuisen	177
12	Individual Response Functions and Correlations Between Judgements W. E. Saris	200
13	Why Biased Answers on Evaluations of Own Job Qualities in Survey Interviews Arise C. Bruinsma and W. E. Saris	215
14	The Measurement of Income Satisfaction L. van Doorn and B. M. S. van Praag	230

Preface

The International Sociological Association held its first international methodology conference in the western hemisphere in Amsterdam from 3 to 6 October 1984. During this conference a large number of papers were presented. In this volume the best papers dealing with data-collection and scaling of social science variables have been brought together.

This volume consists of four parts. Part I deals with data-collection techniques and related problems. 't Hart and Vorst (Chapter 1) discuss the formulation of opinion questions within the survey context. This study is important if one wants to study the effect of public opinion on the opinions of respondents. Dijkstra and van der Zouwen (Chapter 2) show empirical evidence of what goes wrong in the communication between interviewer and respondent in survey research. Bronner (Chapter 3) deals with the problem of interviewing ethnic minorities. This is a growing problem for opinion-poll bureaus in the Western European countries.

Part II is concerned with another data-collection technique, especially with content analysis. Gallhofer and Saris (Chapter 4) provide an example of an elaborate study to develop a content-analysis instrument. Splichal and Ferligoj (Chapter 5) present the results of a study concerned with the amount of ideology in international propaganda. They use in their approach a rather new procedure for analysis which is cluster analysis with constraints. Popping (Chapter 6) gives a classification and an overview of several measures to evaluate the quality of the coding done in content analysis.

The last two parts of this volume are concerned with problems of scaling social science variables. Part III concentrates on scaling variables based on categorical judgements. In Chapter 7 Eggen and van der Linden discuss models which can be used for analysis of data collected according to the well-known paired-comparison procedure; they make a link between this procedure and normally unconnected topics such as the Rasch model and stochastic unfolding. Van Blokland-Vogelesang concentrates on the last model in Chapter 8. In Chapter 9 van Schuur continues the discussion of the unfolding model by introducing a new approach to stochastic unfolding. Sijtsma (Chapter 10) discusses measures for the reliability of the Mokken scale, a topic which has so far not been given much attention.

In Part IV the scaling of continuous variables is discussed. Veldhuisen (Chapter 11) starts with a comparison of different approaches, making comparisons between categorical and continuous-measurement procedures. Saris (Chapter 12) shows that variation in response behaviour might be an important source of error in survey research. On the other hand Bruinsma shows in Chapter 13 that this phenomenon cannot explain error in judgements of individuals about their own position and that other explanations are required. Finally van Praag and van Doorn (Chapter 14) indicate that there is variation in evaluations of income across persons, but that this variation can easily be explained by a very simple model.

WILLEM E. SARIS
IRMTRAUD N. GALLHOFER

Notes on the Contributors

A. W. Blokland-Vogelesang is associated with the Free University of Amsterdam, Netherlands.

A. E. Bronner is Director of the Veldkamp Marketing Research Bureau in Amsterdam, Netherlands.

C. Bruinsma is associated with the Free University of Amsterdam, Netherlands.

W. Dijkstra is affiliated with the Free University of Amsterdam, Netherlands.

L. van Doorn is affiliated with the Dutch Gallup Organization Nipo in Amsterdam, Netherlands.

T. J. H. M. Eggen is associated with the National Institute of Education CITO in Nijmegen, Netherlands.

A. Ferligoj is a mathematician and is Professor for Social Science Research Techniques at the University of Ljubljana, Yugoslavia.

I. N. Gallhofer is Managing Director of the Sociometric Research Foundation in Amsterdam, Netherlands.

H. 't Hart is Professor of Education at the University of Utrecht, Netherlands.

W. van der Linden is Professor of Educational Measurement at the University of Twente in Enschede, Netherlands.

R. Popping is affiliated with the University of Groningen, Netherlands.

B. M. S. van Praag is Professor of Mathematical Economics at the University of Rotterdam, Netherlands.

Notes on the Contributors

W. E. Saris is Professor of Social Science Methods and Techniques at the University of Amsterdam, Netherlands.

W. H. van Schuur is affiliated with the University of Groningen, Netherlands.

K. Sijtsma is affiliated with the Free University of Amsterdam, Netherlands.

S. Splichal is Professor of Mass-Communication at the University of Ljubljana, Yugoslavia.

K. J. Veldhuisen is associated with the Technical University of Eindhoven, Netherlands.

T. Vorst is affiliated with the Open University of Heerlen, Netherlands.

J. van der Zouwen is Professor of Social Science Methods and Techniques at the Free University of Amsterdam, Netherlands.

Part I
Data Collection by Survey Research

1 Noises from the Spiral of Silence: Measurement Errors in Variables, Related to the Assessment of Other People's Opinions

H. 't Hart and T. Vorst

1.1 INTRODUCTION

In 1984 the University of Chicago Press published Elisabeth Noelle-Neumann's book on the Spiral of Silence Theory. In brief this theory states that people who believe that their opinions deviate from those of the general public keep silent. By not expressing their views they reinforce the impression that there is a predominant opinion. This is especially true when the respondents believe that the climate of opinion is developing even further away from their own opinions. In this chapter we shall describe some experiments which were designed to assess the influence of the wording of questions and response categories relating to a climate of opinion.

Public opinion surveys do not only reveal public opinion, they form it. Methodological research on questions asked and answers given in these surveys is concerned, therefore, not only with errors and biases, but also with the contents of public opinion itself. In surveys based on the 'spiral-of-silence' hypothesis we have to proceed from a paradox: we ask respondents what their opinions are, while presuming that some of them will prefer not to express their views in the presence of strangers. We may suppose that this type of respondent is very sensitive to hints inferring what the climate of opinion is. The phrasing of the questions and the response categories provided is therefore of crucial importance: assessment of what the general opinion is can depend on it.

In this chapter we shall deal with three types of question:

1. Questions about opinions.
2. Questions about perceived changes in the climate of opinion.
3. Questions about perceived majority or minority opinions.

We shall deal with two aspects of these questions:

- The inclusion or omission of a 'no-opinion' option.
- The inclusion or omission of a neutral middle category.

1.2 INDIVIDUAL OPINIONS AND NO OPINIONS

Since 1967 (Meilof-Oonk, 1969) we have been involved in research about the climate of opinion. Opinion statements have been used to assess respondents' individual opinions and as a means of inducing them to hazard a guess about the response of the majority of the Dutch public. Five response categories were provided: completely agree, mainly agree, no opinion, mainly disagree, completely disagree. These categories made a distinction between minorities and majorities possible. The meaning of the 'no opinion' option was ambiguous. It could be chosen by those who really did not have an opinion, but also by those who felt 'neutral' on the subject. A first experiment was intended to shed some light on this problem.

1.3 DESIGN AND DATA COLLECTION

In this experiment we used five statements, selected from twelve statements used in an earlier study ('t Hart, 1981). Criteria for selection were:

1. The statements should deal with separate subjects.
2. The distributions of answers should vary.
3. The relationship between perceived difference from majority opinion and willingness to talk about the subject should not be the same.

The following five statements were selected:

A. The death penalty should be introduced.
B. In times of unemployment a man is more entitled to a job than a married woman.
C. Unemployment should be fought by nationalising industries.
D. Tax money should be spent to ensure a reasonable standard of living for foreign workers in The Netherlands.
E. Sunday observance should be re-established. Travelling and working on the sabbath should be forbidden and public places should be closed.

In June 1983 these statements were presented to a nationwide sample of 672 respondents.* A probability sample of household was drawn by NIPO, the Dutch Gallup organisation, which did the field work. Respondents were selected from household members, 17 years and older, by means of the 'first birthday' method. 25 per cent gave no response. Respondents were assigned at random to one of the two conditions of the experiment. 349 respondents were confronted with a questionnaire chart listing five response categories including a 'no opinion' option as the middle category. 323 respondents were confronted with a list of four categories only, the 'no opinion' category being omitted.

We investigated whether the distribution of the following background variables: work status, marital status, sex, education (nominal, 4 categories), educational level (interval, 4 categories), age (nominal, 7 age groups), age in years (interval), religion, self-rating in the political spectrum left/right (interval, 10 categories) and income (interval, 12 categories) differed over the two sample groups. We considered as too large a difference that would have been significant if we had been testing hypotheses (alpha = 0.10). Work status was a case in point. We re-weighted the sample so that the distribution of this variable was the same in each group. The effective sample size (Kish, 1965, p. 430) was reduced to 669.

1.4 INDIVIDUAL OPINION

If it is true that respondents with opinions deviating from those of the majority of the Dutch public prefer to keep their mouths shut rather

---

* The survey was wave 26 of the Continues Surveys of the Political Science Department, University of Amsterdam.

to admitting that they have uncommon views, we would accept a substantial number of refusals to answer. However, the fact that this behaviour is in itself considered unusual, could lead to there being only a small number of 'no answers'.

Sixteen respondents or 2 per cent of the sample did not answer the question about the nationalisation of industries. This was the highest number for any of the five statements. In general, all questions were answered. The number of refusals was too small to warrant further analysis. Moreover, when the percentage of 'no answers' was high, the percentage of 'no opinions' was also high. In further analyses we have treated the 'no answers' as missing values.

The two conditions differed on two points. First, in the first condition there was a 'no opinion' option, missing in the second condition. Second, the 'no opinion' option provided a middle category, while in the other condition choice between agree and disagree could not be avoided. We may suppose that the presence of these two characteristics had a mutually reinforcing effect.

No significant differences were found when the distributions of responses to the five statements were compared. Only in the case of the statement on the 'nationalisation of industries' could a noticeable difference be observed:

Table 1.1 Nationalisation of industries

	Condition I	Condition II	
	%	%	
compl. agree	9	6	compl. agree
mainly agree	14	18	mainly agree
no opinion (presented)	17	12	don't know (volunteered)
mainly disagree	23	20	mainly disagree
compl. disagree	37	45	compl. disagree
total	100	100	
n (weighted)	341	312	

$chi^2 = 9.4$, $df = 4$, $p = 0.05$

N. B. This table shows rounding effects.

In the case of each of the five statements the percentage of 'no opinions' was slightly larger in condition I than in condition II. Surprisingly however, these differences decreased when we added the 'no opinion' and 'no answers' together. The number of 'no answers' in the second condition was consistently larger than in the first. On second thoughts this is not so surprising. In the second condition respondents might have decided not to answer because they were unable to choose 'no opinion'.

On average Schuman and Presser (1981, p. 143) found 22 per cent difference between the percentages of 'no opinions' when this was offered as an alternative and the percentages of 'don't knows', when it was not. Our own results show much smaller differences. However, in their experiments the 'no opinion' option was presented either as a separate filter question or as an integral part of the question. In our experiment the 'no opinion' option was sometimes included in and sometimes omitted as an independent answer.

Schuman and Presser also found that a neutral middle category attracted a considerable number of respondents (pp. 165–8).

If the 'no opinion' category also acted as a neutral middle category, we would expect that when this alternative was not presented, respondents holding a middle position would choose one of the neighbouring categories. This was not the case. The shift was from 'mainly disagree' to 'completely disagree'. No such shift was detected within the 'agree' categories. There is no indication that a 'no opinion' option leads to acquiescence as Bishop *et al.* reported (1983, p. 540).

Our conclusion is that systematic differences in distribution appeared in the two conditions. However, these differences were too small to disturb analyses based on data gathered from either or both conditions.

Proceeding independently from our own data we also reached Schuman's and Presser's finding that 'one would generally draw the same conclusion from the marginals of one form as from the marginals of the other form' (p. 169).

1.5 CHANGES IN THE CLIMATE OF OPINION

The five subjects mentioned in the preceding paragraphs were used as items in a following set of questions. We asked respondents whether they believed that an increasing number of people would come to think as they themselves, or fewer and fewer. The same groups were retained for this experiment. In the second condition we added, 'or do you think the number will remain constant?' No chart was presented for the response categories.

If we consider this experiment as a replica of Schuman and Presser's (pp. 165–9) we would expect that the middle category would attract a substantial number of respondents. Schuman and Presser found that in general the percentage of 'don't knows' was higher when no middle alternative was offered than when one was included. Numerically, however, the difference was small.

Table 1.2 Change in the climate of opinion not known and no change

Condition		Death penalty	Men's right to a job	National-isation of indus.	Tax money f. foreign workers	Sunday observ.
I. forced choice	change not known	% 21	% 17	% 42	% 18	% 26
II. neutral middle category	change not known	10	8	26	13	14
	no change	29	22	35	19	36

Although, in some cases, in the first group 'don't know' might have been used for the same ends as 'remains the same' in the second, on the whole the latter category attracted more adherents. Nevertheless a remarkable number of 'don't knows' remained. The differences between the percentages of 'don't knows' in the two conditions were larger than those found by Schuman and Presser. However we must remember that Schuman and Presser were presenting the results of surveys of actual attitudes. We are concerned with a prediction about the future development of the climate of opinion.

Next we replicated Schuman and Presser's experiments and omitted the 'don't know' and the middle category. We expected no further differences in the distribution of responses in the two conditions. This appears to be near the truth. Only in one case did we find a small but significant difference.

There was no substantial evidence to refute the hypothesis that the middle category attracted respondents from both sides of the continuum, from among those who perceived increase as well as from among those who perceived decrease of support for their opinions.

Table 1.3 Percentage of respondents who perceived a change in the climate of opinion

	Tax money for foreign workers	
	Choice obligatory	Neutral middle category
number of supporters of own personal opinion:	%	%
increase	50	41
decrease	50	59
total	100	100
n (weighted)	281	214

$chi^2 = 4.11$, $df = 1$, sign. (alpha = 0.05)

The addition of a middle category attracts a lot of respondents. This results in an increase in the number of missing values in the analysis of the relationship between being isolated from the trend in the climate of opinion and the willingness to express one's views. On the other hand, if the inclusion of a middle category leads to an increase in the discriminating power of the variables, more is gained than lost. In the near future we will direct our attention to the analysis of this problem.

1.6 PREVAILING OPINIONS IN THE GENERAL PUBLIC AND AMONG ONE'S FRIENDS

The same statements that were used to assess the individual opinions of the respondents were also used to ascertain the perception of the opinions of most of the general public in The Netherlands. First one-third of the respondents in each of the two original groups was assigned to form a new experimental group. The distribution of background variables over the three groups was examined. This time substantial differences were found with the variables work status and sex. Re-weighting reduced the size of the sample used to 657.

The difference between the first two conditions was the same as that between the two conditions in our first experiment. In the second condition choice was forced. In the first condition the experimental group was able to choose 'no opinion', an option that was listed on the chart between the two 'agree' and the two 'disagree' categories.

It is often difficult to know what other people think. So we would expect that the percentage of respondents who did not have an opinion about 'most of the Dutch public' would be higher than the percentage of respondents who professed to have no personal opinion. There was also a chance that occasionally a respondent would use the 'no opinion' option to indicate that most of the Dutch public do not have an opinion on the issue involved.

Indeed the 'most of the public' questions evoked more 'no opinions' than the 'individual opinion' questions, but the differences were small. There were no systematic differences between the two conditions in this respect. No extra respondents were attracted by the 'no opinion' option. The tendency, detected in the previous experiment, to choose 'completely disagree' rather than 'mainly disagree' when choice was forced was also found here. With respect to 'Sunday observance' the difference between the two conditions reached significance (Table 1.4).

Table 1.4 Perception of most of the public's opinions about the reintroduction of sunday observance

	No opinion option	Forced choice
	%	%
mainly/compl. agree	7	5
mainly disagree	51	30
completely disagree	42	65
total	100	100
n (weighted)	215	189

$chi^2 = 21.22$, $df = 2$, sign. ($alpha = 0.05$)

The same procedure was followed with the questions about the perception of the opinions of the respondents' friends. These questions led, unexpectedly, to large numbers of 'no opinions', which were attributed to three factors:

1. Respondents have less information about their friends' opinions than about those of the general public.
2. They are more reluctant to generalise about their friends' opinions.
3. The perception that one does not share the views popular among one's friends is more threatening than not sharing the views of the majority of the Dutch public. It may be that respondents chose the

'no option' category to avoid having to admit that they did not think in the same way as their friends.

The differences in the reactions to the two conditions were again the same as those found in the 'most of the public' questions, although this time they were less pronounced.

Table 1.5 Perception of best friends' opinions about the reintroduction of Sunday observance

	No opinion option	Forced choice
	%	%
mainly/compl. agree	10	13
mainly disagree	25	11
completely disagree	65	76
total	100	100
n (weighted)	210	188

$chi^2 = 13.20$, $df = 2$, sign. ($alpha = 0.05$)

In condition III the question was extended to include the possibility that the numbers of supporters and opponents of the statement are about equal. The respondents were offered three response categories: most people agree, most people disagree, an equal number of people agree or disagree (middle category).

As expected, the middle category attracted more respondents this time than the first and especially the second condition. This happened partly at the expense of the 'don't know' category, although some 'don't knows' did remain.

We found considerable differences in the responses to four out of the five statements in the first condition with the 'no opinion' clause in the middle and the third condition with the 'equal numbers' clause in the middle. The exception was the statement on 'Sunday observance'. In other words, when an 'equal numbers' category was offered it was sometimes chosen instead of one of the substantial categories.

The same did not hold for the 'best friends' questions. Here the only significant difference was the response to the statement about the 'right to work of a man, versus a married woman'. It may be that the middle option was necessary for respondents with as many male friends as female friends. However, this was not the whole story, as shown below in Table 1.6.

It seems that the 'equal-numbers' category attracted adherents from those who, if it had not been included, would have said that

Table 1.6 Perception of best friends' opinions about a man having more right to a job than a married woman

	Condition		
best friends:	I %	III %	best friends:
most agree	53	38	most agree
no opinion (presented)	11	26	equal numbers
most disagree	36	36	most disagree
total	100	100	
n (weighted)	233	195	

$chi^2 = 17.51$, $df = 2$, sign. ($alpha = 0.05$)

most of their friends were in agreement with the statement. This seems to be an example of acquiescence bias. Bishop discovered a similar effect in the percentages favouring the SALT II agreement when he compared responses to filtered and non-filtered questions (Bishop et al., p. 542). His results, however, and ours could be explained as a primacy effect on being obliged to make a choice. By this we mean that if 'most *dis*agree' had been presented first, there would have been an increment in the choice of this alternative in the 'no option' condition.

Our result differs from the majority of the findings presented by Schuman and Presser (1982, p. 169): they found that the inclusion of a middle category did not influence the distributions of substantial responses.

Can we find such effects elsewhere?

To answer this question we examined the differences in distributions between 'most people agree' versus 'disagree' in the first and third condition and the second and third condition:

Table 1.7 Percentages of 'most people agree' (versus 'disagree') in each condition

condition:	Death penalty	Men's right to a job	National-isation of indus.	Tax money f. foreign workers	Sunday observ.
	%	%	%	%	%
I. no opinion opt.	30	68	32*	26	7
II. choice oblig.	35*	67	35*	29*	8
III. equal numbers	20	71	11	19	3

* Significant difference with 'equal numbers' ($chi^2 - alpha = 0.05$).

Similar tendencies in the distributions of answers to all five statements were found when the percentages 'most friends agree' in the first and third conditions were compared. When the percentages in the second and third conditions were compared we found such differences with respect to four out of five statements. However these differences were not significant.

The introduction of a middle category sometimes influenced the choice of substantial categories. When this option was absent this led to higher percentages of 'most people agree'. It is not clear whether this was due to a primacy effect or acquiescence.

1.7 'LOOKING-GLASS PERCEPTION'

Taylor (1982), Eckhardt and Hendershot (1967), and Fields and Schuman (1976), all reported that people often mirror their own individual opinions on the opinions of others. Fields and Schuman introduced the term 'looking-glass perception' to describe this phenomenon. Lack of information about other people's opinions may be one cause. If this were true, then the omission of a 'no opinion' option and a middle position would enhance this looking-glass perception. In the condition with a 'no opinion' option respondents who have no information about other people's opinions were given the opportunity of saying so. The 'equal numbers' options also offered a possible escape: if you do not know, you could hazard a guess that the number of adherents and the number of opponents were about the same.

We may presume that this looking-glass perception was most pronounced when the respondents were forced to make a positive choice and less so when the 'no opinion' option was offered or when a middle category was available.

In Table 1.8 we present Pearson's correlations between personal opinions and opinions ascribed to 'most of the public in The Netherlands'. These correlations were based on double dichotomies: agree versus disagree.

Our hypothesis was not sustained by the data. Correlations do not increase as we proceed down the table.

Table 1.8   Correlations between personal opinions and opinions ascribed to a majority of the Dutch public, agree/disagree only

	Death penalty	Men's right to a job	National-isation of indus.	Tax money f. foreign workers	Sunday observ.
condition:					
I. no opinion opt.	0.44	0.13	0.64	0.40	0.15
III. equal numbers	0.40	0.13	0.51	0.36	0.11
II. choice oblig.	0.43	0.16	0.50	0.39	0.44*

* Only eight people both agreed with this statement and thought that a majority of the Dutch also did.

1.8 HOW MANY DUTCH PEOPLE WERE NEEDED FOR A MAJORITY?

We also asked respondents to indicate what percentage of the public holding an opinion would agree and what percentage would disagree with each statement. Evidently the two percentages should add up to 100 per cent. At least 1 and at most 5 respondents made mistakes in this respect and at least 31 (5 per cent) and at most 73 (11 per cent) could not answer the question. These responses were treated as missing values.

In the 'most of the Dutch public' questions in the first and second conditions a distinction was made between majority and minority opinion. The question whether most of the Dutch public completely or mainly disagree was concerned with the *intensity* of the opinion and not with the *size* of the majority or minority. Still, we may suppose that those people who felt that most of the public agree or disagree completely with a statement perceived a greater majority than those who perceived that most people mainly agree or disagree. Generally speaking this was the case.

It should be noted that, in most cases in which there was no monotonous decline in the figures for the averages of the estimates of the percentages of agreements as we descend the columns, these percentages had been based on a very limited number of observations.

There were no significant differences in mean estimated percentages between the two conditions.

Table 1.9 Mean estimated percentages of the Dutch public thought to be in agreement with the statements in conditions I ('no opinion' option) and II (forced choice) taken together

	Death penalty	Men's right to a job	National-isation of indus.	Tax money f. foreign workers	Sunday observ.
most people					
compl. agree	56 (25)*	68 (69)	63 (18)	48 (13)	76 (6)
mainly agree	57 (102)	62 (205)	56 (98)	56 (93)	48 (23)
mainly disagree	26 (178)	47 (107)	29 (149)	31 (188)	18 (159)
compl. disagree	19 (92)	43 (20)	24 (67)	26 (85)	10 (203)
Total	35 (396)	58 (402)	38 (332)	37 (379)	20 (392)
perc. respds agreeing with statements	32 (638)	62 (637)	27 (558)	51 (601)	10 (638)

* weighted *n*'s

N.B. As a consequence of weighting, the numbers of respondents were rounded off and therefore do not always add up to the totals.

As one may remember, in the first condition a 'no opinion' option was offered and in the third condition a middle category. Did the assessments of the percentages of the Dutch public in agreement with the statements made by those who chose 'no opinion' in the first condition and the assessments made by those who chose the middle category in the third, differ?

Table 1.10 Mean estimated percentages of the Dutch public thought to be in agreement with the statements in conditions I ('no opinion' option) and III ('equal numbers')

	Death penalty	Men's right to a job	National-isation of indus.	Tax money f. foreign workers	Sunday observ.
guess abt most people's opinions: condition:					
I. no opinion	36 (13)*	48 (11)	42 (38)	43 (23)	32 (16)
II. equal numbers	48 (16)	53 (79)	46 (51)	45 (49)	39 (19)

* weighted *n*'s

The 'no opinion' respondents seemed to rate the percentage slightly lower than the 'equal numbers' respondents, but, because of large variances and small numbers, the differences were not significant (alpha = 0.05).

The mean percentages of respondents who answered 'no opinion' to the 'most of the Dutch public' question were in between those for respondents who believed that a majority of the Dutch public agreed with the given statements and those for respondents who believed most of the public disagreed. This also held for those who responded with 'equal numbers'. Now, if those who filled in 'no opinion' on the 'most-of-the-public' question were to estimate the percentage of agreements at random, the mean percentage would also be found somewhere in the middle. In that case the standard deviation of the ratings would be larger than those for the other groups. Our data did not reveal such a pattern.

Respondents who chose 'no opinion' from the categories presented in the 'most-of-the-public' question, in general used 'no opinion' as a middle category. However, on a scale 'no opinion' is closer to the 'disagree' than the 'equal numbers' category.

In Table 1.7 we compared the condition in which a 'no opinion' option was offered and the forced-choice condition with the 'equal numbers' condition. Especially in the forced-choice condition the percentages of respondents who perceived a majority of the Dutch who agreed with the statements 'death penalty', 'nationalisation of industries' and 'tax money for foreign workers' was larger than in the condition in which a middle category was offered. Thus, we would expect that the means of the ratings of those who believed that most of the public agree would be higher in the condition with a middle category than in the forced-choice condition. Figure 1.1 illustrates this hypothesis.

In the case of two statements we find a significant difference in the expected direction (Table 1.11).

We had predicted this difference in the case of 'nationalisation of industries' but not in the case of 'men's right to a job'. The two other predictions were refuted by the results. There was little evidence for our hypothesis.

1.9 SUMMARY

In an investigation into the influence of the perception of the predominant opinion questions were asked about:

Figure 1.1 Hypothetical example of the effect of forced choice on mean ratings of agreement

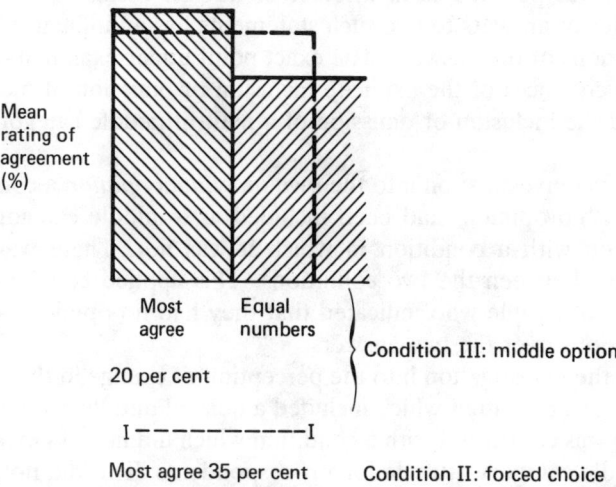

Table 1.11 Mean estimated percentages of the Dutch public, agreeing with two statements in two conditions (respondents who believed most of the Dutch public is in agreement only)

	Men's right to a job	*Nationalisation of industries*
condition:		
2. Forced choice	64	53
3. Equal numbers	68	68
F	3.38 (sign.)*	5.91 (sign.)
df	1;210	1;72
alpha	0.05	0.05

* One-sided test

- own individual opinion
- the opinion ascribed to most of people in The Netherlands
- the opinion ascribed to most of someone's best friends
- the perception of changes in the climate of opinion.

These questions were presented in the form of statements by means of which the respondent could express a greater or lesser degree of concurrence.

In a number of experiments made with the co-operation of Dutch citizens, 17 years of age and older, by means of a questionnaire, the question was pursued as to whether or not the inclusion of certain categories of answers to five such statements has an influence on the distributions of the answers. The exact point under examination was the consequences of the explicit inclusion or omission of 'no opinion' and the inclusion or omission of a neutral middle category.

1. In the investigation into the *own individual opinion* a condition in which 'no opinion' had been included as a middle category was contrasted with a condition in which it was not. There was little difference between the two conditions. This applied equally to the numbers of people who indicated that they had no opinion and the distributions over the two answers.

2. In the investigation into the perception of change in the *climate of opinion* a condition which included a neutral middle category (no change) was contrasted with a condition which did not. As expected, the middle category attracted many respondents. This did not entail that there were no respondents without an opinion. With one exception, the middle category had attracted respondents from both sides of the continuum.

3. Three different lists of answers were tried out with the questions about opinions of *most people in The Netherlands* and questions about *best friends'* opinions. This time the effect of the provision of a 'no opinion' clause as a middle category as well as the effect of the inclusion of a neutral middle category was noted.

3.1 Again, as it turned out, there was not much difference between the conditions in which there was or was not a 'no opinion' category present in the number of respondents who reported that they did not know the answer. In one case the *distributions* over the other answers were influenced: when choice was forced the number of respondents that chose 'completely disagree' was larger, and the number that chose 'mainly disagree' was fewer than when the 'no opinion' option was present. This applied both to the 'most-of-the public' and the 'best-friends' questions.

3.2 The *neutral middle category* was considerably more attractive. This was chosen not only as an alternative to the 'no opinion' option but also for the other possible answers. The former case applied to the questions on 'most people', the latter to both types of question. A forced choice resulted particularly in an increase in the percentages 'most people/friends agree'.

4. Contrary to expectations, a forced choice did not result in an augmentation of the *looking-glass perception*, the tendency to ascribe one's own personal opinion to others. This was apparent from a comparison with a situation in which respondents were presented with a 'no opinion' clause or a neutral middle category.

5. The request to estimate the *percentage of the Dutch public* that agrees with a particular opinion, made a further analysis of the various answers to the question on the perception of the opinion of the majority of the Dutch public possible. 'Most people completely agree' was coupled to a higher mean estimate of the percentage of supporters for the opinion than 'mainly agree'. 'Mainly disagree' was coupled to higher mean estimate than 'completely disagree'. In this instance, 'no opinion' and 'equal numbers' occupied middle positions between 'most of the Dutch public agree' and 'most of the Dutch public disagree'. The percentage estimate of those who chose 'equal numbers' was somewhat higher than that of those who could choose 'no opinion' and took the opportunity of doing so.

6. Only scanty evidence was found for the last hypothesis: respondents who choose the possibility that most Dutch people agree with a statement come, on average, to a higher estimate of the *percentage* of those *in agreement* in the condition in which a neutral middle category is presented than such respondents in the condition in which this is not the case.

1.10 CONCLUSIONS

As stated in Section 1.4 both ways of questioning respondents about their opinions ('no opinion' as against forced choice) led to almost identical distributions of answers. No conclusion about which of the two should be preferred can be drawn from our analysis.

Although the two ways (with or without a middle category) in which we put the question about a change in the climate of opinion did evoke different responses, we still cannot decide, which is better. No significant differences were found between the experimental conditions in the ratio between the number of those who perceived an increase and the number of those who saw a decrease of support for their opinions.

If it is true that being obliged to make a choice leads to acquiescence or primacy effects, we should include a middle position in the 'Dutch public' and 'best friends' questions. By so doing, we might influence the respondents' ratings of the percentages of the Dutch public agreeing with a statement. This would increase the discriminating power of the question.

APPENDIX

The following *statements* were presented on chart 6:
A. The death penalty should be introduced.
B. In times of unemployment a man is more entitled to a job than a married woman.
C. Unemployment should be fought by nationalising industries.
D. Tax money should be spent to ensure a reasonable standard of living for foreign workers in The Netherlands.
E. Sunday observance should be re-established. Travelling and working on the sabbath should be forbidden and public places should be closed.

Question 1

The following question was asked about respondents' personal opinions:

'To what extent do you yourself agree or disagree with each of the statements on this chart?'

There were different response categories for the two subsamples. In subsample 1 (condition I, first experiment) the response categories were:

- completely agree
- mainly agree
- no opinion
- mainly disagree
- completely disagree

In subsample 2 (condition II, first experiment) the response categories were:

- completely agree
- mainly agree
- mainly disagree
- completely disagree

Question 2

Two of the three subsamples (condition I and II, second experiment) were asked the following question:

'To what extent do most of the Dutch public agree or disagree with these statements?'

The first subsample (condition I) had the same response categories as subsample 1 in question 1, the second subsample (condition II) the same as subsample 2 in question 1. For the group in condition III (second experiment) the question was extended with: 'or do you think there are about as many supporters as opponents of this statement?' This necessitated other response categories:

- most of the Dutch public agree with this statement.
- in The Netherlands there are as many supporters as opponents of this statement.
- most of the Dutch public disagree with this statement.

Question 3

All the respondents (condition I, II and III) were asked the following question:

'What is your estimation of the percentage of the Dutch public who agree with the given statement and what is your estimation of the percentage who disagree with it? Please take all Dutch people who have an opinion on the subject into consideration. Together the percentages should add up to 100%.'

Respondents were shown the following response categories on chart 6:

- percentage that agrees with the statement   =   %
- percentage that disagrees with the statement   =   %

together = 100%

Question 4

The following question was put to two of the three subsamples (condition I and II, third experiment):

'Do your best friends agree or disagree with the given statements?'

The response categories for the condition I subsample were the same again as in question 1 for this condition, for the condition II subsample they were the same again as for condition II in question 1. For the group in condition III (third experiment) the question was extended in the same way as in question 2. The response categories were:

- most of my friends agree with this statement.
- among my friends are as many supporters as opponents of this statement.
- most of my friends disagree with this statement.

Question 5

Subsample 1 (condition I, fourth experiment) were asked the following question:

> 'With respect to the statements in front of you do you think that an increasing number of people will come to think like you in the future or fewer and fewer?'

For the second group (condition II, fourth experiment) the question was extended with: 'or do you believe this number will remain constant?'

Figure 1.2 Subsamples

QUESTIONS	Condition I n = 239	Condition II n = 110 + n = 107	Condition III n = 216
1. own opinion	'no opinion' presented	forced choice	
2. most people	'no opinion' presented	forced choice	neutral middle category
3. estimation	estimation of the opinion of the Dutch public in %		
4. best friends	'no opinion' presented	forced choice	neutral middle category
5. change in climate	no neutral middle category	neutral middle category	

REFERENCES

BISHOP, G. F., OLDENDICK, R. W. and TUCHFARBER, A. J., 'Effects of Filter Questions in Public Opinion Surveys', *Public Opinion Quarterly*, **47** (1983) 528–46.

ECKHARDT, K. W. and HENDERSHOT, G., 'Dissonance–Congruence and the Perception of Public Opinion', *American Journal of Sociology*, **73:2** (1967) 226–34.

FIELDS, J. M. and SCHUMAN, H., 'Public Beliefs about the Beliefs of the Public', *Public Opinion Quarterly*, **40** (1976) 427–48.

'T HART, H., 'People's Perceptions of Public Opinions', paper presented at the Fourth Annual Scientific Meeting of the International Society of Political Psychology (Mannheim, June 1981).

KISH, L., *Survey Sampling* (New York: Wiley, 1965).
MEILOF-OONK, S., *Meningen over Homosexualiteit (Opinions about Homosexuality)*, I. ('s-Gravenhage [The Hague]: Staatsuitgeverij, 1969).
NOELLE-NEUMANN, E., *Öffentliche Meinung: Unsere Soziale Haut* (Frankfurt-am-Main: Ullstein, 1982).
―― *Public Opinion: Our Social Skin* (Chicago: University of Chicago Press, 1982).
SCHUMAN, H. and PRESSER, S., *Questions and Answers in Attitude Surveys* (New York: Academic Press, 1981).
TAYLOR, D. G., 'Pluralistic Ignorance and the Spiral of Silence: a formal analysis', *Public Opinion Quarterly*, **46**, (1982) 311–35.

2 Types of Inadequate Interviewer Behaviour in Survey-Interviews

W. Dijkstra and J. van der Zouwen

2.1 THE PROBLEM

Researchers have long been aware that the information gathered by means of survey-interviews is probably distorted. Perhaps Rice (1929) was the first who was able to show, as early as 1929, that interviewers can affect the respondent's answers in a definite way. Since that time the number of studies on information-distortion in interviews has constantly increased (see for example Sudman and Bradburn, 1974; Dijkstra and van der Zouwen, 1982). By now there is clear evidence that the respondent's answers can be the result of numerous factors other than the respondent's opinion, attitude or whatever the investigator is interested in.

This evidence has led some researchers to conclude that the survey-interview in its present form should not be used as a method of data collection (e.g. Phillips, 1973). Others argue that the interview-situation should be structured in such a way, that the possibility of distortion is reduced. This approach has led to the development of a number of techniques, such as Randomised Response Techniques (RRT), or Computer Assisted (Telephone) Interviewing (CA(T)I). Such techniques however, are usually applicable in a limited range of situations only.

In our opinion, in order to prevent or correct for interview-distortions, one should first have a clear understanding of the different factors that influence the respondent's answers during the interview, and the manner in which such factors exert their influence. Previous research (Dijkstra and van der Zouwen, 1982) revealed us that, among other factors, the interviewer in particular appears to affect the answers given by the respondent. For example, it is well known that different interviewers tend to obtain different response-distributions from their respondents (e.g. Freeman and Butler, 1976;

O'Muircheartaigh, 1976). Moreover, existing research has shown that notwithstanding all efforts to standardise the interviewers' conduct through selection, training and supervision, their behaviour varies considerably across interviews (e.g. Bradburn and Sudman, 1979; Brenner, 1982).

It remains unclear which differences in interviewer behaviour should be held responsible for the variance in answers. The results of one of our own research projects (Dijkstra, 1983) suggest that interviewers differ especially with respect to the adequacy of their performance, and that inadequate performance can lead to information-distortion. Examples of such inadequacies are talking about irrelevant matters, deviations from the question as worded in the questionnaire, and directive probing. They also include inadequate control, or inadequate correction of poor respondent performance. On the basis of these observations we decided:

(a) to develop a coding scheme, which would enable us to trace both the adequate and the inadequate interactions between interviewer and respondent;
(b) to attempt to distinguish between various types of interviewer inadequacies;
(c) to relate the occurrence of particular types of inadequate interviewer behaviour to other interviewer characteristics, as well as to the (non)occurrence of a particular respondent behaviour;
(d) to attempt to estimate the impact of inadequate interviewer behaviour on the outcomes of the survey.

2.2 THE DATA

Our data came from 384 audiotaped interviews concerning satisfaction with housing conditions and social relations with neighbours. The respondents were randomly selected from the adult inhabitants of Amstelveen, a recently developed urban area near Amsterdam. Equal numbers of male and female respondents were randomly assigned to 16 interviewers. Half of these interviewers were trained in a so-called 'socio-emotional' style of interviewing. These interviewers were informed that a good relationship with the respondent is a prerequisite for the respondent's willingness to provide the information asked for. They were taught to react to the respondent's answers in a warm and understanding manner. For example, the interviewer could make personal statements such as 'I understand what moving to this house meant to you' or 'How nice for you!'; and so on.

The other 8 interviewers were trained in a so-called 'formal' style. These interviewers were instructed to behave in a neutral, business-like manner and to restrict understanding and empathic reactions to a socially acceptable minimum. These interviewers were told that too much attention to personal matters would distract respondents from their task and thus lead to useless or inadequate responses. They were trained to attend only to the information-gathering aspect of the interview, and to act in a polite but essentially neutral fashion.

For all 16 interviewers a considerable part of the training was devoted to learning adequate interviewer performance. For example, all interviewers were instructed to read questions as worded in the questionnaire, to probe non-directively, to give positive feedback if the respondent's answer was adequate (e.g. 'Thank you') and not to answer for the respondent. The number of male and female interviewers (randomly) assigned to each interviewing style, was balanced.

The present study is based on the verbatim transcriptions of 7 questions and the responses to these questions. These 7 questions were added to the questionnaire for the purpose of this analysis. All the question–answer sequences under investigation here had roughly the same structure. First (phase 1) the respondent was requested to choose one alternative from a set of response-alternatives. The selection of an alternative by the respondent was included in this phase. Next (phase 2) the respondent was asked to motivate this choice, whereupon (in phase 3) the interviewer requested the respondent to further elucidate this motivation, if the motivation was considered insufficient. A fourth phase covered actions of the interviewer and respondent that were no longer relevant to the question as formulated in the questionnaire.

Due to limited resources it was impossible to transcribe the question–answer sequences of all 384 interviews. Eighteen interviews were randomly selected from each of our 16 interviewers. Thus we had transcriptions of $16 * 18 * 7 = 2016$ question–answer sequences at our disposal.

2.3 PROCEDURES

The verbal behaviour of interviewer and respondent was decomposed into speech acts. A speech act is any meaningful question, answer or other verbal utterance. The average question–answer sequence involved approximately six speech acts by the interviewer and seven by the respondent. This resulted in over 26 000 speech acts, namely 13 times the 2016 question–answer sequences. Next, these 26 000 speech acts were coded according to a number of variables regarding form and content. Our coding procedure was based on schemes developed by Cannell, Lawson and Hauser (1975), and Brenner (1982). The first variable identified the actor, that is, the person who uttered the speech act, usually the interviewer or the respondent, but occasionally a third person, or 'bystander'. Second, the speech act was classified as either a question, an answer, a reaction, or a neutral remark. Reactions applied, for example, to repetitions, explanations of the purpose of the survey and so on. Neutral remarks concerned speech acts that were irrelevant to the interview, as for instance the question 'Would you like a cup of coffee?' The third variable expressed the phase of the sequence, as explained in the previous section. The fourth and fifth variable pertained to more detailed distinctions between different types of questions, answers or reactions. For example, a distinction was made between directive and nondirective questioning. One of the manners in which answers were classified was according to whether they concerned factual information or attitudinal information. As to reactions, distinctions were made between repetitions, feedback, empathic reactions and so on. Finally, the sixth variable concerned the relation between the content of the question and the response alternatives, as formulated in the questionnaire on the one hand, and the actual content of the speech act on the other hand.

An example illustrates the essentials of our coding system. Consider the following part of a question–answer sequence.

(1) IQ1KNF: How satisfied are you with your home?
(2) IQ1ANF: Would you say dissatisfied, neither satisfied nor dissatisfied, satisfied or very satisfied?
(3) RA1KJO: Well, I'm quite satisfied.
(4) IQ1ANS: Yes, is it satisfied or very satisfied?
(5) RA1KJS: Very satisfied.
(6) IQ2ONF: Can you tell me what makes you satisfied with this home?
(7) RA2OFS: Well, it's quite large, . . .
   (etc.)

The first speech act (1) is posed by the interviewer (I) and it is a question (Q) from the questionnaire (phase 1). The question is a closed one (K), and posed non-directively (N). Moreover, it is posed exactly as worded in the questionnaire (F). The second speech act (2) consists of the presentation of the response alternatives by the interviewer; the only difference with the codes of the previous speech act is the letter A, to signify that it concerns the presentation of response alternatives. Next (3), the respondent (R) provides an answer (A); still within phase 1, because this speech act is an immediate answer to the interviewer's phase 1 question. Moreover, it is an answer to a closed question (K), and it concerns an attitudinal statement. To indicate that the answer does not fit one of the proposed response alternatives, the code O is used. The interviewer then repeats two of the response alternatives (4). Code S is used because the interviewer repeats only two, and not all four response alternatives.

The respondent replies (5) with 'Very satisfied', and because this fits one of the response alternatives, the code S is used. Next the interviewer asks the respondent to motivate the choice, and with this speech act (6) phase 2 of the question–answer sequence is entered. The question is an open one (O), posed non-directively (N) and within the scope of the question as formulated in the questionnaire. The respondent motivates (7) the choice with factual information (F), that applies to part of the subject of the original question, namely, a specific aspect of the own home: code S, etc.

These coding activities resulted for each question–answer sequence in a pattern of codes, representing the very question–answer sequence. Each coded question–answer sequence was preceded by numbers, enabling us to identify the interviewer, respondent and question, and thereby to connect it with additional information, such as the coded answer (the score) as it appeared in the questionnaire, the adopted interviewing style, and so on. For example:

051436 IQ1KNF IQ1ANF RA1KJO IQ1ANS RA1KJS IQ2ONF RA2OFS . . . (etc.)

It is obvious that the coding was a complex and difficult task. It was carried out by two coders. To assess the inter-coder reliability, sixteen interviews were independently coded by both individuals. Correcting for agreement by chance as measured by Kappa (Cohen,

1960), coefficients ranging from 0.74 to 0.98 for the six previously mentioned variables were obtained, which we considered very satisfactory.

The very detailed coding system enabled us to identify a large number of different verbal behaviours. As pointed out before, we focused on inadequate interviewer behaviour. The coded sequences made it possible to locate precisely where in the sequence the inadequacies occurred, and what preceded and followed the inadequate behaviour. Moreover, we could distinguish interviewers who exhibited many inadequacies of a particular type, from interviewers who showed fewer such inadequacies, and subsequently compare the responses they obtained.

2.4 RESULTS

2.4.1 Types of Inadequate Interviewer Behaviour

The following four types of inadequate interviewer behaviour were observed.

Type 1: Deviation from the Questionnaire

This type refers to the situation where the interviewer deviated from the formulation of the question (or the set of response-alternatives) as it appeared in the questionnaire. It was found that this type of behaviour usually occurred when the interviewer, who first posed the question correctly, obtained an inadequate answer from the respondent. This type of deviation from the questionnaire can be viewed as a form of 'adaptive behaviour'. For example:

I: Do you have many social contacts in the neighbourhood?
R: Well, I have good neighbours.
I: Do you have many contacts with them?
 Would you say a few, many, . . . (etc.)

A more harmless example is the following. On the basis of previous answers indicating that the respondent was quite satisfied with his or her home, the interviewer was likely to present only part of the set of response alternatives, such as: 'Would you say satisfied or very satisfied.'

These deviations, which occurred in about 4 per cent of all question–answer sequences, appeared to be unrelated to the style of interviewing. The proportion of question–answer sequences containing deviations varied between interviewers however, and ranged from 1 to 9 per cent.

Type 2: Irrelevant Behaviour

Irrelevant interviewer behaviour concerns questions posed, or information provided by the interviewer about matters that were not at all related to the items from the questionnaire. This behaviour can be conceived as inattentiveness, whereby the interviewer appears to have forgotten the purpose of the interview, namely, to obtain information from the respondent, on topics defined by the researcher. As a result, part of the time intended for data collection is spent on irrelevant matters, making the interview less efficient, at least from the viewpoint of the researcher.

Analysis of the sequences containing irrelevant interviewer behaviour showed that while irrelevant questioning was clearly prompted by irrelevant answers on the part of the respondent, providing irrelevant information was independent of respondent behaviour. Irrelevant interviewer behaviour occurred in about 8 per cent of all question–answer sequences. The number of sequences containing irrelevant behaviours in the socio-emotional style was three times as large as in the formal style.

Type 3: Hinting

Hinting applies to situations where the interviewer asked leading questions, or suggested a particular answer. This was the most prevalent type of inadequate interviewer behaviour. Questions from the questionnaire were posed in a suggestive manner in approximately 10 per cent of the sequences. These figures were 19 per cent (378 sequences) for questions about motives, and 11 per cent (233 sequences) for requests to elucidate these motives.

These findings indicate that leading questions were asked especially when the interviewees were requested to motivate their particular response selection. At first we assumed the reason to be that respondents were sometimes unwilling or unable to provide a motive. This, however, proved to be incorrect because it was observed in only 4 out of the 378 sequences mentioned earlier.

An alternative explanation is that interviewers asked leading questions because they learned that it produced 'quick results'. In line with this explanation one should find that interviewers posed more leading questions as the interview-campaign progressed. Our analysis indeed showed that, on average, interviewers probed in a suggestive manner in 15 per cent of the sequences from the nine interviews they conducted during the first half of the interview-campaign, with the percentage increasing to 23 per cent for the interviews they conducted during the second part.

Hinting occurred more frequently in the socio-emotional style of interviewing than in the formal style. In addition, there were very large differences among the interviewers with respect to the prevalence of suggestive probing. For example, the percentage of sequences per interviewer within which one or more leading questions were used, ranged from 7 to 71 per cent.

Type 4: Choosing Behaviour

The fourth type of inadequate interviewer behaviour is called 'choosing'. In the event the respondent did not select one of the response-alternatives presented, the interviewer was instructed to pose the question again and to insist that a proper choice was made. What often happened, however, was that the interviewer failed to follow this instruction, and, without repeating the question, marked one response alternative in the questionnaire, probably on the basis of previous remarks of the respondent. Choosing behaviour occurred in 327 sequences, that is in more than 16 per cent of all 2016 sequences. This type of behaviour was equally frequent in both styles of interviewing, but again there were large differences among the interviewers.

In the majority of cases (namely 212 of the 327 sequences) the interviewers based their choice on an inadequate response alternative of the respondent. In the other cases (115 sequences) the respondent failed to make a choice. It is quite remarkable that, if respondents gave no, or only inadequate, response alternatives, the interviewers rarely encouraged the respondent to as yet make a proper choice. Apparently they preferred the less bothersome procedure of drawing inferences from the information at hand about the choice of a response alternative, and filling in this part of the questionnaire on their own.

2.4.2 Effects of Inadequate Interviewer Behaviour

We also attempted to estimate the impact of the four types of interviewer inadequacies on the research results. Actually this would have required so-called 'validating information', which is often difficult to obtain, especially in the case of attitudinal data. Our point of departure here was that it is reasonable to expect specific categories of respondents to differ with respect to their answers to particular questions. Thus we examined whether interviewers who exhibited relatively few inadequacies of a particular type, and interviewers who exhibited relatively many such inadequacies obtained similar answer patterns for the specific categories of respondents.

To this end each respondent was classified either as living with a partner or as living single. We presumed that these categories of respondents would differ according to (first) the number of social contacts they mentioned, and (second) how lonely they perceived themselves in comparison with other people (cf. de Jong-Gierveld, 1984). The interviewers were divided in two groups, on the basis of the degree of inadequate behaviour, and for each type of inadequate behaviour respectively, using the median as a cutting-point. Analysis of variances were performed to investigate whether different relations between type of respondent on the one hand, and the respondent's answers on the other, were found for the two groups of interviewers. The results are shown in Table 2.1.

In all eight cases the observed differences between the individuals living with a partner and the individuals living on their own, were larger for respondents questioned by interviewers showing relatively few inadequacies, than for respondents questioned by interviewers showing relatively many inadequacies. These differences were significant at the 5 per cent level in three of the eight cases. Choosing behaviour on the part of the interviewer appeared to have the least effect on the observed relations between respondent type and respondent answers.

In our view the results obtained by the interviewers with relatively few inadequate behaviours correspond best with reality. Interviewers who engage in irrelevant talk, deviate from the questionnaire or probe suggestively, may communicate to the respondent that they are inattentive to the task requirements of the interview. Consequently the respondents may feel distracted from their task, or they may answer less carefully.

Table 2.1 The differences between respondents living without and with partner with respect to (a) number of social contacts, and (b) feelings of loneliness, as indicated by data gathered by interviewers exhibiting relatively few, respectively many inadequacies of a certain type

(a) Number of social contacts (1 = no contacts; 5 = many contacts)

Type of interviewer inadequacy		Type of respondent Living single / with partner		Significance level of interaction term
1. Deviations	few	2.47	2.95	
	many	2.66	2.82	$p = 0.249$
2. Irrelevancies	few	2.35	2.92	
	many	2.84	2.85	$p = 0.024$ *
3. Hinting	few	2.47	2.92	
	many	2.69	2.86	$p = 0.264$
3. Choosing	few	2.50	2.90	
	many	2.65	2.87	$p = 0.549$
		$N = 68$	$N = 301$	

(b) Loneliness (1 = nonlonely; 5 = very lonely)

Type of interviewer inadequacy		Type of respondent Living single / with partner		Significance level of interaction term
1. Deviations	few	2.59	1.79	
	many	2.31	2.08	$p = .037$ *
2. Irrelevancies	few	2.51	1.83	
	many	2.32	2.04	$p = .161$
3. Hinting	few	2.56	1.76	
	many	2.28	2.11	$p = .026$ *
3. Choosing	few	2.55	1.83	
	many	2.31	2.05	$p = .105$
		$N = 68$	$N = 314$	

* significant at the 5 per cent level

2.5 CONCLUSIONS

We distinguished four kinds of inadequate interviewer behaviours: deviations from the questionnaire, irrelevant behaviours, hinting and choosing. Interviewers who exhibited many of these inadequate behaviours obtained responses which suggested quite different relationships between variables such as the presence of a partner on the one hand, and feelings of loneliness or the number of contacts on the other hand. Apparently the interviewer can determine to a considerable degree, whether particular research hypotheses about relationships between variables should be rejected or not.

In an earlier research project (Dijkstra, 1983) we found that a socio-emotional style of interviewing appeared to motivate the respondent better, than a formal style of interviewing. The results of the present study show, however, that a socio-emotional style also enhances the risk of inadequate interviewer performance, especially irrelevant behaviour and hinting, which in turn may lead to information-distortion. We therefore conclude that a socio-emotional style should be preferred to a formal style of interviewing, provided that interviewers are carefully selected, trained and supervised. For instance, interviewers could be instructed, and even encouraged, to show personal interest in the respondent, and to give empathic reactions, if this is called for by the respondent's answers. However, in training and supervision it should be stressed by the researcher that they should not digress from the interview topic, or engage in irrelevant talk with the respondent, let alone probe in a suggestive manner.

REFERENCES

BRADBURN, N. M. and SUDMAN, S., *Improving Interview-Method and Questionnaire Design* (San Francisco: Jossey-Bass, 1979).
BRENNER, M., 'Response Effects of "Role-restricted" Characteristics of the Interviewer', in: DIJKSTRA, W. and ZOUWEN, J. van der (eds) *Response Behaviour in the Survey-interview* (London, New York: Academic Press, 1982) 131–65.
CANNELL, C. F., LAWSON, S. A. and HAUSER, D. L., *A Technique for Evaluating Interviewer Performance* (Ann Arbor, Mich.: The University of Michigan, 1975).
COHEN, J., 'A coefficient of agreement for nominal scales', *Educational and Psychological Measurement*, **20** (1960) 37–40.

DIJKSTRA, W., *Beinvloeding van Antwoorden in Survey-interviews* (Dutch). Dissertation, Free University Amsterdam (Delft, 1983).
DIJKSTRA, W. and ZOUWEN, J. van der, *Response Behaviour in the Survey-interview* (London, New York: Academic Press, 1982).
FREEMAN, J. and BUTLER, E. W., 'Some Sources of Interviewer Variance in Surveys', *Public Opinion Quarterly,* 40 (1976) 79–91.
O'MUIRCHEARTAIGH, C. A., 'Response Errors in an Attitudinal Sample Survey', *Quality and Quantity,* 10 (1976) 97–115.
JONG-GIERVELD, J. de, *Eenzaamheid* (Dutch) (Deventer: Van Loghum Slaterus, 1984).
PHILLIPS, D. L., *Abandoning Method* (San Francisco: Jossey-Bass, 1973).
RICE, S. A., 'Contagious Bias in the Interview: A Methodological Note', *American Journal of Sociology,* 35 (1929) 420–3.
SUDMAN, S. and BRADBURN, N. M., *Response Effects in Surveys* (Chicago: Aldine, 1974).

3 Surveying Ethnic Minorities
A. E. Bronner

3.1 INTRODUCTION

More than half a million foreign residents, mainly from Turkey and Morocco, live in The Netherlands. The practice of Dutch research institutes is to include individuals of these groups in their samples only if they speak the Dutch language. It will be clear that consequently there is a lack of statistical knowledge about these residents. As the notion is growing that their stay is likely to be permanent there is an increasing interest for social research in this field. Many of the foreign residents originally came as temporary 'guest workers', but this post-war migration has resulted in the permanent settlement of substantial cultural and ethnic minorities in West European countries. In general this first generation (the people who came to Holland) has a poor educational and socio-economic level and there is also a great cultural distance between them and the Dutch community (see van den Berg-Eldering, 1978; Heijke, 1979; Shadid, 1979). Entzinger (1984) characterises the situation of many immigrants by three elements: (1) a weak legal status (often combined with insecurity of residence), (2) a socially deprived position, and (3) a different ethnic origin. Because of this last aspect the immigrant groups are sometimes referred to as 'ethnic minorities'.

These problems, together with the acknowledgement of permanent settlement, have created the need to gather information about these groups. In this framework the following question is relevant: 'Is it possible to apply our traditional "Western" data-collection techniques to these groups?' In the last two years we have gained experience in surveying Turks, Moroccans, Italians, Spaniards, Portuguese and people born in Surinam. Research problems differ considerably for the Mediterranean workers and their families at one side and Moluccans, Surinamers and Antilleans at the other side. The last group is able to speak the Dutch language and 90 per cent has the Dutch nationality. It is a culturally, but not linguistically different group. Furthermore they have more religious similarities with the Dutch than, for example, Islamitic Mediterranean groups. For reasons of clarity I limit the illustrations in this paper to culturally *and* linguistically different groups. The emphasis is on the comparison between the autochton Dutch and the Mediterranean group. Within the last population a distinction can be made between Islamitic (Turks, Moroccans) and non-Islamitic (Italians, Spaniards, Portuguese) minorities. In this paper the possibilities and pitfalls involved in surveying ethnic minorities will be illustrated.

3.2 PROBLEM

As everybody can imagine, surveying ethnic minorities means that the researcher has to adapt the traditional data-collection procedures followed in his daily practice of social reasearch. Language problems, cultural differences and a low socio-economic level are the main factors contributing to a diverging approach.

Adapting procedures means that there arise differences between interviewing ethnic minorities and the Dutch. It will be these differences we will treat in this paper. A selection is made of seven aspects of survey-interviewing:

(a) different interviewers
(b) different days for interviewing
(c) different response rates
(d) different respondents
(e) different order of questions
(f) different questions
(g) different length of the interview

Each of these points will be illustrated in turn with some examples, mainly based on experiences in two large surveys which were carried out in 1983 and 1984. The first survey will be characterised as the political knowledge study, the second as the buying-behaviour study. In Section 3.3 a short description of these projects will be given.

3.3 DATA-BASES

In 1986 the Dutch Government gave the vote to foreign residents in The Netherlands in order to give them the possibility of influencing their own situation on a local level. To evoke a maximum participation the Department of Internal Affairs started a campaign levelled at the different ethnic groups living in our country. This campaign was based on and evaluated by means of social research. Our institute has been invited to carry out a longitudinal research programme limited to the most important ethnic minorities, like Turks and Moroccans. In 1983 the first phase of this project was completed (Veldkamp/ Marktonderzoek/VNG, 'Minderheden meer toekomst', 1983). A comparable study was done in Sweden (Hammar, 1977). Furthermore the publications of the British Commission for Racial Equality were very helpful (see, for example, Anwar, 1981). In Table 3.1 more details about the study are presented.

In 1984 we carried out a large-scale survey for the Ministry of Economic Affairs, the aim of which is to gain insight into the buying behaviour and selection of shops of these ethnic minorities.

In order to be able to make an adequate comparison it was necessary to have an homogeneous supply structure. This was the reason for limiting the research to a few districts in the four largest cities in The Netherlands. For more details we once again refer to Table 3.1.

Now that the data-bases have been introduced the different aspects of data-collection can be considered.

3.4 ASPECTS OF DATA-COLLECTION: differences between ethnic minorities and the Dutch

3.4.1 Different Interviewers

Surveying ethnic minorities means building up a new interviewer corps. The well-trained Dutch interviewers normally employed for this purpose cannot operate in the field, mainly because of language problems. The situation in The Netherlands differs for example from the UK and USA because many ethnic minorities do not master the

Table 3.1 More details concerning the data-bases

	Political knowledge and participation study	
		n =
respondents:	Moroccans	70
	Turks	85
	Italians	70
	Spaniards	85
	Portuguese	20
		330
carried out in:	Amsterdam, Rotterdam, Eindhoven, Hengelo, Bussum, Emmen (variation according to region and urbanisation)	
sample:	Moroccans, Turks: head of household	18+
	Italians, Spaniards, Portuguese: random	18+
date:	March–May 1983	

	Buying behaviour study	
		n =
respondents:	Moroccans	222
	Turks	266
	(people born in) Surinam*	241
	Dutch	206
		935
carried out in:	Amsterdam, Rotterdam, Utrecht, Den Haag (four largest cities), old nineteenth-century districts in the centre	
sample:	Moroccans, Turks: head of household 18+ (together with partner)	
	(people born in) Surinam, Dutch: person primarily responsible for the household duties such as shopping, 18+	
date:	April–June 1984	

*In this paper no results of this group will be presented (see for a justification, Section 3.1).

language of the country they live in. Knowledge of the Dutch language varies greatly among the different groups. To give one example, in Table 3.2 we present the results of the questions 'Do you ever listen to the newsreports on the Dutch radio?' – 'Do you understand these reports well, a little, hardly at all?'

Table 3.2 Illustration of understanding the Dutch language

	Mor.	Turks	Ital.	Span.*
% that listens to and understands Dutch news reports on the radio	20	13	56	45

* Estimated Dutch figure: 60–80 per cent.

Comparable questions about reading Dutch newspapers, language barriers in shops and so on show the same results: Italians and Spaniards are able to understand the Dutch language much better than do Turks and Moroccans. One of the reasons for this is that Italians and Spaniards are more integrated into Dutch society: for example, about 50 per cent of the Italians has a Dutch partner, and only 2 per cent of the Turks. But all of these groups have at different levels, problems with speaking and understanding Dutch, and there is no significant relationship between the number of years members of the first generation have spent in The Netherlands and matters such as level of education, the ability to communicate in the Dutch language, the ability to understand programmes on Dutch television or radio and the ability to read Dutch newspapers (see Wentholt, 1982, p. 8).

So as a result of language problems we need to employ other interviewers, who use for the sake of uniformity fully a prior translated questionnaires. Working with a translated questionnaire requires a very careful translation process. Interpreters should realise that they participate in social science research, which implies simple, easy understandable formulations. The best interpreter for a more formal text is not necessarily the best for a questionnaire.

One of the first questions to answer is, what is preferable: to enlist Dutch interviewers who speak the specific foreign language, or to employ fellow countrymen to carry out the interviews? A reason for not enlisting Dutch interviewers is to avoid the friendliness-bias. Although we have no empirical results concerning this point, discussions with experts have revealed that ethnic minorities are more honest (and critical) about their situation in the presence of non-Dutch interviewers. Another important fact as regards this point is: the more integrated an ethnic minority is, the easier it is to approach specific persons within the group with Dutch interviewers who speak the foreign language. For some groups like Moroccans and Turks male interviewers should be employed.

Our experiences are very similar to multi-cultural research in other countries. Guthrie and Guthrie (1984) conclude about the Australian situation that it is necessary to use interpreters who engage in social and cultural backgrounds. They state that social research undertaken by persons with a totally different social, cultural and work background results in questions not fully understood by the persons studied, and answers that are often given to please the interviewer.

3.4.2 Different Days for Interviewing

If somebody enters the fieldwork staff of a market research agency one of the first lessons is: do not let interviewers carry out interviews on Sundays and only in exceptional cases on Saturdays. In Table 3.3 the preference of 'average' Dutch interviewers for interviewing on specific days is shown. The best days for interviews are Monday and Tuesday, only 5 per cent mentions the weekend.

Table 3.3   Preference for certain days for interviewing of 'average' Dutch interviewers

	most-preferred day for interviewing (100% = 1630)*
	%
Monday	35
Tuesday	44
Wednesday	8
Thursday	6
Friday	2
Saturday	5
Sunday	0

* 1630 interviewers from seven research agencies were questioned in 1983 about their fieldwork-behaviour.

This 'iron law of interviewing' does not automatically apply to all ethnic minorities, as is shown in Table 3.4

Table 3.4 Days for interviewing Moroccans and Turks (political knowledge study)

	Mor. (100%=70)	Turks (100%=85)
	%	%
Monday	17	11
Tuesday	11	14
Wednesday	14	15
Thursday	9	21
Friday	9	12
Saturday	11 } 40	7 } 27
Sunday	29	20

30 to 40 per cent of the interviews are held at the weekend. If we take a Dutch survey like the National Readership Survey no interviews are held on Sunday and only 8 per cent on Saturday. So it can be concluded that there is a large difference between the Dutch and ethnic minorities as regards the days preferred for interviewing. The weekend is excellent for interviewing ethnic minorities.

3.4.3 Different Response Rates

A careful introduction, an approach on a suitable day and at a suitable time, and the employment of well-trained interviewers are all requirements to attain response rates which are much better than in the Dutch interview situation. In the introduction phase one should take care to stress the rules for privacy. Respondents must be assured of the anonymity of the data if honest answers are to be expected; you have to stress the fact that their identity will not be disclosed and make clear that the government of their native country is not in any way involved in the survey. In Table 3.5 response rates which were attained are shown.

In the buying-behaviour study the response rate within the Turkish group was nearly double the Dutch rate (83 per cent v. 44 per cent). One should keep in mind that it was the same questionnaire, the same period and the same districts! A more integrated group like the Italians exhibits response-figures comparable with Dutch ones. A further striking aspect is that the most frequent reason for non-cooperation of Moroccan and Turkish groups is that they were not at

Table 3.5 Response rates ethnic minorities compared to Dutch ones

Response rates, political knowledge study (six cities spread over the country)

	Mor.	Turks	Ital.	Span.	Dutch (estimated)
% response	72	76	64	75	60

Response rates, study on buying behaviour (old districts, four largest cities)

	Mor.	Turks	Dutch
% response:	66	83	44

Table 3.6 Reasons for non-response (buying-behaviour study)

	Mor. %	Turks %	Dutch %
Reasons for non-response:			
– ill	2	1	4
– not at home (3x)	16	8	19
– refusal	13	7	32
– other reasons	3	1	1
Total non-response	34	17	56
Response	66	83	44

home on three different occasions. The Dutch score higher in all categories for non-cooperation: they are ill more often, they are out more often and have a higher rate of refusal. But the most frequent reason for non-cooperation seems to be a plain refusal (Table 3.6).

3.4.4 Different Respondents

Taking the Turkish and Moroccan cultural tradition into account, the best entrance is to approach the head of the household. The introductory letter should be addressed to him and the interviewer should approach him. At the moment this is the only way to get insight into the knowledge, attitudes and feelings of these groups. Of course where generalisation is concerned this is a very unsatisfactory procedure. In order to obtain information about the partner and children of the respondent other methods are required. Some solutions are briefly sketched in points (1) to (3):

(1) Group discussions with women and young people. Wentholt (1982) used this method: 'This form of discussion, in addition to the individual approach, was deemed necessary, as the latter has considerable limitations, certainly in the case of Mediterranean cultures.' (p. 6)
   In many cases he used existing groups which operate independently of the head of the household, for example sewing-circles, school-classes, general courses and so on.
(2) At the end of the interview one can ask the head of the household if it is possible to pose some questions to other members of the family. Interviewers have to estimate their chances of success. If, for example, the housewife was not allowed to be present during the interview, the chances of approaching other members of the family are very slight.
(3) At the end of the interview with the head of the household one can ask him to answer some questions on the behaviour of other members of the family ('Which radio programmes does your wife listen to?', 'If your wife had the right to vote, do you think she would vote?', 'Do you know anything about the reading habits of your children?').

Of course this is the present picture. The general expectation is that in the next ten years there will be some cultural adaptation, which will make it easier to gain access to interviewing women and young people (second-generation) for individual interviews.
   Related to this problem is the treatment of these different groups. Should one treat these different groups as a part of the Dutch population or as different populations? If a single sample may contain many language and cultural groups, to what population are we able to generalise? My suggestion is to treat the ethnic groups as different populations. For example, regression analysis on some variables should be applied for each group separately. Generalisations should be made per subgroup.

3.4.5 Different Order of Questions

Concerning the order of the questions, a social researcher has to forget some classical lessons. Let me take as an example the income question. The traditional procedure in survey-research is to end the questionnaire with the income question. The assumption is that it is a delicate and private question which can disturb and influence the interview. To minimise this effect the question is kept until the end of the interview.

In the pilot study of the buying-behaviour research the income question was in the traditional place at the end of the interview. In the session during which the results of the pilot were discussed the Turkish and Moroccan interviewers remarked that they were astonished about this stupidity. They said: 'If you start with the income question people will reply more honestly to questions concerning expenditure: the respondent is aware that the interviewer knows the income situation and therefore will not give a misrepresentation of his buying behaviour.' They said that the problem of privacy is not in itself a problem. So we changed the place of this question in the questionnaire.

The main research confirmed this decision: there was hardly any non-response to the income question and earnings and expenditure were more compatible than in the pilot study.

3.4.6 Different Questions

The advice is to use simple and short questions. A rule which comes from practical experience is: Design a questionnaire which you would use in a Dutch interview situation for an interview by telephone and adapt the resulting questionnaire to a face-to-face situation. It is impossible to use cards or other visual aids which are normally used in an interview situation. Especially among Moroccans there is a high degree of illiteracy (25 per cent of the head of households) which prohibits the use of any self-completion procedure. So traditional European semantic differentials or other rating scales cannot be used. The maximum is a three-point verbal scale. (See, for a discussion about illiteracy and scales, Morris and van der Reis, 1980.) For reasons of comparability the selected procedures should be suitable for use among literates and illiterates, which implies a uniform procedure adapted to the most illiterate group.

3.4.7 Different Length of Interview

No rules can be found in literature for multiplication of the length of an average Western face-to-face interview to the length of a questionnaire for ethnic minorities. Our projects give some insight, as is shown in Table 3.7.

If the questionnaire were to be used for interviewing Moroccans it

Table 3.7 Mean interview time of ethnic minorities compared to the Dutch

Mean interview time – political knowledge study

	Mor.	Turks	Ital.	Span.	Dutch (estimated)
minutes:	88	73	65	62	45
% interviews which took > 90 minutes	31%	17%	10%	2%	

Mean interview time – buying-behaviour study

	Mor.	Turks	Dutch (real time)
minutes:	96	78	44
% interviews which took > 90 minutes	59%	25%	1%

would take about twice as long, and if used for interviewing Turks about 1.6 to 1.8 times as long. In the case of the more integrated minorities, about 40 per cent more time will be required.

Among the Moroccans there is a large portion of very long interviews: 59 per cent took more than 90 minutes, and 5 per cent more than 150 minutes. One of the factors causing this length is that you need a little extra time for the opening social rituals and generally for 'coming to the point'. We have also seen from experience that the 'thankyous and good-byes' take more time than in the usual Dutch survey.

3.5 CONCLUSION

Our basic question was: Is it possible to use survey-techniques in data-collection among ethnic minorities living in an industrialized West European country?

A poor ability to speak and understand the Dutch language, a low educational level and different cultural traditions (especially the Islamitic groups) prohibit the straight transplantation of traditional survey techniques. Data-collection by ethnic minorities means abandon a lot of primary methodological lessons. We have shown that interviewing ethnic minorities compared to the Dutch implies:

- building up a new interviewer corps
- choosing different days for interviewing
- higher response rates, provided that the necessary adaptations are made
- limiting the primary approach to the heads of households
- changing the usual order of questions
- using simple questions without the traditional cards or visual aids
- a larger interview time.

Our main conclusion is that survey techniques can only be used, if the necessary provisions are made. Of course there are considerable limitations (length, complexity, respondents) which imply that other techniques like group discussions are deemed necessary in addition to the individual approach in order to round off survey results.

REFERENCES

ANWAR, M., *Votes and Policies: Ethnic Minorities and the General Election 1979* (London: Commission for Racial Equality, Feb. 1981).
BERG-ELDERING, L. van den, *Marokkaanse Gezinnen in Nederland* (Alphen a/d Rijn: Samson, 1978).
ENTZINGER, H. B., *Het Minderhedenbeleid* (Meppel: Boom, 1984).
GUTHRIE, R. V. and GUTHRIE, P. M., 'The Delta Factor: Verification of Participant Observation and Survey Research in Multi-cultural Societies'. Paper given at First International Conference on Methodological Research (Amsterdam: Oct. 1984).
HAMMAR, T., *The First Immigrant Election* (Stockholm: Department of Political Science, 1977).
HEIJKE, J. A. M., 'Sociaal-economische Aspecten van Gastarbeid' (Erasmus Universiteit, Rotterdam, diss., 1979).
MORRIS, N. and REIS, A. P. van der, 'The Transferability of Rating Scale Techniques to an African Population', *Proceedings 33rd ESOMAR Congress, Monte Carlo* (1980) 417–36.
SHADID, W., 'Moroccan Workers in the Netherlands', (Leiden, diss., 1979).
WENTHOLT, H., *Mass Media and Migrant Workers in The Netherlands* (NOS-publication, Feb. 1982).

Part II
Data Collection by Content Analysis

4 A Coding Procedure for Empirical Research of Political Decision-making

I. N. Gallhofer and W. E. Saris

4.1 INTRODUCTION

Large numbers of documents are available in which decision-makers explain their choices. Examples of such documents include minutes of meetings, speeches in the parliament, telegrams of embassies, correspondence between officials, diaries, etc.

The speech of a Dutch Minister of Foreign Affairs is presented below, relating to a decision during a session of the Council of Ministers in October 1914, at the beginning of the First World War. The Dutch government had to choose whether or not to abandon its policy of neutrality in the face of the impending occupation of Antwerp by the Germans.[1]

> The Minister of Foreign Affairs agrees with the Chairman and dissuades firmly to ask the question neither in the way the Ministers of Navy and War proposed nor in the amended version of the Minister of Agriculture.[2]
> Our own interests have not been threatened yet; we only can guess, but do not know, how the war will end. This is therefore not the right moment to take sides with one or another of the belligerent parties, although our interests are closer to the British, especially with respect to our colonies.
> In case that we ask the question it looks like a call to stop or a taking sides. It is inconceivable that Germany will answer categorically at this stage of the war that it will not keep Antwerp or that it will only occupy it temporarily. Although it is unlikely that Germany will wish to incorporate Belgium, it will either answer evasively, or politely give us to understand that Germany's intentions are no concern of us.
> Shall we lay this statement on the table or shall we insist on a clear answer?
> The latter could cause trouble, perhaps even war, and certainly would shake German confidence in our neutrality, which is of paramount importance.
> To change our official position of neutrality now would not be in our best interests, especially since we declared it so loudly and since Germany

explicitly said that it would respect our position. The Minister of War's plan to grant the guarantors of Belgium's neutrality access to our neutral territory in order to force back the German army is even less justifiable. Although it is unlikely that the British would even consider entering the Western Scheldt to relieve Antwerp, any British warship that tried would be sent to the bottom by the German artillery.

Actually it is unclear what we would gain at the final peace settlement by pressing the Germans now. If we have to enter the war and Germany wins the war, we have to pay the piper. If the British are victorious then we can not expect much reward, at most an equivalent piece of land from Germany in exchange for Dutch Flanders and the Scheldt, which will be given as compensation to Belgium.

If the war ends no clear winner, then we are left with a partially destroyed country and a shaken confidence on the part of our Eastern neighbour on whom we depend so much economically. The occupation of Antwerp is in no case worth any of these things.

That we would get in trouble with the British if we do not speak at all is not to be expected.

There are several problems in analysing such texts in order to determine the speaker's argument.

First of all there is the problem of choosing the concepts one should use. Second, the problem arises whether different readers (coders) of a document using the same concepts obtain the same results (coder reliability or agreement). In a long-term study of such texts the authors of this chapter have tackled these problems (Saris and Gallhofer, 1975; Gallhofer, 1978; Gallhofer and Saris, 1979c).

For the choice of concepts a vast literature of normative decision-making is available to borrow ideas from (e.g. Fishburn, 1964; Keeney and Raiffa, 1976). As in the normative studies, the structure of the decision situation as formulated by a decision-maker can be represented by a decision tree. We also have made use of this representation. Given the decision trees we have tried to discover the rules which can predict the choices of the government officials. In our studies the decision rule turned out to be surprisingly simple and different from the rules put forward in the normative studies (Gallhofer and Saris, 1979a, b). The major problem in this approach to political decision-making at the moment is intercoder agreement.

We therefore undertook a separate study in order to investigate how the agreement between the coders could be improved.

We focused on three relevant factors:

(1) the use of teams of two coders instead of individual coders;
(2) the use of more extensive instructions than those used in the past;
(3) the selection of proficient coders.

This chapter describes how the different factors influenced the results, and also presents what we consider to be the most practical and successful procedure.

In the following the construction of decision trees and the task of the coders will be introduced.

4.2 THE CONSTRUCTION OF DECISION TREES

Figure 4.1 gives an example of a scheme of a decision tree. It consists of a chronological sequence of the actions available to the decision-maker, the possible actions of the other party(-ies), and the possible outcomes which may occur. The values of the possible outcomes as well as the probabilities of the actions of the other party(-ies) and the outcomes are also indicated in Figure 4.1. Such a pattern of actions, and reactions is generally called a 'strategy'.

Figure 4.1 General scheme of a decision tree

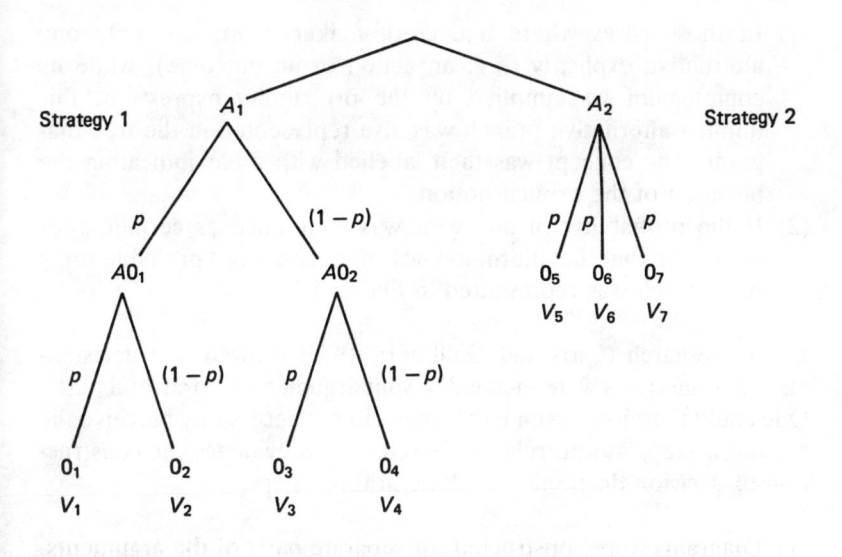

Where A_i = action i of the decision-maker; $i = 1, 2$
AO_j = action j of the other party(-ies); $j = 1, 2$
O_k = outcome k; $k = 1, \ldots, 7$
V_k = value of outcome k
p = probability of AO_j or O_i

Figure 4.1 illustrates a decision-maker disposing of two strategies. If he uses A_1 then he must account for two possible reactions of the other party(-ies), AO_1 or AO_2, which can lead either to 0_1, 0_2, 0_3 or 0_4. Using A_2, 0_5, 0_6, or 0_7 can occur. Based on the values assigned to the several outcomes, the probabilities of occurrence of the outcomes and the actions of the party(-ies), he can decide which action should be adopted.

Obviously this scheme represents a trivial argument. The objective of the study, therefore, was to determine whether it is possible to represent complex decisions with high reliability using tree diagrams (Figures 4.1–4.3).

4.3 THE CODING INSTRUCTIONS

The coders were instructed to represent the structure of the decision situation in a tree, based on the concepts they had encountered in a document. Two additional rules for the construction of trees were given:

(1) In those cases where a decision-maker mentioned only one alternative explicitly (e.g. an action or an outcome), while its complement was implied by the probability expression, this implicit alternative branch was also represented in the tree diagram. The concept was then labelled with a bar indicating the negation of the explicit notion.
(2) If the probability of an event was mentioned as certain, thus indicating that the alternative was not considered probable, only one branch was represented in Figure 4.1.

Earlier research (Saris and Gallhofer, 1975) showed that decision-makers sometimes were inclined to split arguments into several parts. One could therefore assume that they did not necessarily perceive the reasoning steps as interrelated. Based on this evidence the construction of decision diagrams was done in three steps:

(1) Diagrams were constructed for separate parts of the arguments.
(2) Trees of interrelated arguments were combined into larger diagrams.
(3) Finally, an attempt was made to combine the diagrams from steps 1 and 2 into a larger overview tree.

The coding reliabilities of steps 1 and 2 were very satisfactory. The median agreement score both for individuals and groups was 1.0 (Gallhofer and Saris, 1979c). The agreement scores of step 3, which produced the data for the analysis, were less satisfactory, however: the mean agreement scores for individuals were 0.41.

The problems the coders encountered with this task were mainly the following:

- Which subtrees (parts of the argument) have to be linked together?
- Where to link them in the overview structure?

Most coders tried to link too many subtrees together without taking into account the general structure of the discourse. Sometimes they even ignored verbal connectors indicating linkages for the overview structure. Where verbal connectors were missing, some coders did not make sufficient use of the extra-linguistic information they were provided with in order to decide whether or not a certain subtree should be brought into the overview diagram (examples of overview diagrams are presented in Figure 4.2). To increase coder agreement we developed a new coding instruction,[3] taking into account as many of the problems mentioned above as possible. Since the coders seemed to pay little attention to the underlying structure of a document we first made them focus on the structure. After reading the document carefully they had to give a brief summary of each paragraph, indicating whether it contained an elaboration of a strategy or not. This could be either (a) an entire strategy; (b) the beginning of a strategy; (c) the end of a strategy as continuation of an earlier paragraph; (d) a specification of a strategy mentioned earlier; (e) a summary of one or more strategies mentioned previously in the document. This last possibility frequently occurs at the end of documents and indicates the overview structure; that is, the totality of strategies a decision-maker considered relevant.

Starting the coding activity with this task we hoped that coders would become more aware of the essential parts of the arguments and could more easily discern which parts functioned as rhetorical repetitions to increase the persuasive element. The coders then analysed the paragraphs that contained elaborations of strategies. The instructions were the same as those mentioned at the beginning of this section. The entire procedure was also illustrated with an example. Before starting the actual coding the judges had to work through this example, and the steps that they found problematic were discussed during training sessions.

4.4 A MEASURE OF AGREEMENT BETWEEN CODERS[4]

Decision diagrams (see, e.g., Figure 4.2) of different coders relating to arguments in a specific text may differ with respect to:

(1) *The supposed chronological sequence.* Coders select the same number of branches with identical concepts but then differ in the arrangement of these branches. In this case the chronological sequence of events is not explicitly indicated in the documents and the coders make their own inferences about it.
(2) *The selection of concepts.* This may be due to different ways of categorising the same textual units, or different ways of decomposing portions of the text (see Gallhofer, 1978).

Figure 4.2 Representation of two decision diagrams from different coders and computation of the agreement measure

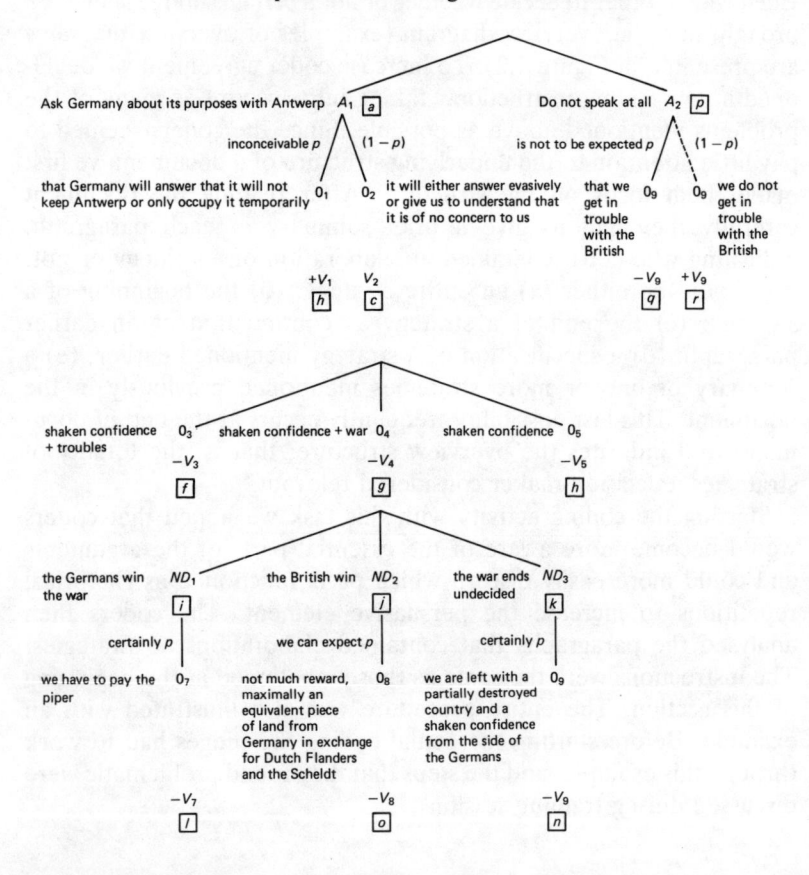

Ask Germany about its purposes with Antwerp A_1 $\boxed{a}$			Do not speak at all A_2 $\boxed{p}$	
inconceivable p	$(1-p)$		is not to be expected p	$(1-p)$
that Germany will answer that it will not keep Antwerp or only occupy it temporarily O_1	O_2 it will either answer evasively or give us to understand that it is of no concern to us		that we O_9 get in trouble with the British	O_9 we do not get in trouble with the British
$+V_1$ $\boxed{h}$	V_2 $\boxed{c}$		$-V_9$ $\boxed{q}$	$+V_9$ $\boxed{r}$

shaken confidence + troubles O_3	shaken confidence + war O_4	shaken confidence O_5
$-V_3$ $\boxed{f}$	$-V_4$ $\boxed{g}$	$-V_5$ $\boxed{h}$

the Germans win the war ND_1 $\boxed{i}$	the British win ND_2 $\boxed{j}$	the war ends undecided ND_3 $\boxed{k}$
certainly p	we can expect p	certainly p
we have to pay the piper O_7	not much reward, maximally an equivalent piece of land from Germany in exchange for Dutch Flanders and the Scheldt O_8	we are left with a partially destroyed country and a shaken confidence from the side of the Germans O_9
$-V_7$ $\boxed{l}$	$-V_8$ $\boxed{o}$	$-V_9$ $\boxed{n}$

I. N. Gallhofer and W. E. Saris 57

(3) *The number of branches.* In this case one coder omits branches considering them as not essential to the argument while the other judges them as essential. It may also be due to a different categorisation so that a greater or lesser number of branches are available to the coder.
(4) *Combinations of 1, 2 and 3.*

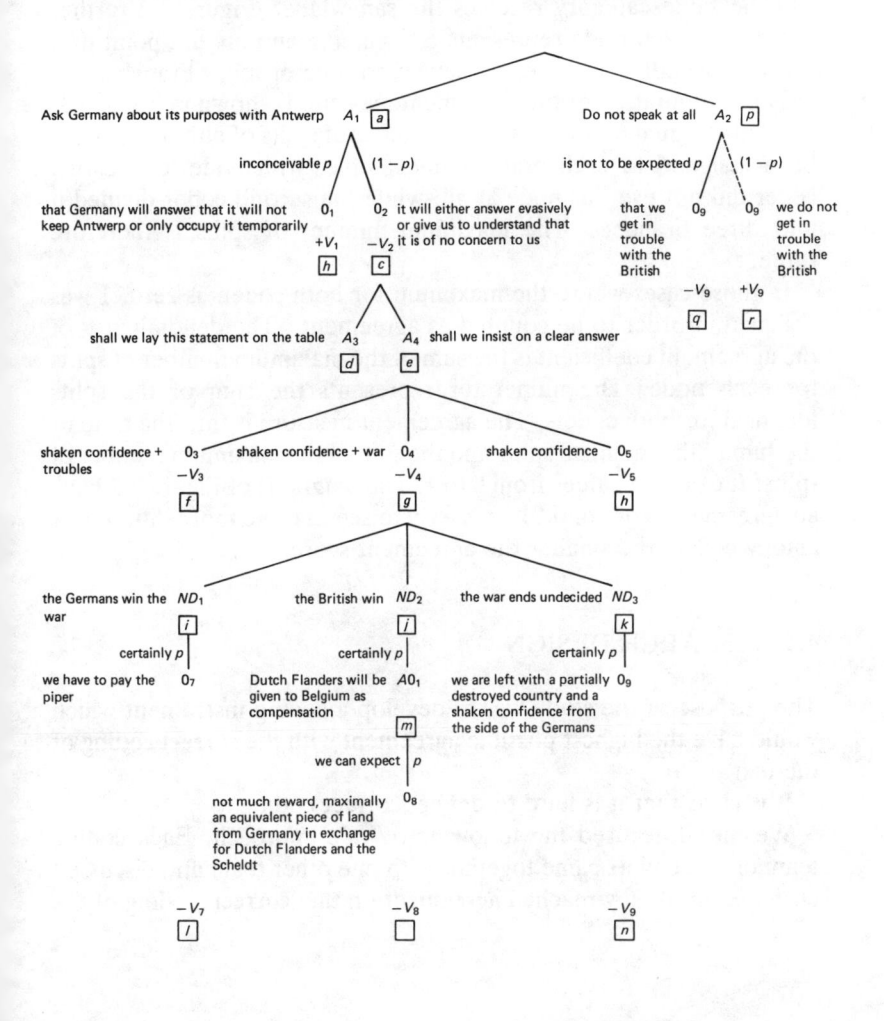

In the following the computation of the agreement measure, which takes the above-mentioned differences into account, is illustrated by an example. Figure 4.2 displays two decision diagrams from two different coders based on the text quoted above. The two representations of the argument are quite similar, except that coder 2 used three more branches than coder 1. Coder 2 inserted after the statement of having received an evasive answer or a polite denial (0_2) two actions the Minister considered (A_3, A_4). Under the condition that the British would win the war (ND_2), he made use of the statement that Dutch Flanders and the Scheldt would be given as compensation to Belgium ($A0_1$). Since the original coding data of coder 1 showed that he did categorise A_3, A_4, he probably did not consider them as essential to the argument, and $A0_1$ was not at all categorised in his coding. The potential sources of differences mentioned under (3) earlier apply to these coding examples.

In order to compute the agreement measure each node at the beginning and the end of a branch provided with the same text unit and the same category receives the same label. Figure 4.2 further shows that each node represents a beginning and an end-point of a branch. A node can therefore have zero, one or more branches.

The computation of the agreement measure is shown in Table 4.1. A number equal to the maximum number of splits of either coder has been assigned to each node. For example, with node 'e' the first coder did not use this node at all, while the second coder divided it into three branches. The maximum number of splits is therefore three.

In those cases where the maximum for both coders is zero, 1 was assigned in order to be counted as agreement.[5] The denominator of the agreement coefficient is the sum of the maximum number of splits for each node. The numerator represents the sum of the splits identical for both coders. The agreement measure is thus the ratio of the sum of the identical splits and the sum of the maximum number of splits. It can take values from 0 to 1. The diagrams of Figure 4.2 have an agreement score of 0.71. It is easy to see that the more differences among coders the smaller the agreement score.

4.5 RESEARCH DESIGN

The purpose of the study was to develop a coding instrument which would have the highest possible agreement with the correct coding of the text.

It is clear that it is hard to define 'correct coding'.

We therefore used the following *ad hoc* approach. Each coding team of two coders came together with one other team and discussed each text until they reached agreement on the 'correct' coding of the

Table 4.1 Computation of the agreement measure relating to the decision trees of Figure 4.2

Labels	Number of identical splits	Maximum number of splits
a	2	2
b	1	1
c	0	2
d	0	0
e	0	3
f	1	1
g	3	3
h	1	1
i	1	1
j	0	1
k	1	1
l	1	1
m	0	1
n	1	1
o	1	1
p	2	2
q	1	1
r	1	1
Total	17	24

Agreement coefficient = $\dfrac{\text{number of identical splits}}{\text{maximal number of splits}} = \dfrac{17}{24}$

text. Thus these 'correct' codings are based on the joint efforts of four coders. That the correctness of the results is not perfect can be seen in Table 4.2 where the measure of agreement is shown for four texts obtained between two groups of four coders that independently defined their 'correct' coding for each text. Table 4.2 clearly shows that the agreement for the different texts varies considerably. The explanation for this fact might be the variation in the ambiguity of different texts.

It should be clear that we cannot expect the coders or teams of coders to reach higher agreement scores with these 'correct' codings than the scores mentioned in this table. So the scores in Table 4.2 represent the upper bound of the agreement obtainable for these four texts, given our approach. In order to study the effect of the instruction and the team-coding on the agreement between the obtained coding and the 'correct' coding, these two factors have been varied. We thought that it was not possible, because of memory effects, to

Table 4.2 Agreement of coding results of two teams of coders

Text	Coefficient of agreement
1	0.80
2	0.77
3	0.93
4	0.62

ask the same coders to analyse the same text twice using different coding instructions. We therefore used two new texts for the test of the new coding instruction. The design is given in Table 4.3.

Under condition 1 the simple instruction was used, and coders 1, 2, 3 and 4 coded the texts 1 and 2 individually. The averaged agreement of the four coders over the two texts with the two possible 'correct' codings of the two teams of four coders is denoted by $\bar{y}_1$. Condition 2 differs on only one point from condition 1, namely, that coders 1 and 2 on the one hand, and coders 3 and 4 on the other, formed a coding team, and that each of the two teams produced its own coding. The mean agreement under this condition is represented by $\bar{y}_2$. Condition 3 also differs on only one point from condition 1 which is the fact that not texts 1 and 2 but the texts 3 and 4 are coded. Condition 4 differs in exactly the same way from condition 2. Condition 5 also differs on only one point from condition 1, namely, that under this condition the coding is not done by coders 1, 2, 3 and 4, but by coders 5, 6, 7 and 8. And in the same way condition 6 differs from condition 2. Finally, conditions 7 and 8 differ in two points from conditions 3 and 4. First of all, other coders have been used and, second, a more elaborate instruction is used.

Condition 1 can be seen as the control situation and the agreement in this situation is denoted by β_0. The effect of team coding compared to individual coding is denoted by β_1. The effect of instruction is denoted by β_2, the effect of the difference in texts by β_3, and the effect of the difference in sets of coders by β_4. Using this notation the means under the different conditions can be described as functions of these parameters as presented in Table 4.3. In this formulation interaction terms are ignored, which means that the fit will not be perfect but good enough for our purposes.

It can be checked by comparison of the means that all parameters can be estimated. In this study the model has been re-formulated in a regression model with dummy variables (Kerlinger and Pedhazur,

Table 4.3 Research design and model part one

Instruction	Simple		Elaborate	
Set of Coders	1, 2, 3, 4		5, 6, 7, 8	
Set of Texts	1, 2	3, 4	1, 2	3, 4,
Individual coding	condition 1 $\bar{y}_1 = \beta_0$	condition 3 $\bar{y}_3 = \beta_0 + \beta_3$	condition 5 $\bar{y}_5 = \beta_0 + \beta_4$	condition 7 $\bar{y}_7 = \beta_0 + \beta_2 + \beta_3 + \beta_4$
Team Coding	condition 2 $\bar{y}_2 = \beta_0 + \beta_1$	condition 4 $\bar{y}_4 = \beta_0 + \beta_3 + \beta_1$	condition 6 $\bar{y}_6 = \beta_0 + \beta_4 + \beta_1$	condition 8 $\bar{y}_8 = \beta_0 + \beta_1 + \beta_2 + \beta_3 + \beta_4$

1973) and the parameters have been estimated by ordinary least squares. It was expected that only the effect of the instruction (β_2) and of the team coding versus individual coding (β_1) would be significantly different from zero. Since we also expected differences between individual coders, between different teams and between different texts within each condition, we shall estimate these differences in the same way after correction of the agreement scores for the effects mentioned here.[6] In the first analysis these factors are cancelled out by use of means over individuals and texts.

Table 4.4 'Estimates of the effects outlined in Table 4.3

Description	Coefficient	Estimated value	t-value
Agreement in the control condition 1	β_0	0.338	6.72
The effect of team coding	β_1	0.196	3.90
The effect of the new instruction	β_2	0.194	2.05
Coder set effect	β_3	0.019	0.29
Text set effect	β_4	0.070	1.05

4.6 THE EFFECTS OF THE INSTRUCTION AND THE TEAM CODING

In Table 4.4 the estimates of the different effects are given together with the *t*-values. This table indicates that, as expected, only the effect of the instruction and the team coding versus individual coding were significantly different from zero. Since the coder set factor, the text set factor, and the instruction factor are correlated by design, the effect of the instruction factor changes slightly by fixing the other two effects at zero, being not different from zero. By doing so the instruction effect was 0.254. Thus the new instruction increases the agreement of codings with the correct codings on the average by 0.254. The estimate of β_3 also changes a bit because different data were combined in the first condition. The new estimate was 0.368. The effect of the team versus individual coding remained the same: 0.196. Thus with team coding the average agreement was 0.196 higher than it was for individual coding. The consequences of this analysis with the coder set effect and the text set effect fixed at zero are presented in Table 4.5. This table clearly indicates that team

Table 4.5 Observed and predicted agreement scores under four conditions

Instruction	Simple	Elaborate
Individual coding	$\bar{y}_1 = 0.369$ $\hat{y}_1 = \beta_0$ $= 0.368$	$\bar{y}_3 = 0.616$ $\hat{y}_3 = \beta_0 + \beta_2$ $= 0.622$
Team coding	$\bar{y}_2 = 0.559$ $\hat{y}_2 = \beta_0 + \beta_1$ $= 0.564$	$\bar{y}_4 = 0.829$ $\hat{y}_4 = \beta_0 + \beta_1 + \beta_2$ $= 0.818$

where $\bar{y}_i$ = the observed agreement in the ith condition and $\hat{y}_i$ = the predicted agreement in the ith condition

coding combined with an elaborate instruction is superior to the other approaches.

It is unlikely that the procedure can be improved since the average agreement between the two 'correct' codings according to Table 4.2 is 0.775, which seems to be the upper bound of the agreement for these four texts. As we have already obtained (by chance) a slightly higher agreement with the elaborate instruction and team coding further improvement does not seem to be possible.

4.7 DIFFERENCE BETWEEN CODERS OR CODERS TEAMS AND BETWEEN TEXTS

On the average the elaborate instruction and team coding seem to be the best. The question remains however, whether which coders are chosen and how they have been combined in a team makes a difference. To study this point we corrected the agreement scores obtained by the coders or teams for each text by subtracting the expected average agreement for the specific condition in which the coding took place.[7] The residual agreement scores so obtained can vary for three reasons. First, because of differences between coders and teams of coders. Second, because of different levels of complexity of the texts and third, because of the fact that the agreement is computed with the 'correct' coding of the group of which the coder is himself a member or not.

We hoped that this last factor would not matter. This turned out to be correct; and therefore the last factor was ignored in the rest of the

Table 4.6 The coder, team and text specific effects on the agreement scores obtained from the residual scores after correction for instruction and team coding effects

Description	Estimated value	t-value
deviation of coder 1 on text 1 from the expected agreement	0.127	1.80
deviation in agreement from coder 1 for coder		
2	−0.011	−0.13
3	0.071	0.80
4	−0.295	−3.30
5	−0.097	−1.09
6	0.169	1.90
7	−0.173	−1.94
8	−0.264	−2.96
deviation in agreement from coder 1 for team		
1	−0.035	−0.39
2	−0.148	−1.66
3	−0.060	−0.68
4	−0.057	−0.63
deviation in agreement from text 1 for text		
2	−0.144	−2.80
3	0.075	1.46
4	−0.138	−2.67

analysis.[8] The sizes of the different-effect parameters are estimated in exactly the same way as in the last section. The results of the analysis are presented in Table 4.6.

Table 4.6 indicates that coders 4, 7 and 8 are significantly worse than the first coder, while the other coders are not significantly better or worse than this coder.[9] It is also remarkable that although individual differences exist, the teams of coders do not vary much. Only team 2 is somewhat worse than the other teams. The result indicates that the individual coders correct each other's errors so well in the team coding sessions that hardly any differences between the teams remain.

It should be said, however, that combining two bad coders and two very good coders has not been done. Team 2 had a moderately good and a bad coder while the best team had two moderately good coders.

With respect to differences in difficulty between the different texts the results in Table 4.6 indicate that text 2 and text 4 are more complex or ambiguous than the other two. This phenomenon was already mentioned when we interpreted the results of Table 4.2.

4.8 A CODING PROCEDURE AND THE SELECTION OF CODERS

Given the results presented in Section 4.6 the following procedure should be used for the coding of decision texts:

(1) One should use teams of two coders who first code the texts independently and then produce a joint coding. This approach is superior to individual coding as we have seen, especially with complex texts.
(2) One should use instructions which require the coders to concentrate first on the general structure of the argument given in the text before they study the text in detail. It has been shown that these more elaborate instructions lead to greater agreement than instructions that direct the coder to start immediately with the details.

With respect to the selection of the coders Section 4.7 has shown that there is no proof of an effect of the quality of the coders as the team coding corrects many of the mistakes made by the coders. Nevertheless, it seems reasonable to try to use superior coders. For this purpose we wanted to choose for selection purposes a text that was as unambiguous as possible so that all coders could do a good job if they took sufficient time and worked carefully. As can be seen in Tables 4.2 and 4.6, text 3 fulfils this requirement. We therefore chose text 3 as the selection text. In fact this is the text that was given as an example in Section 4.1. Even with this unambiguous text, however, the agreement scores of the coders varied considerably.[10] The best coders obtained agreement scores above 0.8 with this text. Moderately good coders obtained scores between 0.6 and 0.8 on text 3. Their scores were lower mainly because they worked less carefully than the first group of coders. A third group of coders obtained scores below 0.6. In this study there were two such coders. We had the impression that they could not think in decision terms although they did their best. Given this situation we decided that the coders should have scores above 0.8 on this text to become coders of new texts.

The consequences of these selection criteria in our recent studies have been that four coders out of the six who did the test had scores above 0.8 on text 3. These four coders coded 18 more new texts. For these 18 texts we can of course only report the agreement scores the two coders of each team obtained comparing the two individual codings. For 11 texts the agreement score was 1. For five texts it was between 0.8 and 1, and for two texts the agreement was between 0.6 and 0.8. If we take into account that team coding adds about 0.2 (see Table 4.4) to the agreement score, it can be expected that in 16 out of the 18 cases approximately perfect agreement has been obtained, whereas in two cases the agreement was somewhat less but probably also close to the upper limit of the agreement obtainable for these two texts given their ambiguity.

These results show that the selection was rather successful, and it is clear that such a selection procedure should be used if enough coders are available. We have no proof, however, that the results would have been less favourable if we had used the other two coders whom we did not select. Their scores on text 3 were between 0.6 and 0.8. Certainly it would have required more training time since the main difference between them and the other coders was the accuracy with which the work was done. But in general such mistakes due to lack of sufficient attention will be corrected by team coding.

4.9 CONCLUSIONS

The procedure for coding decision texts that we have proposed in Section 4.8 can be used with approximately optimal intersubjective agreement. The selection of the coders, although not proven to be necessary, also seems to be useful in practice. Given the quality of the measurement procedure as it now stands, we think that it opens the possibility for a systematic study of the arguments of decision-makers. The first few studies we did led to a different decision rule than the rules recommended in the normative decision literature (Gallhofer and Saris, 1979 a, b). Decision-makers were not maximising their benefits but trying to avoid risks. Many kinds of texts can be analysed with this procedure. It is not restricted to foreign-policy decision-making, but can be used for any kind of decision documents. It can probably also be used with open-ended questions that contain reasons why a respondent has made certain decisions like a decision for divorce or a choice of a certain school or job.

NOTES

1. The document is published in *RGP IV, Bescheiden betreffende de buitenlandse politiek van Nederland*, 1895–1919, p. 156.
2. The Ministers of Navy and War proposed keeping the Germans off balance by allowing England and France, the guarantors of Belgium's neutrality, access to Dutch territory if they requested it, while the Minister of Agriculture proposed asking Germany about its purposes with Antwerp.
3. Gallhofer, Saris and Melman, eds, 1986, Appendix 3.
4. R. J. M. Does and F. J. A. Overweel of the Mathematical Centre of Amsterdam developed the measure.
5. The constructors of the measure pointed out that, however arbitrary this choice was, it worked satisfactorily.
6. The whole analysis could have been done in one run, but in order to obtain the contrast we wanted we have chosen this two-steps approach.
7. The following scores have been used:

$$Y_{ijk} - \hat{Y}_{ij} = Y_{ijk} - (0.368 + 0.196\ C_i + 0.254\ I_j)$$

where Y_{ijk} is the agreement score obtained by the kth coder or team in the coding condition i (team or individual) and with the jth instruction.
8. This effect was equal to 0.047 and the t-value was equal to 1.29. We therefore have ignored this effect in the further analysis.
9. One should be careful with the interpretation of the t-values, as they depend on the contrast chosen, although the differences between the coders are not affected by the choice of the contrast.
10. We have computed the expected score for all coders on this text, given the estimates of the parameters. This procedure was necessary since the first four coders coded only according to the simple instruction.

REFERENCES

FISHBURN, P. C., *Decision and Value Theory* (New York: Wiley, 1964).
GALLHOFER, I. N., 'Coder's reliability in the study of decision-making concepts, replications in time and across topics', *Methoden en Data Nieuwsbrief van de Sociaal-Wetenschappelijke Sectie van de Vereniging voor Statistiek* (1978), **1**, 58–88.
—— and SARIS, W. E., 'The Decision of the Dutch Council of Ministers and the Military Commander in Chief relating to the Reduction of Armed Forces in Autumn 1916', *Acta Politica* (1979a), **1**, 95–105.

—— and SARIS, W. E., 'Strategy Choices of Foreign Policy Decisionmakers: The Netherlands 1914', *Journal of Conflict Resolution* (1979b), **23**, 425–445.
—— and SARIS, W. E., 'An Analysis of the Argumentation of Decisionmakers using Decision Trees', *Quality and Quantity* (1979c), **13**, 411–29.
GALLHOFER, I. N., SARIS, W. E. and MELMAN, M. (eds), *Different Text Analysis Procedures for the Study of Decision Making* (Amsterdam: Sociometric Research Foundation, 1986).
—— SARIS, W. E. and VALK, B. M. de, 'Een begrippenapparaat voor de beschrijvingen van redeneringen van politici', *Acta Politica* (1978) **3**, 371–82.
KEENEY, R. L. and RAIFFA, H., *Decisions with Multiple Objectives, Preferences and Value Trade Offs* (New York: Wiley, 1976).
KERLINGER, F. N. and PEDHAZUR, E. J., *Multiple Regression in Behavioral Research* (New York: Holt, Rinehart & Winston, 1973).
NAMENWIRTH, Z. J. and KLEIJNNIJENHUIS, J., 'Contrasting Themes among Different Types of Phrases in a Dutch Ministerial Debate concerning the German Attack on Antwerp', *Methoden en Data Nieuwsbrief,* van de Sociaal-Wetenschappelijke Sectie van de Verenigning voor Statistiek (1978), **1**, 89–107.
NAMENWIRTH, Z. J., SARIS, W. E., GALLHOFER, I. N. and KLEIJNNIJENHUIS, J., 'In Search of Semantic Characteristics for Machine Coding', *Methoden en Data Nieuwsbrief*, van de Sociaal-Wetenschappelijke Sectie van de Vereniging voor Statistiek (1978), **1**, 75–88.
RGP IV, *Bescheiden betreffende de buitenlandse politiek van Nederland, 1895–1919* (The Hague:Nijhoff, 1974).
SARIS, W. E. and GALLHOFER, I. N., L'application d'un modèle de décision à des données historiques *Revue Française de Science Politique* (1975), **XXV**, 473–501.

5 Ideology in International Propaganda: A Clustering Approach for Content Analysis Data

S. Splichal and A. Ferligoj

5.1 INTRODUCTION

International propaganda clearly shows a tendency of rapid growth since its first institutionalisation in the Sacra Congregatio de Propaganda Fide of Pope Gregory XV in the seventeenth century. In different historical periods and social systems (and likewise in different communication and political theories) diverse and even controversial concepts of propaganda have been developed. Although there is no commonly accepted definition of propaganda, a large majority of definitions have some identical elements (e.g. that it attempts to influence people's opinions, attitudes, values, actions). However, there does not exist an agreement about the *essence of propaganda* and its specific characteristic in relation to communication in general, to ideology, class struggle and other key social phenomena. The relationship of propaganda to ideology seems to be the most ambiguous. On the one hand, controversies result from the *concept of ideology* itself (e.g. differences between Marx's, Lenin's, Mannheim's and other considerations of ideology). On the other hand, conceptual differences are related to the development of a specific kind of social communication – mass communication and mass media. The general characteristic of *mass communication as public communication*, which supposedly goes beyond particular interests because of its 'universality', conceals the ideologic-legitimising function of mass media. This concealment could be best exemplified by those definitions of mass communication, by which the public nature of communication or the publicity of the mass media is operationally defined as their accessibility to everyone (and anyone). Precisely because of this formally 'quite technical' character, the mass media seemingly appear to be most appropriate for achieving social integration of all classes and layers which, in reality, makes them particularly appropriate for the transfer of ideology, and for the stabilisation of ideological norms, values and meanings.

With the transfer of propaganda into the sphere of mass communication, the mass media became, along with the family, church and school, the most important agents of mass socialisation (at first mainly for secondary socialisation, today increasingly for primary as well). The development of writing and the ability to write initiated a process of enlarging temporal and spatial horizons, and surpassing natural existential conditions which had determined Man's relations in production, as well as his relation to language as a form of natural belonging to some collectivity. In propaganda this historical process turned into its opposite – into the growth of alienation which, in turn, appeared to him as something self-understood, so-to-speak natural.[1]

Due to their subordination to politics (through propaganda) and to the commodity economy (through advertising), the communication media have been abused, as Williams put it, for political control or for commercial profit, as a new instrument of government or a new opportunity for trade.[2]

5.2 RESEARCH AIMS AND HYPOTHESES

External radio broadcasting is, even now, in the age of satellite communication and other new means of communication, considered as one of the most significant agents in international communication. Largely due to its technical ability to cover a large part of the globe, and to relatively low costs of transmission and reception, it has been in use for decades as one of the most influential and efficient propaganda instruments in international relations. At any rate, external broadcasting shows clearly a tendency of growth; after the Second World War it more than doubled within each decade.

A rough analysis indicates that broadcasting is too important to be left to the broadcasters. On the one hand, national stations are subject to state control in the sense that they are directed to operate within, and to share and maintain, the basic assumptions of a given political system. On the other hand, it seems that external radio broadcasting is considered in many official quarters as essential in carrying out foreign policy and it is allotted a large slice of the state budget, since there is no other way of financing this kind of activity.

To protect their societies against alien propaganda some countries even try to filter or halt incoming propaganda messages. This is possible to a certain extent in the case of press, journals, books, films and even television, but becomes unrealistic when trying to stop radio signals. That is why the modern concept of international propaganda includes external radio broadcasting as one of its essential components and operative instruments.

What then is the role of international radio, of external broadcasting in the contemporary world, in relations between different societies and nations?

This was the original point of departure for the present study, which is a part of a long-run research project on international propaganda. The main aim of the project is to reveal (different) ideological systems (re)presented by propaganda and their stability v. variability through time. Furthermore, it attempts to compare external radio broadcasting to Yugoslavia with the contents and dominant ideology of Yugoslav radio programmes, in order to come to inductive conclusions about the potential (dis)socialisation effects of foreign propaganda programmes upon Yugoslav listeners.

According to our assumptions that international propaganda is a means of universalisation of particularistic 'national' interests, it was hypothesised that contents' variability through time was subordinated to and less significant than elements of constancy in propaganda programmes. Or, in other words, differences between single radio programmes were assumed to be relatively stable through time.

Second, if ideology is the dominant dimension of (international) propaganda, then content analysis of external radio propaganda will produce specific 'capitalist' and 'socialist' clusters of programmes.

Finally, ideological systems propagated by foreign radio stations to the Yugoslav listeners were expected to differ significantly from the predominant Yugoslav ideology as presented in the Yugoslav radio programmes.

Given the current state of propaganda analysis, our study was also aimed at subjecting the data obtained by content analysis to different statistical analysis in order to validate them.

5.3. CONTENT ANALYSIS

In various historical periods and societies, as well as today, various concepts of propaganda were upheld in theory and practice. It would therefore make little sense to look for a generally accepted (not to say upheld) definition of propaganda, because the identical elements in various definitions mostly say little or nothing about the essence of propaganda. Such a search for a 'common denominator' in definitions usually turns out as an empty set of definitive elements or else it ends by losing specificity – propaganda is reduced and simplified to 'attempts at influencing human opinion, attitudes, values and behaviour'.

Because of difficulties in defining propaganda, it is very often denoted (in fact, exemplified) by its extremes, by its most evident forms – e.g. by the most satiated forms of evaluative-ideological orientation of communications, or else by formal-organisational criteria (as external radio broadcasting in international communication).

For several reasons, cross-cultural or international-comparative studies revealed a wide range of methodological problems, which are not at stake when research is focused on a 'unified' cultural (and political, economical . . .) context. Fortunately, in exploring external radio broadcasts to a single country, transmitted in the language of the target-country, which should be the principal subject of our analysis, methodological problems related to the cross-cultural character of the analysis do not appear to a great extent at all. This at least holds true for the three basic problems which usually lessen the validity of international comparative research, namely:

1. adequacy and comparability of descriptive categories because all the transmissions under study are in the same, Serbo-Croatian language,
2. functional equivalence of the phenomena (they are all intended for Yugoslav listeners), and
3. equivalence of research procedures (identical procedures were performed on all the materials).

Our model of propaganda analysis is derived from the concept of *archaisation of values*,[3] which determines the relationship between communicators and recipients (including potential effects in propaganda). The term 'arche' (pl. archai) is taken from Greek: for Anaximander, arche was the ultimate source and first principle. In our model, arche is defined as the ideal objectivisation, which is generally accepted by all or by a majority of members of a given social group (nation, class, etc.), and functions as a blockade in the communication process, forecloses rational discourse, but also renders possible the establishment of a communication act at all. Since concrete archai as ideal objectivisations cannot be defined (although they can be projected more or less reliably on to the primary dimension of evaluative orientation, i.e. good-bad dimension, and described), they can be operationalised only by exemplification (enumerating and describing of archai). Such an exemplification, however, can never be exhaustive, because there is no standard to distinguish between ideal objectivisations ('pure values'), values- (material) goods and non-evaluative concepts. The class character of international relations provides an additional standard: the ideological character of values is in an inverse relationship with their general validity (acceptedness) in the world because (in as much as) archai regulate particularism in international relations. This is precisely the supposed dominant function of propaganda. For international propaganda, thus, archai could be operationalised as those values whose projection on the primary evaluative dimension (good-bad) is significantly discriminated in at least two of all the analysed propaganda programmes. The use of such an operational rule is naturally preconditioned by knowledge of a sufficient number of different programmes, i.e. by preliminary explorative analysis. When identified, such values were called 'symbols'.

The primary (good-bad) and secondary categories of evaluative orientation,[4] which are projectable on to the primary dimension and whose projection on this dimension is commonly accepted (i.e. does not differ in different programmes), are standards for *evaluation* of symbols and subjects. Although it is possible to grade categories of evaluative orientation (good, better, the best; honest, more honest, the most honest, etc.), it is not possible to project (to map) such gradations unanimously on to the primary dimension (is 'more honest' equivalent to 'good', 'better' or to 'the best'?). This is so not only because such a mapping would differ through time, but also because evaluative categories and values in the strict sense cannot be measurably quantified.[5] Hence *evaluation* in our model has only two categories (variate values): good (positive) and bad (negative). 'Neutral evaluation' (in fact non-evaluativeness) denotes that the information does not suffice for mapping symbols on an evaluative dimension.

The third key element of the analytical model are *the subjects of international relations*: (a) as subjects to which *symbols* or *evaluations* are referred (i.e. the evaluation of subjects), or (b) as subjects that actively (as *actors*, as a driving force), or passively (as *targets*, as objects or results of an action) determine or define a concrete activity of its result.[6] Messages that do not contain either Subjects or Symbols are to be left out of the analysis; however, in the sample chosen for the analysis there were no such messages.

The basic unit in the model of propaganda analysis is *the message*. The message is defined as a part of the total (sample of) broadcast which is not directly dependent on other parts. Its inclusion or exclusion from the analysis has no implications on the inclusion/exclusion of other units. The basic analytical unit has physically determined boundries (e.g. an article).

The *systematic* (also recording) unit is a part of the basic unit or equal to it (but never transcending it) as defined by four combinations of three key elements (Subject, Symbol, Evaluation):

1. radio station – source / *Actor* / connector / *Target*
2. radio station – source / *Subject* / connector / *Evaluation*
3. radio station – source / *Subject* / connector / *Symbol*
4. radio station – source / *Symbol* / connector / *Evaluation*

In each basic unit (message) there could be any number of systematic units of all four types, but at least one systematic unit. If we denote Actor, Target, Subject, Symbol and Evaluation as *variables* than it holds that the systematic unit is a part of the basic unit determined by the combination of variate values of two and only two variables. Systematic units can be connected among each other as, for example, in the statement: Yugoslavia, India and Egypt (three different variate values of the variable Subject) founded non-alignment (Symbol). The *connector* denotes the associative or dissociative relation among the variate values of two variables (constitutive elements of a given type of systematic unit).[7]

By the first type of systematic unit we examined the *distribution of attention* of radio stations to various actions of various subjects in the world as they are operationally defined by the interaction of at least two subjects of international relations. (Only in the case in which an empty set results from application of the other three types of systematic unit on the message, would the same subject necessarily appear in the 'role' of actor and target at the same time.) By the following three types of systematic unit, three dimensions of *evaluative-ideological orientation* of radio stations are explored: (2) evaluation of subjects on the primary (good–bad) evaluative dimension, (3) application of symbols to subjects, and (4) evaluation of symbols by means of the primary evaluative dimension.

5.4 DATA MATRIX FOR MULTIVARIATE STATISTICAL ANALYSIS

Due to a large number of variate values of Symbol and Actor/Target (Subject) variables, combinations from the first and the third types of systematic unit were not included in the data analysis. With ten subjects, we already get a hundred combinations of actors and targets; but in the analysed radio programmes, 114 different subjects of international relations were identified. If we add to this the number of analysed radio stations (six in two time periods) it becomes quite understandable that we had to eliminate combinations as a specific measure in the analysis of distribution of attention and evaluative orientation. Due to this limitation only the following variables were included in the data analysis: Station, Source, Actor, Target, Subject as reference of Symbol, Symbol as attributed to Subject, Evaluation of Subject and Evaluation of Symbol (see Table 5.1)

Since all variables, when studying their (frequency of) appearance, were 'measured' by nominal scales (e.g. 114 categories of the variable Subject), a set of dummy variables was created by treating each category of a nominal variable as a separate variable and assigning a score 1, for its appearance and zero score for its absence. For the categories of variables Subject in the second type of systematic unit and Symbol in the fourth type of systematic unit, a coefficient of evaluation C was calculated. For multivariate analyses the initial data matrix was transformed into a new matrix by determining frequency of appearance (presence) for each dichotomous dummy variable and calculating the coefficient of evaluation for categories of subjects and symbols for each of the radio stations as a whole. The obtained frequencies were normalised (divided by the number of all systematic units of a given type in the programme of a given radio station). The matrix form is shown in Table 5.1.

5.5 SAMPLE OF EXTERNAL RADIO PROGRAMMES TO YUGOSLAVIA

In the first time period of analysis of international radio propaganda (1973) all foreign radio broadcasts in the Serbo-Croat language intended for Yugoslavia were taken into account. There are 14 foreign countries broadcasting regularly 15 external broadcasting programmes to Yugoslavia, in the Slovenian and Macedonian languages as well as in Serbo-Croat. Only Radio Madrid, which could

Table 5.1 Data matrix for multivariate analysis

Radio Station	← Frequency of appearance →				Evaluation	
	Actor $1,\ldots,a$	Target $a+1,\ldots,t$	Subject $t+1,\ldots,s$	Symbol I $s+1,\ldots,k$	Symbol II $k+1,\ldots,l$	Subject Symbol $l+1,\ldots,m$
1	$f_{1,1}$	...		$f_{1,k}$	$v_{1,k+1}$	$v_{1,m}$
.	.			.	.	.
.	.			.	.	.
n	$f_{n,1}$	...		$f_{n,k}$	$v_{n,k+1}$	$v_{n,m}$

where:
a of various categories of Actor, $(t-a)$ of Target, $(s-t)$ of Subject, $(k-s)$ of Symbol I, $(l-k)$ of evaluated Symbol II and $(m-l)$ of evaluated Subject;
f_{ij} the frequency of appearance of the jth variable (individual category of Actor, Target, Subject, Symbol) in the ith station;
v_{ij} coefficient evaluation of jth variable (individual category of Subject, Symbol) in the ith station;
$$v_{ij} = \frac{a-b}{a+b+c},$$ where a is the frequency of positive, b the frequency of negative and c the frequency of neutral evaluations of the individual subject or symbol in a given station.

not be heard sufficiently clearly in both Ljubljana and Belgrade, and Radio Vatican, due to its peculiar religious content, which could not be analysed by the methods adopted, were not included in the sample. In the period from the 8th to the 14th of September 1973, 7700 minutes of broadcasting content were analysed from a total of 13 foreign radio stations, to which the external programme of Radio Yugoslavia (Belgrade) was added for comparison.

In the second period of analysis (1977) six radio stations were selected on the basis of the results obtained in the first phase[8] – i.e. the 'representatives' of the relatively homogeneous groups as obtained by Q factor analysis:

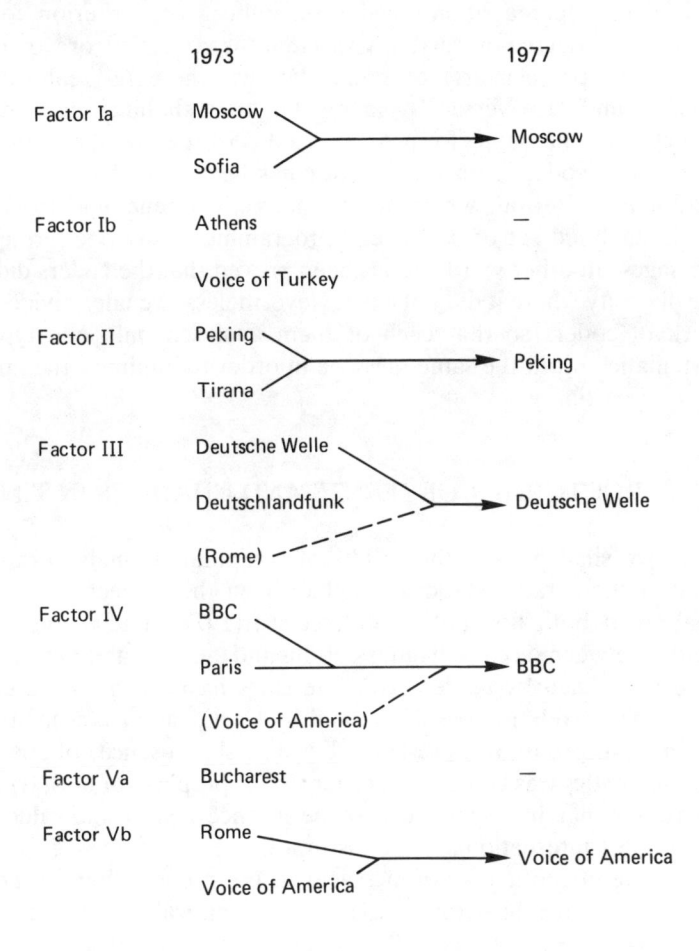

	1973	1977
Factor Ia	Moscow Sofia	Moscow
Factor Ib	Athens Voice of Turkey	— —
Factor II	Peking Tirana	Peking
Factor III	Deutsche Welle Deutschlandfunk (Rome)	Deutsche Welle
Factor IV	BBC Paris (Voice of America)	BBC
Factor Va	Bucharest	—
Factor Vb	Rome Voice of America	Voice of America

The reduction of sample size was based on stations' loadings on oblique rotated factors. The selected radio stations' programmes were analysed from the 4th to the 10th of February 1977. This time Radio Ljubljana replaced Radio Belgrade as the representative of the target-country in the sample of analysis.

5.6 RELIABILITY TEST

The reliability of analysis was tested on a partial sample of 20 messages analysed by seven coders. The reliability test showed a satisfactory degree of intercoder reliability. The criterion for an appropriate degree of reliability was that the coders' error would not create groups (clusters) of radio stations where no real clusters existed, and vice versa. By factorising the reliability data matrix (which had the same form as in Table 5.1 except that 'stations' referred to coders), only one factor has been obtained by Kaiser–Guttman's criterion, which meant that coders generated from one single analysed set of messages ('programme') only one 'group' of messages. In other words, it has been proved that the coders did not see diversity where it did not exist. Nevertheless, we later divided the work of coders so that each of them analysed only one type of systematic unit in the same message in order to minimise the impact of their partiality.

5.7 STRUCTURAL CONSTANTS AND CHANGES IN TIME

Here we shall present the results of comparative analysis through time of those radio stations that had been the subjects of content analysis at both first (1973) and second (1977) time points. Similarities between six chosen radio stations and their variabilities through time as defined by content characteristics have been measured by Pearson's correlation coefficient and by Euclidean distance. In both instances not only the presence, but also the absence, of specified characteristics was taken into account. This property of both types of measurement is important because the absence of *particular* values and subjects of international relations in a given set of messages, when appearing in another set of messages, is not random, but rather – at least hypothetically – consciously and systematicaly produced. However, when using the correlation coefficient, as well as Euclidean distance, the rule of *non-negativity of definitions* has to be satisfied, though it is not included in the very logic of measurement: Determining similarities on the basis of too large a number of absent characteristics leads to 'confirmation' of *apparently* similar units or homogeneous clusters which have in common the absence and not the presence of given characteristics. In order to avoid this error we measured changes in time of radio programmes only on those characteristics that were present in at least eight units (thus at least in the programmes of two radio stations in both time points), and whose total frequency of appearance (presence) was at least $f = 20$, which should assure the non-randomness of their presence. Because of the large sample of messages the first criterion already implied the second. Taking into account both conditions, 123 variables were included in the data analysis.

The results of cross-time comparative analysis consistently reveal the rigidity of structural relations between the six radio stations regarding their evaluative-ideological orientations. The assessment that ideology represents the dominant dimension of propaganda is not to be interpreted in the sense of its absolute unchangeability through time, but rather in the sense of the persistence of basic evaluative or ideological premises and the variability of 'tactical' evaluative orientations that are, on the one hand, dependent on changes of actual social relations through time and, on the other hand, determined by a relatively permanent communicative competence of communicators. Time comparison shows that the elements of permanence predominate over the elements of variability of propaganda, which is one of its *'differentium specificum'* as we define it in regard to mass communication.

The factor matrix (Q-factor analysis) of six propaganda stations at two time points (12 units altogether) more precisely explains the above given general claim. Among five factors derived by the criterion of the number of eigenvalues greater than one, in four factors (the first, third, fourth and fifth) which jointly explain 53 per cent of the total variance, constancy in propaganda broadcasts is in the limelight. Variability of the analysed programmes is clearly indicated only by the second factor, explaining 15.7 per cent of the total variance.

From the obtained factor scores matrix we can perceive that the first factor is determined by variables of obviously evaluative-ideological character, primarily by the frequency of appearance and evaluation of *symbols Socialism, Freedom, Imperialism, Reaction,*

Table 5.2 The factor matrix of foreign radio stations (1973 and 1977)

Radio Station	Year	I	II	Factors III	IV	V	Communalities
Deutsche Welle	1973	0.54	0.50	0.04	−0.32	0.31	0.74
Deutsche Welle	1977	0.64	−0.19	0.10	−0.51	0.32	0.82
Belgrade	1973	−0.50	0.17	0.68	0.07	−0.01	0.74
Ljubljana	1977	−0.45	−0.28	0.60	−0.39	−0.06	0.78
BBC	1973	0.18	0.42	0.20	0.53	−0.01	0.54
BBC	1977	0.34	−0.56	−0.02	0.09	−0.44	0.64
Moscow	1973	−0.55	−0.25	−0.14	0.33	0.27	0.56
Moscow	1977	−0.26	−0.32	−0.42	0.17	0.68	0.83
Peking	1973	−0.22	0.58	−0.40	−0.20	−0.28	0.66
Peking	1977	−0.42	0.26	−0.56	−0.24	−0.25	0.68
VOA	1973	0.49	0.33	0.14	0.52	0.01	0.64
VOA	1977	0.38	−0.56	−0.22	0.15	−0.26	0.61
Percent of explained variance		18.9	15.7	13.3	11.2	9.6	68.7

Disarmament and by evaluation of two *subjects*, the *Soviet Union* and *USA*. These symbols and subjects are frequently presented by both groups (the Western and the Eastern one) but from different evaluative or ideologic points of views. The second factor is determined by those variables which 'defined' world events, i.e. by the perceived actors and targets. In the first period of time (1973) the attention of radio stations was focused mainly on the contrarevolution against Allende in Chile, the visit of the French president to China and the meeting of GATT in Japan; in the second, more peaceful period (1977), besides relations between the USA and the USSR, events in Portugal, Lebanon, Italy and Czechoslovakia came to the forefront. The shift in accent from one to the other group of subjects in international relations is accompanied by a partial change of the repertoire of symbols, but in its entirety maintaining the basic ideological split of radio stations into two clusters.

Variability through time is most significant in the case of the BBC and the Voice of America, while the other four stations (and, particularly, the Eastern ones) are more static in their evaluative-

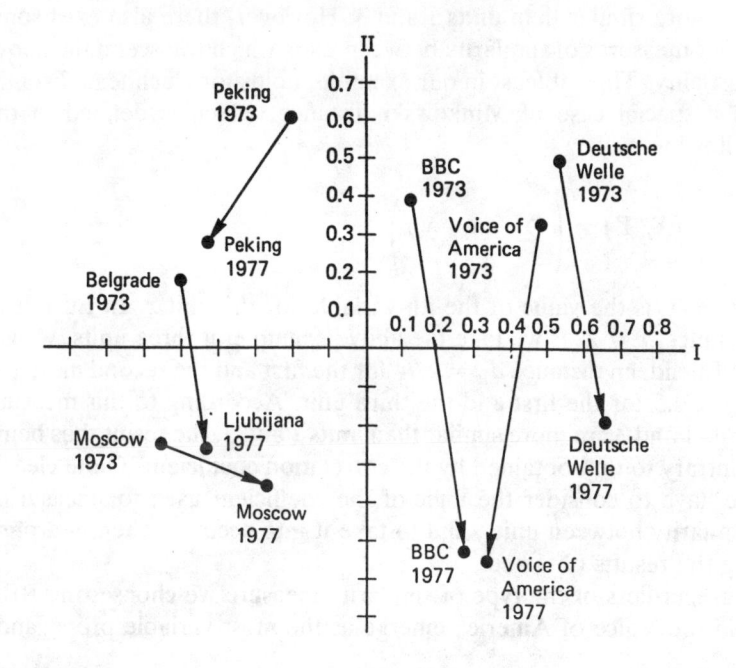

Figure 5.1   Changing positions of six radio stations from 1973 to 1977: presented in the space of factor I and factor II

ideological orientations. Stability v. variability through time in regard to content orientation of each individual station at both time points (defined by the above-mentioned 123 variables) can be measured either by a correlation coefficient (r) or by Euclidean distance (e). Though a correlation coefficient is the most common measure of the similarity between units, it is actually valid only when we are interested in measuring the similarity of the *form* of distributions of units and not in measuring the similarity between units according to their *actual values*.[9] The correlation coefficient is equal to 1 when two forms of distribution are parallel regardless of how apart from each other they are. If we take as an example three units determined by five variables, where the values of the second unit are twice the values of the first plus one, and the values of the third unit the same as those of the first one, except the value of the fifth variable:

1. -1 $-1/2$ 0 $-1/2$ -1
2. -1 0   1   2   3
3. -1 $-1/2$ 0 $-1/2$ 3/2

then the correlation coefficient for units 1 and 2 is equal to $r_{12} = 1$, and for units 1 and 3 to $r_{13} = 0.986$, thus indicating that units 1 and 2 are more similar than units 1 and 3. However, there also exist some other measures of similarity between units which transcend the above partiality. This, at least in our example, holds for Euclidean distance as a special case of Minkowski distance, which is defined in the following way:

$$d(X, Y) = \left(\sum_{i=1}^{n} (x_i - y_i)^r \right)^{1/r}$$

where x_i is the value of the ith variable for the unit x. In Euclidean distance, $r = 2$. If we take the above example of three units, we get an Euclidean distance $d_{12} = 2.74$ for the first and the second unit, and $d_{13} = 0.5$ for the first and the third unit. According to this measure units 1 and 3 are more similar than units 1 and 2, the result thus being contrary to that obtained by the correlation coefficient. Quite clearly we have to consider the logic of the coefficient used for measuring similarity between units, and to take it into account when interpreting the results obtained.

Regardless of the type of similarity measure we choose, the BBC and the Voice of America emerge as the most variable propaganda

Table 5.3 Similarity of programmes of individual radio stations transmitted in 1973 and 1977 – (a) measured by correlation coefficient, (b) by Euclidean distance

Radio Station	Similarity 1973–7 measured by			
	correlation coefficient		Euclidean distance	
	r	Rank (r)	e	Rank (e)
Belgrade/Ljubljana	0.355	2	15.03	3
Moscow	0.273	3	13.07	2
Peking	0.269	4	15.32	4
Deutsche Welle	0.361	1	11.96	1
Voice of America	0.067	5	16.10	5
BBC	–0.079	6	16.11	6

stations, according to changes of their programme content through time (i.e. when measuring similarity of contents of one station-unit between the two time periods).

More precisely the relationship between constancy and variability in the contents of propaganda broadcasts can be determined by clustering radio stations with the local optimisation clustering method according to chosen variables.[10] In our example, Ward's criterion function was used:

$$P(R) = \sum_{C \in R} \sum_{\substack{X,Y \in C \\ X > Y}} d(X,Y)/|C|$$

where X and Y are units, C cluster, R the clustering, $d(X,Y)$ the dissimilarity between the Xth and Yth units and $|C|$ the number of units in cluster C. Radio stations were clustered according to the both types of dissimilarities mentioned above (Euclidean distance and dissimilarity d_{ij} obtained from Pearson's correlation coefficient: $d_{ij} = (1-r_{ij})/2$). As with Pearson's coefficient, the Euclidean distance was also calculated on the basis of the values of 123 variables, i.e. the characteristics of propaganda messages of six stations at the first (1973) and the second (1977) time points.

One among the heuristic approaches to determining the most accurate number of clusters is a review of the values of the criterion

Table 5.4 Values of Ward's Criterion Function of the best obtained clustering $P(R^*)$ for different number of clusters

Number of clusters	The value of the criterion function of the best obtained clustering		Decrease of the value of the criterion function	
	Euclidean distance	Correlation coefficient	Euclidean distance	Correlation coefficient
1	89.51	4.048		
2	78.24	3.535	11.3	0.513
3	67.31	3.060	10.9	0.475
4	57.59	2.633	9.8	0.427
5	48.57	2.232	9.0	0.401
6	40.81	1.866	7.7	0.366

function at the best obtained clusterings with different numbers of clusters. Here the most appropriate number of clusters is defined as the greatest degree of decrease in the value of the criterion function from the clustering with n clusters to the neighbouring clustering with $(n+1)$ clusters.

According to the above criterion, clustering into two clusters might be denoted as the most appropriate. The dominant characteristic of the two-clusters solution is that the value of Ward's criterion function is much lower (and closer to the local minimum value) when stations are clustered according to their general evaluative-ideological orientation (Western v. Eastern stations) than in the case of clustering according to the first and the second time points. Thus, we could claim that evaluative-ideological orientations distinguish propaganda stations more strongly than do characteristics of variability through time. By clustering propaganda stations into Eastern and Western clusters for both periods of time, the value of the criterion function is $P_e(R) = 78.36$ (Euclidean distance) or else $P_p(R) = 3.542$ (Pearson's r) – thus only 0.12 or 0.007 respectively greater than the value of the Ward's criterion function of the best obtained clustering with two clusters $P(R^*)$ (Figure 5.2). By clustering stations into two clusters, one consisting of stations in 1973 and the second of the same stations in 1977, $P_e(R) = 79.22$ (Euclidean distance) or else $P_p(R) = 3.577$ (Pearson's r) – thus 0.98 or 0.042 respectively above $P(R^*)$. In other words, evaluative-ideological constants dominate over variability through time in foreign radio programmes.

The minimum value of Ward's criterion function for clustering into

Table 5.2 The best-obtained clustering (two clusters) by Ward's local optimisation method, where dissimilarity between stations is measured by Euclidean distance; $P_e(R^*)=78.24$, and by correlation coefficient; $P_r(R^*)=3.535$.

	Euclidean distance	Correlation coefficient
Cluster I	BBC 1973 Deutsche Welle 1973 Deutsche Welle 1977 BBC 1977 Moscow 1977 Voice of America 1973 Voice of America 1977	BBC 1973 Belgrade 1973 Deutsche Welle 1973 Ljubljana 1977 Moscow 1973 Peking 1973 Peking 1977 Voice of America 1973
Cluster II	Belgrade 1973 Ljubljana 1977 Moscow 1973 Peking 1973 Peking 1977	Deutsche WElle 1977 BBC 1977 Moscow 1977 Voice of America 1977

two clusters is obtained by excluding Radio Moscow from the cluster of Eastern stations (Euclidean distance) or by excluding Radio Peking and Radio Ljubljana (Pearson's r) from the cluster of radio broadcasts in the second time period. Ideology and changes in time help us in explanation: Eastern stations (Peking, Moscow, Ljubljana or Belgrade) are less subject to changes over time than are Western stations, while in regard to the ideological factor Radio Moscow approaches (from 1973 to 1977), at least in some aspects, ideological orientations characteristic for Western stations.

Since the first two factors (Table 5.2) explain together only one-third of the total variability of information (in other words, they are determined only by one-third of all the messages' characteristics), while in the clustering procedure all the information is used, it is not possible to compare the factor and the clustering solutions. On the other hand, the results of both clusterings with two clusters (Figure 5.2) could be, at the first glance, interpreted as completely incongruent: The first clustering is seen to be based on the ideological dimension (clusters of Eastern and Western stations), the second one on the time dimension (clusters of programmes in 1973 and in 1977). In fact, however, the dominant ideological dimension that is shown by clustering on the basis of Euclidean distance is not in contradiction with the changing-through-time dimension as the dominant dimension in clustering on the basis of Pearson's correlation coefficient.

The reason for this apparent contradiction of two clusterings stems from the different logic of measuring (dis)similarities by Euclidean distance and correlation coefficient. While the first measures dissimilarity by distance between the values of variables for individual stations, the second measures dissimilarity by dissimilarity of forms of distribution of variables' values between the stations.

We have already established that, through time, the attention paid by the stations to subjects of international relations changes to a greater degree than does their repertoire of symbols. In other words, the form of distribution of attention to subjects changes more through time than does the form of distribution of symbols and the subject's evaluation in individual station (which is particularly significant in programmes of Western stations). Because of the property of Pearson's r discussed above, it is understandable and *in harmony* with the results of clustering on the basis of Euclidean distance, that clusters are formed mostly by that which determines the *form* of distribution, i.e. by time or, more concretely, by events (subjects of international relations, perceived either as actors or as targets of events), by which both time periods are specifically designated.

For that reason, we can conclude that the results of both clustering procedures confirm our hypotheses, namely that (1) evaluative-ideological orientations are relatively constant in time and significantly different between Western and Eastern stations, and (2) that distribution of attention to international events and their subjects (Actors, Targets), significantly varies through time, but does not significantly differentiate Eastern and Western stations. In his article on ideology and international politics Benko concludes the analysis of such a change, in which the present cannot be freed from the power of the past, with the thought of the Serbian poet Vuk Karadžić: 'All is the same, but still a bit different.'[11]

The degree of adaptability ('pragmatism') in directing the attention of radio stations to the objective changes through time is best revealed by the clustering of stations into five clusters. As factor analysis has already shown, the Western stations (the BBC, the Voice of America and Deutsche Welle) are far more 'sensitive' to changes in time; in journalistic jargon we could say that the content of their transmissions is more 'newsworthy' or at least more up to date. From both matrices of dissimilarities (once formed from Pearson's correlation coefficients and secondly from Euclidean distance) the clustering procedure turns out in the identical clustering of radio stations into five clusters.

Figure 5.3 The best-obtained clustering of radio stations into five clusters by Ward's local optimisation method. Identical clustering was obtained when measuring dissimilarity by Euclidean distance – $P_e(R^*)=48.57$ – or by correlation coefficient – $P_r(R^*) = 2.232$.

Cluster I:	Cluster II:
BBC 1973	BBC 1977
Deutsche Welle 1973	Deutsche Welle 1977
Voice of America 1973	Voice of America 1977

Cluster III	Cluster IV
Moscow 1973	Belgrade 1973
Moscow 1977	Ljubljana 1977

Cluster V
Peking 1973
Peking 1977

The ideological dimension, though dominant in the programmes of all the analysed stations, is relatively more significant for determining differences within the cluster of Eastern stations than within the cluster of Western stations. Because of discrete time points (1973, 1977) the results of different procedures in data analysis – though perfectly consistent – do not allow a conclusion as to whether changes through time denote only a delay in co-orientation (as one could – too quickly! – deduce from the 'sequential movement' of Peking, Moscow and Belgrade/Ljubljana in Figure 5.1) or whether they are subject to a persistent and explicit differentiation between stations. In the first case the content differences through time would denote a tendency toward lessening ideological differences, while in the second case the same differences could only be interpreted as assuring the given ideological structure and differences between the stations. At any rate the content orientations of Western stations are more subject to oscillations in time, and thus also the relations (distances) between the stations (as the result of integrational and disintegrational tendencies in the Western hemisphere and within its dominant 'subjects' – the European Economic Community and the North Atlantic Treaty Organization). Yet these oscillations take place within given 'limits of tolerance' determined by the opposite pole – the 'Eastern group'. In the latter, limits of oscillation are less tolerable and more determined by within-group contradictions than by relations with the West.

5.8 CONCLUSION

Results from the present study provide support for our general hypothesis, that – due to the ideological determination of propaganda – international radio propaganda is characterised by relatively stable agenda-setting profiles over time. (1) Radio stations seek to convince listeners as to what, from their ideological point of view, are the most important issues; thus, the dominant subjects and symbols are rather unchangeable over time. (2) The same holds true for the structural relations between individual radio programmes: though they slightly change over the two analysed time periods, their variabilities have no significant impact on differences (distances) between the programmes. However, as revealed in the present study by factorising as well as by hierarchical clustering content analysis data, unchangeability of the contents is more significant for the Eastern radio stations than for the Western ones, which are more 'sensitive' to the objective changes through time. Finally, the content characteristics of individual radio stations and/or ideological clusters differ from the characteristics of the Yugoslav stations in both periods, thus indicating incongruency with the prevalent Yugoslav ideology and potential dissocialising effects upon Yugoslav listeners.

The findings of the research confirm the significance of the ideological dimension of propaganda and, moreover, they also reveal clearly how different data analysis designs deflect the results (e.g. correlation coefficient v. Euclidean distance as the measures of similarity and Q-factor analysis v. hierarchical clustering as the methods for obtaining 'typical groups'). But, when considering the specific logic of different approaches used in our study, formally (or even apparently) different results as obtained by different methods become nothing but different attempts to measure the same concept, which refer to the confirmation of convergent validity of the research.

NOTES AND REFERENCES

1. The Concept, propaganda, is theoretically elaborated in more detail in Slavko Splichal, *Mlini na eter* (*Air-Miles*) (Ljubljana: Partizanska knjiga, 1984).
2. Raymond Williams, *Communications* (Harmondsworth: Penguin Books, 1976) 10–11.
3. Cf. Kathleen Jamieson Hall, 'Archai and National Identity', paper at the

Fulbright Conference on Communication, Society and Culture (Dubrovnik, 1982).
4. For details see Agnes Heller, *Vrednosti i potrebe* (*Values and Needs*) (Beograd: Nolit, 1981) 35.
5. Osgood and associates hold that it is possible to decompose the perception of any 'attitude object' with a satisfactory degree of attitude objects' discrimination along three dimensions: positive–negative (evaluative), strong–weak (potency) and active–passive (activity), irrespective of culture. Even if such a notion would hold (we doubt it), the three-dimensional space changes through time and thus three-dimensional denotations are not comparable. See Ch. Osgood, 'Studies of the Generality of Affective Meaning System', *American Psychologist* **17** (1962) 10–28; and O. R. Holsti, *Content Analysis for the Social Sciences and Humanities* (Reading, Mass.: Addison-Wesley, 1969) 167–8.
6. The subject is an individual, a group, an organisation or any other part of the 'subject of international relations' as defined by international law (states, governmental and non-governmental international organisations). Only exceptionally the category of Subject, Actor or Target variable could be defined narrower than at the state level so that more than one subject exist within one state or international organisation. The following rule was adopted for coding procedure: If in one state (such examples did not exist within international organisations at the time of analysis) there exist two or more organised political groups that in regard to each other, and publically, do not acknowledge the legitimate right or sovereignty of government, then each of such groups is a separate subject (e.g. Allende and Pinochet in Chile, Sikhanuk and Lon Nol in Kampuchea, North and South Vietnam in 1973, or different groups in Lebanon in 1977).
7. Fuller report of the content-analysis methodology is published in *External Radio Broadcasting and International Understanding* (Ljubljana: Faculty of Sociology, Political Science and Journalism, 1975) 21–81.
8. The full report on the analysis in 1973 has been published in *External Radio Broadcasting and International Understanding – Broadcasting to Yugoslavia* (Paris: Unesco Reports and Papers in Mass Communication, 1977) no. 81.
9. Brian Everitt, *Cluster Analysis* (London: Heinemann, 1977) 54–77.
10. Anuška Ferligoj, *Clustering* (Ljubljana: Faculty of Sociology, Political Science and Journalism, 1982).
11. Vlado Benko, 'Ideologija in zunanja politika' (Ideology and International Politics), *Teorija in praksa* (1972) no. 5.

6 On Agreement Indices for Nominal Data
Roel Popping

6.1 AGREEMENT

In empirical research certain measurements are frequently performed. Measurement is the assigning of numbers to subjects to denote a property. These measurements take place at a level of measurement: nominal, ordinal, interval or higher. Especially in the social sciences, the assignment to a category is very often based on the judgement of an expert and not on an objective and clear criterium. Still it is desirable that the 'scientists agree', i.e. the assignment will not or scarcely differ if another rater had performed the assignment task. So it is of importance that there is agreement among the raters. There is agreement when raters assign an entity to the same category. Agreement is not only investigated within the social sciences, but in general also in the fields of biology and medicine.

It is remarkable how often it is said that agreement is of importance for those investigators who collect their data by means of content analysis, and how little attention is given to agreement in the handbooks on content analysis. Most of the time nothing is said, or a few remarks are made, and only one or two types of agreement-indices are mentioned, mostly the coefficient used by Dice (van Cuilenburg, 1982), or the *pi* suggested by Scott (Lisch and Kriz, 1978; Krippendorff, 1981). The book by Krippendorff is the most informative one with regard to agreement.

In this text it will be investigated in how far agreement indices fulfil a number of requirements. These will be indices used when there are nominal data. For an introduction to measures to be used at a higher level of measurement see Bartko and Carpenter (1976).

Agreement is very often considered as a special kind of association. There are differences however. It is important to determine the similarity of the content of behaviour (in a broad sense) between raters in general with the degree of identity of this behaviour. The behaviour of one rater does not have to be predicted from that of the other. In case of association the strength of the linear relationship between the variables is investigated. Here the goal is to predict the values of one variable from those of the other.

There are a few assumptions that should be satisfied if one is willing to compute nominal scale agreement. These assumptions are: (1) the statements or subjects are independent; (2) the categories of the nominal scale are independent, exclusive and exhaustive; and (3) the raters operate independently. Furthermore the categories should be used more or less with the same frequency.

A simple application of agreement is the following: in an investigation it is necessary to assign a sample of statements or subjects to the categories in favour or against something. This is done by two raters. When they have finished their task the assignments are compared. The number of times they both assigned a statement to the same category is a starting-point for computing the reliability. If this reliability is sufficient, the investigator can continue using the assignments by one of the two raters. If he were to use the assignments by the other rater, he would get (nearly) the same results.

6.2 *A PRIORI* VERSUS *A POSTERIORI* METHODS OF CODING

If one is willing to compute the agreement in assignments, one research situation is of great importance, and will be mentioned here, separate from possible other empirical research situations. It has to do with whether or not the response categories are known when the raters start their assigning task.

If the categories are known, they are equal for all raters, and all subjects would be assigned to one of these categories. A different situation occurs when the response categories have to be developed by the raters during the assigning process. In this situation each rater may finish with a different number and set of categories. This situation arises in pilot studies, where the investigator wishes to find a set of response categories that will be used in the main investigation.

In the first situation it is said that the *a posteriori* method of coding is applied: assigning starts when the set of categories has been determined. In the other situation the *a priori* method of coding is applied assigning starts even before the sets of categories have been determined (Montgommery and Crittenden, 1977). Both methods demand that agreement is determined in another way, because the categories may differ if the *a priori* method of coding is used.

6.3 REQUIREMENTS TO BE FULFILLED BY AGREEMENT INDICES

Empirical investigators have not paid much attention to the statistical properties of agreement indices. According to Bartko and Carpenter 'too often a reported reliability reflects an association between pairs of raters rather than an accurate assessment of agreement between ratings. Furthermore, practices such as: (a) devising special reliability measures for a particular study which precludes scientific generalisability and therefore does not permit comparisons with other studies; (b) failure to take chance agreement into account; and (c) reporting reliability without an associated test of statistical significance are commonplace' (Bartko and Carpenter, 1976, p. 307).

$$I(0) = O,$$

where O is the observed amount of agreement between the raters. The minimum value this index can take is 0, the maximum value is equal to the number of observations. Indices of this type can hardly be compared, therefore they are normed so that their values are in a certain range. The following types of indices can be distinguished:

$$I(1) = O / M,$$

where M is the maximum possible amount of agreement. This index takes values in the range 0 to +1. A second type of index is:

$$I(2) = (O - \tfrac{1}{2}M) / (\tfrac{1}{2}M),$$

where the possible values are in the range −1 to +1. The final type of index is:

$$I(3) = (O - E) / (M - E),$$

where E is the amount of agreement to be expected by chance (to be defined). This index takes the value +1 in the case of perfect agreement, and the value 0 if the observed agreement is equal to the amount of expected agreement by chance. The index takes a value less than 0 in case the observed agreement is less than the expected agreement. The lower limit is $-E/(M-E)$; if $E = \frac{1}{2}M$ this value is -1. This last type of index is to be preferred, as will be explained later.

The requirements, in the literature mostly found, are in general terms or for the measurement of comparable notions, will be presented here for agreement indices for nominal data, disregarding whether they are obtained by means of the *a priori* or the *a posteriori* method of coding. Use is made of the requirements for statistical indices that are found in the literature. This literature will not be considered in detail.

First the requirements will be mentioned. They are followed by a keyword. Next, explanations will be given with regard to some of the requirements. More details are given in Popping (1983b).

1. the maximum possible value of the index is 1, regardless of the number of raters or categories (MAX);
2. in the case of independence given the marginals, the index takes the value 0 (IND);
3. each rater agrees perfectly with himself (PERFSELF);
4. perfect agreement is a transitive relationship (PERFTRANS);
5. permutations of categories may not lead to other results. Because the data are measures on a nominal scale, the order of the categories is arbitrary, and does not influence the results (PERMUT);
6. the estimated value of the index is independent of the number of observations (NOBS);
7. if there are more than two categories, it should be possible to compute the amount of agreement for all categories together, but also per single category (CATEG);
8. if there are more than two raters, it should be possible to compute the amount of agreement for all raters together, but also per single rater (RAT);
9. the index should be symmetrical with respect to the raters involved, and in such a way that the value of the index does not depend on the number of raters (SYMMETR);
10. the sampling distribution of the index, or at least the variance, should be known (VAR);

11. the index should be robust (ROBUST);
12. the index should be simple and interpretable (SIMPLE);
13. the index should be valid (VALID).

Now some of the requirements will be explained.

MAX: in the case of perfect agreement, the marginals of the raters are equal, so there is no doubt about the maximum. But how to define it if there is no perfect agreement? The maximum can be defined as dependent or independent of the marginals. In the latter case the maximum is reached when all subjects in an agreement-table are on the diagonal of that table (after the ordering of the nominal sets of categories). In the former case, however, the reasoning is that a certain cell on the diagonal can never contain more subjects than the lowest frequency in the corresponding marginals, so this frequency is a determinant for the maximum. In the case of agreement, however, perfection is demanded: the categories assigned by the raters must have an equal content, there is no question of predicting a category from one of the raters from a category given by another. This means that only the maximum that is independent of the marginals is of importance.

INDEP: Indices can take extreme values, either because there is no correction for the actual minimum value they can take, or because there is no correction for the results that can be expected based only on independence (Mokken, 1971, p. 55). In the above-mentioned type of index $I(3)$ there is a correction for chance agreement.

With regard to the amount of agreement that is to be expected by chance given independence, it is assumed that all subjects are drawn from one population; the independent classification according to chance is specified on this population. There is no reason to accept that the separate categories are all used with the same frequency by all raters, so that all marginals are symmetric. However, for perfect agreement this is necessary. It is the distinguishing mark of raters that they use categories with different frequency.

In the choice of a transformation formula the demands 'null in the case of independence', 'fixed maximum', 'fixed minimum' are in general conflicting; the last demand is usually dropped. Arguments for this are that the minima often concern a pathological situation, while agreement less than expected by chance is not interesting for criteria concerning the content, and hardly ever occurs. Very often extreme results are possible (Mokken, 1971, p. 56). In indices where there is a correction for chance these extreme results are removed. Therefore indices of this type are preferred.

A disadvantage of these indices is, however, that they cannot handle some very extreme situations: in the unusual and in general undesirable situation that a rater has assigned all subjects to one and the same category, it is not possible to investigate the difference between observed and expected values. Given one alternative these two are always equal. One can wonder whether in future assignments there will also be at least one rater who assigns all subjects to just one category, 'the measurement is not sensitive enough to warrant any decision about constancy' (Galtung, 1979, p. 111). In practice this problem will hardly ever occur. The best is to norm for chance, given independence.

SYMMETR: if one rater is standard the index need not be symmetrical.

The other requirements seem to be clear. Popping (1983b) contains a more extensive treatment. The estimated value of the index is dependent on the number of categories that has been used.

6.4 FIELDS OF APPLICATION

A number of empirical situations can be distinguished on the grounds that they require different kinds of agreement indices. One important aspect of these situations concerns the coding process, as was already shown in a previous paragraph. Other aspects of empirical situations that have to be distinguished include:

- whether the identity of the rater per observation is registered (if not, the term 'agreement between judgements' is used, rather than 'agreement between raters');
- the number of raters or judgements;
- the definition of agreement (pairwise, simultaneous, majority);
- whether there is a standard rater to which the others are compared;
- use of weights based on the seriousness of disagreement between category pairs;
- the amount of agreement for a fixed category;
- the amount of (dis-)agreement for two different fixed categories;
- the amount of agreement within a category, computed by taking one of the raters as a standard;

- the number of judgements per subject;
- missing values;
- the number of categories.

In practice these situations do not appear separately, but in combination with each other.

6.5 INDICES THAT SATISFY THE REQUIREMENTS

6.5.1 Indices for the *a posteriori* Method of Coding

In this paragraph the agreement indices, that should be used with the *a posteriori* method of coding, are compared; the categories were known to the raters when they started assigning the subjects. The results are presented in Table 6.1. More details on this comparison are in Popping (1983b). With regard to the variance of an index it must be noted that a + sign is only given if the variance was found in the literature. This does not imply, however, that this is the reference mentioned after the name of the index; the variance of SI, for example, was determined by Elston *et al.* (1982), who developed an index equal to SI, but who do not refer to Hawkins and Dotson (1975). The variance of some indices was not found, though it is quite easy to compute it.

In Table 6.1 a reference is given after the name of the index; this is not necessarily the only reference there is. In general it is to the paper in which the index was proposed.

The indices that satisfy best are the *kappa*-index (Cohen, 1960), and the S-index (Janson and Vegelius, 1979). The variance of this last index must be computed. However, *kappa* is to be preferred. A disadvantage of S is that it is not exactly an index of type $I(3)$, as mentioned in paragraph 3, and it has only been presented for the comparison of the assignments by two raters (this, however, holds for most indices). Extensions of *kappa* have already been developed for the empirical research situations mentioned in paragraph 4. This is done by means of adaptation of the formulas for observed and expected agreement. *Kappa* also has the advantage that it permits weighting. The indices that have been developed for more than two categories can be used so that they satisfy the requirement CATEG: all categories except one are combined. When agreement is computed now, it is the amount of agreement with regard to this one category.

Table 6.1 Comparison of agreement indices to be used when the *a posteriori* method of coding is applied with the requirements 1 = MAX, 2 = IND, 3 = PERFSELF, 4 = PERFTRANS, 5 = PERMUT, 6 = NOBS, 7 = CATEG, 8 = RAT, 9 = SYMMETR, 10 = VAR

requirement	1	2	3	4	5	6	7	8	9	10
index										
kappa (Cohen, 1960)	+	+	+	+	+	+	+	+	+	+
kappa (Fleiss, 1971)	+	+	+	n	+	+	+	n	+	+
V (Crittenden and Hill, 1971)	+	−	n	n	+	+	+	+	+	+
M (Clement, 1976)	+	−	n	n	+	+	n	n	n	−
C (House et al., 1981)	−	−	n	−	−	−	n	n	n	−
P(o)	+	−	+	+	+	+	+	+	+	+
II (Hawkins and Dotson, 1975)	+	−	+	+	+	+	n	+	+	+
SI "	+	−	+	+	−	+	n	+	+	+
UI "	+	−	+	+	−	+	n	+	+	+
mean SI UI "	+	−	+	+	+	+	n	+	+	−
WI (Sloat, 1978)	+	−	+	+	+	+	n	+	+	−
OI (Hopkins and Hermann, 1977)	−	−	+	+	−	+	n	+	+	+
voting concordance (Rae and Taylor, 1970)	+	−	+	+	+	+	n	+	+	−
solidarity "	+	+	+	+	−	+	n	+	+	−
M (Harris and Lahey, 1978)	+	−	+	+	+	+	n	+	+	−
S(d) (Dice, 1945)	+	−	+	+	−	+	n	+	+	−
A2 (Rogot and Goldberg, 1966)	+	−	+	+	+	+	n	+	+	−
A1 "	+	−	+	+	+	+	n	+	+	−
G (Holley and Guilford, 1964)	+	−	+	+	+	+	n	+	+	+
RE (Maxwell, 1977)	+	−	+	+	+	+	n	+	+	+
RE (Janes, 1979)	+	−	+	+	+	+	+	+	+	+
S (Bennett et al., 1954)	+	−	+	+	+	+	+	+	+	+
pi (Scott, 1955)	+	−	+	+	+	+	+	+	+	+
pi (Flanders, 1967)	+	−	+	+	+	+	+	+	+	−
pi (Garrett, 1975)	+	−	+	+	+	+	+	+	+	−
lambda (Goodman and Kruskal, 1954)	+	−	+	+	+	+	+	+	+	−
r (1,1) (Maxwell and Pilliner, 1968)	+	+	+	+	+	+	n	+	+	−
S (Janson and Vegelius, 1979)	+	+	+	+	+	+	+	+	+	−
occurrence *kappa* (Kent and Foster, 1977)	−	−	+	+	−	+	n	+	+	−

continued on page 98

Table 6.1 continued

requirement	1	2	3	4	5	6	7	8	9	10
non-occurrence *kappa* (Kent and Foster, 1977)	−	−	+	+	−	+	n	+	+	−
C (Cicchetti, 1972)	−	+	+	+	+	+	+	+	+	+
I (Woodward and Franzen, 1948)	−*	−	+	+	+	+	+	+	+	−
r(*) (Fleiss, 1965)	+	−	+	+	+	+	n	−	+	−
y(1) (Elston, *et al.*, 1982)	−	−	−	+	−	+	n	+	+	+
y(3) "	+	−	+	+	−	+	n	+	+	+
A (Cartwright, 1956)	+	−	+	+	+	+	+	n	+	+
MAI (Armitage *et al.*, 1966)	+	−	n	+	+	+	n	n	+	+
MPDI "	−*	−	n	−	−	−	n	n	+	+
SDAI "	−	−	n	−	−	−	n	n	+	−

+ satisfies
− does not satisfy
n not appropriate

* In the case of perfect agreement, the index takes the value 0.

This can be done for both *kappa* and S. It is also possible to consider the observed and expected agreement in a category as a fraction of the mean number of assignments per rater to that category. *Kappa* is also defined within these terms. The requirement RAT is satisfied when the mean is taken of all pairs of raters. Here an alternative is to use the means of observed and expected agreement, and to enter these into the formula of *kappa*. Now a high or a low amount of agreement between a pair of raters is taken in this ratio in the mean. The S-index is a generalisation of the *phi*-coefficient.

Suppose that, for the computation of *kappa*, N subjects have been assigned to c categories by two raters. The number of subjects assigned by one rater to category i is denoted $f(i,.)$, and the number of subjects assigned by the other rater to category j by $f(.,j)$. The number of assignments by the first rater to category i and by the second one to category j is denoted $f(i,j)$. The formula for *kappa* is:

$$K = (Po - Pe) / (N - Pe)$$

where

$$Po = \sum_{i=1}^{c} f(i, i)$$

and

$$Pe = \sum_{i=1}^{c} f(i,.) f(.,i) / N$$

In this formula *Po* is the amount of observed agreement, *N* the maximum possible amount and *Pe* the expected amount of agreement.

6.5.2 Indices for the *a priori* Method of Coding

If the *a priori* method of coding is used, the sets of response categories, as developed by the raters, can refer to different contents. Therefore it is not possible just to consider the subjects on the diagonal of the agreement-table. Instead, pairs of subjects have to be compared. The $N (N - 1) / 2$ pairs of subjects per rater can be assigned to the classes: 'same' category and 'different' categories. Now the pairs can be placed in a 2 * 2 table in which the cell 'same-same' denotes the pairs on which there is agreement between the raters. Here this cell denotes the amount of observed agreement.

All agreement indices that are mentioned in Table 6.2 are based on the above principle. In the table the same holds for the + sign at the variance, as in the previous paragraph.

Table 6.2 Comparison of agreement indices to be used when the *a priori* method of coding is applied with the requirements 1 = MAX, 2 = IND, 3 = PERFSELF, 4 = PERFTRANS, 5 = PERMUT, 6 = NOBS, 7 = CATEG, 8 = RAT, 9 = SYMMETR, 10 = VAR

requirement	1	2	3	4	5	6	7	8	9	10
index
A' (Brennan and Light, 1974)	−	−	+	+	+	−	−	+	+	+
A" (Light, 1973)	+	−	+	+	+	−	−	+	+	+
gamma (Hubert, 1977)	+	−	+	+	+	+	−	+	+	+
J (Janson and Vegelius, 1982)	+	+	+	+	+	+	−	+	+	+
Yule's Q (Montgommery and Crittenden, 1977)	+	−	+	−	+	+	−	+	+	−
Rand (Anderberg, 1973)	+	−	+	+	+	−	−	+	+	−
Dot "	−	−	+	+	+	−	−	+	+	−
Jaccard "	+	−	+	+	+	−	−	+	+	−
Dice "	+	−	+	+	+	−	−	+	+	−
ss1 "	+	−	+	+	+	−	−	+	+	−
pm "	+	−	+	+	+	+	−	+	+	−
K "	+	−	+	+	+	−	−	+	+	−
ss2 "	+	−	+	+	+	−	−	+	+	−
D2 (Popping, 1983a)	+	+	+	+	+	+	+	+	+	+

+ satisfies
− does not satisfy

When the *a priori* method of coding is used, the best agreement indices are the *D*2-index (Popping, 1983a) and the *J*-index (Janson and Vegelius, 1982). The *D*2-index has been extended to several empirical research situations, by adapting the definitions of observed, expected and maximum possible agreement. The *J*-index is not of the type $I(3)$ as mentioned in Section 6.3. In the index there is no such correction for chance agreement. Therefore *D*2 is preferred.

Since the raters could have used not only categories referring to a different content, but also a different number of categories, it is assumed that one rater used c categories, and the other one r categories. *D*2 is defined as:

$$D2 = (Do - De) / (Dm - De)$$

where

$$Do = \sum_{i=1}^{c} \sum_{j=1}^{r} f(i,j)(f(i,j) - 1)/2$$

and

$$De = \sum_{i=1}^{c} \sum_{j=1}^{c} t(i,j)$$

with

$$t(i,j) = g(i,j)(h(i,j) - \tfrac{1}{2}g(i,j) - \tfrac{1}{2})$$

where

$$h(i,j) = f(i,.)f(.,j)/N$$

and

$$g(i,j) = \text{entier}(h(i,j)).$$

Further

$$Dm = \max.(Dc, Dr),$$

where

$$Dc = \sum_{i=1}^{c} f(i,.)(f(i,.) - 1)/2,$$

and

$$Dr = \sum_{j=1}^{r} f(.,j)(f(.,j) - 1) / 2.$$

6.6 CONCLUSIONS

The agreement indices to be used when data are measured on a nominal scale have been investigated. If the *a posteriori* method of coding is used, the response categories are known before and are equal for all raters, the index *kappa* (Cohen, 1960) is to be preferred. If the *a priori* method of coding is used, the raters also have to determine the set of categories, then the $D2$-index (Popping, 1983a) deserves attention. Both indices have been extended so that they can be used in many empirical research situations. These extensions are based on adapted definitions of observed, expected and maximum agreement. There is no one model that can be applied in all empirical situations, and such a model would be very complicated.

This does not mean that all problems have been raised. Two important general problems must be mentioned:

1. the investigator has to determine when the amount of agreement found is sufficient. In the literature the value 0.80 is often mentioned as a 'rule of thumb' for *kappa*. It is not correct just to accept this value;
2. skewed distributions always have a strong influence on the results. If there are such distributions, the investigator should at least also report the observed and expected agreement. Further he should give extra attention to these situations, and ask himself why they occur.

There is another problem that only arises when agreement is determined after the *a priori* method of coding is used. The investigator is interested in the answer to the question: why is there no perfect agreement? Is this mainly due to the differences in the sets of categories as developed by the raters, or is it due to differences in assigning? In Popping (1983b) it is shown that especially differences in assigning contribute to disagreement. A final problem for the investigator now is how to determine the set of categories to be used in the main investigation. One method for this is given in Popping (1983b).

Nothing has been said about the requirements ROBUST, SIMPLE and VALID so far. Popping (1983b) has shown that both *kappa* and *D*2 are robust. By not extending the indices to a complicated model which can handle all research situations, but by using an adapted version of the index for each situation, it is guaranteed that the index is simple and interpretable.

It is not possible to indicate exactly when an index is valid. The following should hold: when any group of raters has to classify a sample of subjects, and any other group, from the same population, in both cases for the computed amount of agreement, it is necessary to be (about) the same. It is possible, however, to make a number of recommendations to increase the validity. The procedure that is used is of great importance. The raters have to be well-instructed, they have to know exactly what is expected of them. They cannot be allowed to interpret their task in different ways. The investigator has to take care of a correct choice of the set of categories that will be used, this set has to exclude all possible alternatives, have one interpretation only and should be clear. If weights are used, they should be well-chosen. The investigator should also have chosen the correct alternative of the index (in the final report it should be explained why the alternative is chosen). It is important that the index contains a correction for the expected value under the null-model of independence, because now a possible bias of the results is excluded. Correction for the maximum possible result is necessary in order to make the results interpretable and comparable.

If all these points are taken into consideration, then the validity will be increased.

If one is willing to compute indices of the *kappa*- or *D*2-type, a computer program is available which can handle all the relevant situations mentioned above (Popping, 1984).

REFERENCES

ANDERBERG, M. R., *Cluster Analysis for Applications* (New York: Academic Press, 1973).

ARMITAGE, P., BLENDIS, L. M. and SMYLLIE, H. C., 'The Measurement of Observer Disagreement in the Recording of Signs', *Journal of the Royal Statistical Society (A)*, **129** (1966) 98–109.

BARTKO, J. J. and CARPENTER, W. T., 'Methods and Theory of Reliability', *Journal of Nervous and Mental Disease*, **163** (1976) 307–17.
BENNETT, E. M., BLOMQUIST, R. L. and GOLDSTEIN, A. C., 'Response Stability in Limited Response Questioning', *Public Opinion Quarterly*, **18** (1954) 218–23.
BRENNAN, R. L. and LIGHT, R. J., 'Measuring Agreement when Two Observers Classify People into Categories not Defined in Advance', *British Journal of Mathematical and Statistical Psychology*, **27** (1974) 154–63.
CARTWRIGHT, D. S., 'A Rapid Non-parametric Estimate of Multijudge Reliability', *Psychometrika*, **21** (1956) 17–29.
CICCHETTI, D. V., 'A New Measure of Agreement Between Rank-Ordered Variables', *American Psychological Association. Proceedings of the 80th Annual Convention*, **7** (1972) 17–18.
CLEMENT, P. G., 'A Formula for Computing Interobserver Agreement', *Psychological Reports*, **39** (1976) 257–8.
COHEN, J., 'A Coefficient of Agreement for Nominal Scales', *Educational and Psychological Measurement*, **20** (1960) 37–46.
CRITTENDEN, K. S. and HILL, R. J., 'Coding Reliability and Validity of Interview Data', *American Sociological Review*, **36** (1971) 1073–80.
DICE, L. R., 'Measures of the Amount of Ecological Association between Species', *Ecology*, **26** (1945) 297–302.
ELSTON, R. C., SCHROEDER, S. R. and ROJAHN, J., 'Measures of Observer Agreement when Binomial Data are Collected in Free Operant Situations', *Journal of Behavioral Assessment*, **4** (1982) 299–310.
FLANDERS, N. A., 'Estimating Reliability', in AMIDON, E. J. and HOUGH, J. B. (eds) *Interaction Analysis: Theory, Research and Applications* (Reading, Mass.: Addison-Wesley, 1967) 161–6.
FLEISS, J. L., 'Estimating the Accuracy of Dichotomous Judgements', *Psychometrika*, **30** (1965) 469–79.
――― 'Measuring Nominal Scale Agreement Among many Raters', *Psychological Bulletin*, **76** (1971) 378–82.
GALTUNG, J., 'Measurement of Agreement', in GALTUNG, J. (ed.), *Papers on Methodology. Theory and Methods of Social Research*, vol. II (Copenhagen: Christian Eijlers, 1979) 82–135.
GARRETT, C. S., 'Modification of the Scott Coefficient as an Observer Agreement Estimate for Marginal-form Observation Scale Data', *Journal of Experimental Education*, **43** (1975) 4, 21–6.
GOODMAN, L. A. and KRUSKAL, W. H., 'Measures of Association for Cross-classifications', *Journal of the American Statistical Association*, **49** (1954) 732–64.
HARRIS, F. C. and LAHEY, B. B., 'A Method for Combining Occurrence and Non-occurrence Interobserver Agreement Scores', *Journal of Applied Behavior Analysis*, **10** (1978) 523–7.
HAWKINS, R. P. and DOTSON, V. A., 'Reliability Scores that delude: An Alice in Wonderland Trip Through the Misleading Characteristics of Interobserver Agreement Scores in Interval Recording', in RAMP, E. and SEMB, G. (eds) *Behavior Analysis: Areas of Research and Application* (Englewood Cliffs, N.J.: Prentice-Hall, 1975) 359–76.
HOLLEY, J. W. and GUILFORD, J. P., 'A Note on the G-index of

Agreement', *Educational and Psychological Measurement*, **24** (1964) 749–53.
HOPKINS, B. L. and HERMANN, J. A., 'Evaluating Interobserver Reliability of Interval Data', *Journal of Applied Behavior Analysis*, **10** (1977) 121–6.
HOUSE, A. E., HOUSE, B. J. and CAMPBELL, M. B., 'Measures of Interobserver Agreement: Calculation Formulas and Distribution Effects', *Journal of Behavioral Assessment*, **3** (1981) 37–57.
HUBERT, L. J., 'Nominal Scale Response Agreement as a Generalized Correlation', *British Journal of Mathematical and Statistical Psychology*, **30** (1977) 98–103.
JANES, C. L., 'Extension of the Random Error Coefficient of Agreement to N * N tables', *British Journal of Psychiatry*, **134** (1979) 617–19.
JANSON, S. and VEGELIUS, J., 'On the Generalization of the G-index and the Phi Coefficient to Nominal Scales', *Multivariate Behavioral Research*, **14** (1979) 255–69.
____ and ____ 'The J-index as a Measure of Nominal Scale Response Agreement', *Applied Psychological Measurement*, **6** (1982) 111–21.
KENT, R. N. and FOSTER, S. L., 'Direct Observational Procedures: Methodological Issues in Naturalistic Settings', in CIMINERO, A. R., CALHOUN, K. S. and ADAMS, H. E. (eds) *Handbook of Behavioral Assessment* (New York: Wiley, 1977) 279–328.
KRIPPENDORFF, K., *Content Analysis. An Introduction to its Methodology* (Beverly Hills: Sage, 1981).
LIGHT, R. J., 'Issues in the Analysis of Categorical Data', in TRAVERS, R. M. W. (ed.) *Second Handbook of Research Teaching* (Chicago: Rand-McNally, 1973) 318–81.
LISCH, R. and KRIZ, J., *Grundlagen und Modelle der Inhaltanalyse* (Reinbek: Rororo, 1978).
MAXWELL, A. E., 'Coefficients of Agreement Between Observers and their Interpretation', *British Journal of Psychiatry*, **130** (1977) 79–83.
MAXWELL, A. E. and PILLINER, A. E. G., 'Deriving Coefficients of Reliability and Agreement for Ratings', *British Journal of Mathematical and Statistical Psychology*, **21** (1968) 105–16.
MOKKEN, R. J., *A Theory and Procedure of Scale Analysis: With Applications in Political Research* (The Hague: Mouton, 1971).
MONTGOMMERY, A. C. and CRITTENDEN, K. S., 'Improving Coding Reliability for Open-ended Questions', *Public Opinion Quarterly*, **41** (1977) 235–43.
POPPING, R., 'Traces of Agreement: On the Dot-product as a Coefficient of Agreement', *Quality and Quantity*, **17** (1983a) 1–18.
POPPING, R., 'Overeenstemmingsmaten voor Nominale Data', unpublished PhD thesis, University of Groningen (1983b).
POPPING, R., 'AGREE, a package for Computing Nominal Scale Agreement', *Computational Statistics and Data Analysis*, **2** (1984) 182–5.
RAE, D. W. and TAYLOR, M., *The Analysis of Political Cleavages* (New Haven: Yale U.P., 1970) 115–45.
ROGOT, E. and GOLDBERG, I. D., 'A proposed Index for Measuring Agreement in Test–retest Studies', *Journal of Chronic Diseases*, **19** (1966) 991–1006.

SCOTT, W. A., 'Reliability of Content Analysis: The Case of Nominal Scale Coding', *Public Opinion Quarterly*, **19** (1955) 321–5.
SLOAT, K. M. C., 'A Comment on "Correction for Bias Present in a Method of Calculating Interobserver Agreement"', unpublished manuscript. Kamehomela Early Education Program, 1978.
VAN CUILENBURG, J. J., 'Inhoudsanalyse', in SWANBORN, P. G. and RADEMAKER, L. (eds), *Sociologische Grondbegrippen 2* (Utrecht: Het Spectrum, 1982) 150–67.
WOODWARD, J. L. and FRANZEN, R., 'A Study on Coding Reliability', *Public Opinion Quarterly*, **12** (1948) 253–7.

Part III
Scaling Categorical Data

7 The Use of Models for Paired Comparisons with Ties

T. J. H. M. Eggen and
W. J. van der Linden

7.1 INTRODUCTION

The method of paired comparisons has a long tradition which has been caused not only by its simplicity and statistical elegance, but also by its wide applicability. Among the most important applications are its uses in areas as taste testing, personnel rating, consumer testing, the psychological study of preference and choice behaviour, attitude measurement and tournaments.

Although the method was used first by Fechner (1860) in psychophysics, it can be stated that the introduction of probability models for comparisons of objects by Thurstone (1927) and Zermelo (1929), and in particular the independent discovery of Zermelo's model by Bradley and Terry (1952), were the starting-points of an extensive series of publications on the method of paired comparisons. Valuable reviews of the literature have been given by David (1963) and Bradley (1976), while Davidson and Farguhar (1976) have provided an extensive bibliography.

In the original papers the attention was focused mainly on designs with an equal number of repetitions for each comparison and for which independence of all comparisons could be assumed. For this case procedures for parameter estimation and test of model fit were given by Mosteller (1951) and Bradley and Terry (1952). Nowadays the situation has changed completely. Not only have alternative models been developed (e.g. by Thomson and Singh, 1967) but also a great many extensions of the basic models and designs have become available. Some of these are models for unbalanced designs – i.e. unequal numbers of repetitions of comparisons – (Dijkstra, 1960), models that account for effects of the order of presentation of the objects in a pair (Beaver and Gokhale, 1975; Davidson and Beaver,

1977; Kousgaard, 1979), and models permitting the occurrence of ties in comparisons (Glenn and David, 1960; Rao and Kupper, 1967; Davidson, 1970; Kousgaard, 1976). Furthermore, the theory of paired comparisons has been generalised to triple comparisons, factorials in comparisons, and multivariate paired comparisons (see e.g. Bradley, 1976, and the references therein). Some statistical tests for dependence between comparisons have been provided by Molenaar (1973). Finally, graph-theoretic and combinatorial studies on tournaments have provided all kinds of designs for paired comparison experiments.

In this chapter we restrict ourselves to models for paired comparisons with ties. In the first part of the chapter a review of models with special parameters for ties will be given. In particular attention will be payed to extensions of the Bradley–Terry model and to models with individual tie parameters. This part of the chapter also deals with statistical issues in parameter estimation and shows how the method of conditional maximum-likelihood can be used to remove the individual tie parameters from the estimation equations so that consistent estimates of the object parameters are obtained. The second part of the chapter deals with a special application of models with tie parameters. As already noted by Gridgeman (1959), an obvious advantage of such models is that they can handle more response formats and are able to distinguish between abilities of respondents or judges. It is the contribution of this chapter to point at a less obvious application of models with tie parameters, namely the analysis of completely different experiments and models for which it can be shown that a transformation of the data exists that induces a paired-comparisons experiment with ties. The original experiment does not need to have ties or even comparisons. We will illustrate this with the analysis of binary test items with the Rasch (1960) model. Analysis of the induced experiment instead of the original has some notable advantages.

7.2 MODELS WITH TIE PARAMETERS

Thurstone's (1927) basic model applies to the following situation. There are n objects (treatments, stimuli, etc.) that are presented in pairs to respondents who are asked to express preference for one object of the pair with respect to some attribute. The model assumes that the probability of preferring object i to j is governed by

$$P(X_i > X_j) = \frac{1}{\sqrt{2\pi}} \int_{-(u_i-u_j)}^{\infty} \exp(-y^2/2) \, dy = \Phi(u_i - u_j),$$

$$i \neq j, \ldots, n \quad (1)$$

where X_i is the random variable denoting the response to object i ($i = 1, \ldots, n$) with location u_i on the attribute and $\Phi(.)$ denotes the standard normal distribution function.

Replacing the normal density in Equation (1) by the logistic, the Bradley–Terry model is obtained:

$$P(X_i > X_j) = \frac{1}{4} \int_{-(\ln\pi_i - \ln\pi_j)}^{\infty} \operatorname{sech}^2(y/2) \, dy = \Psi(\ln\pi_i - \ln\pi_j)$$

$$= \pi_i/(\pi_i + \pi_j), \quad i \neq j = 1, \ldots, n \quad (2)$$

now π_i represents object i's location with $\pi_i > 0$ and $\sum_{i=1}^{n} \pi_i = 1$ and $\Psi(z) = 1/(1 + e^{-z})$ is the logistic distribution function.

Glenn and David (1960) were the first to present a modification of the Thurstone model that makes provision for the possibility for judges to state an indifference between objects. These differences are called 'ties'. In Thurstone's model it is assumed that differences between the responses X_i and X_j – however small – are discernible by the respondent, who, consequently, is always able to state a preference. Glenn and David, however, postulated that when the absolute difference lies below a certain threshold value, i.e. when $X_i - X_j$ lies between $-\tau$ and τ, a respondent will not be able to give a preference and a tie occurs. For normally distributed response variables X_i with expectation u_i and variance 1, Glenn and David's model follows as in Figure 7.1.

Algebraically, the model can be given as:

$$P(i|i,j) = P(X_i - X_j > \tau) = \Phi(u_i - u_j - \tau)$$

$$P(j|i,j) = P(X_i - X_j < \tau) = \Phi(u_j - u_i - \tau) \quad (3)$$

$$P(0|i,j) = P(-\tau < X_i - X_j < \tau)$$

$$= \Phi(u_i - u_j + \tau) - \Phi(u_i - u_j - \tau),$$

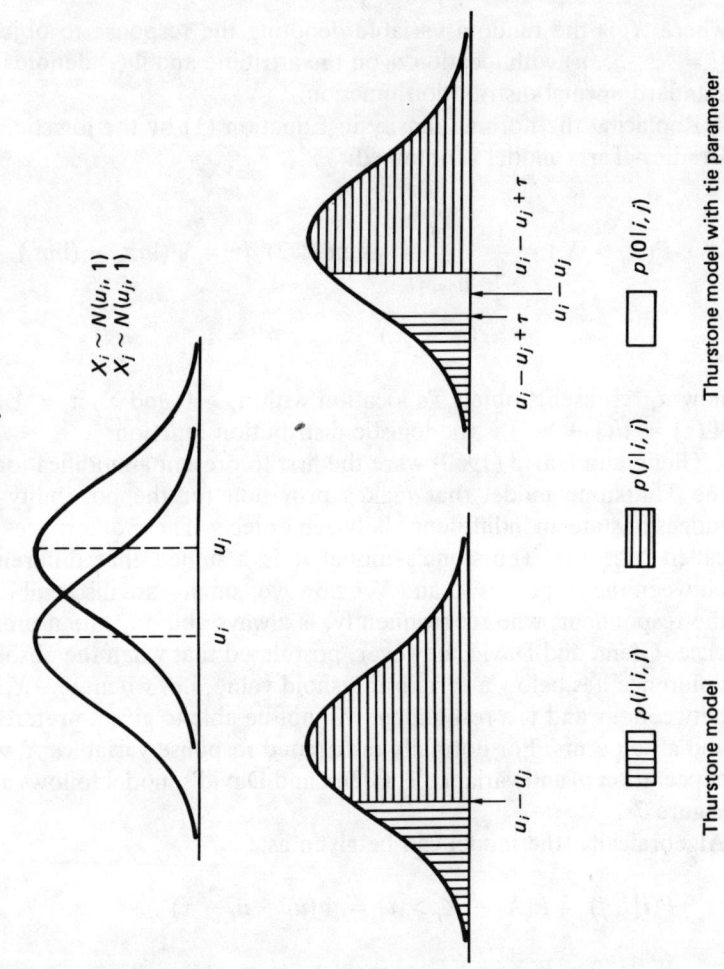

Figure 7.1 Thurstone model with and without tie parameter in a standard normal density

where $P(\cdot|i, j)$ are the probabilities that i is preferred, j is preferred or a tie occurs. It should be noted that τ, the threshold or tie parameter, can be interpreted as the judges' ability to discriminate between objects and that Thurstone's model is obtained for $\tau = 0$.

The second model for paired comparisons with ties is the one by Rao and Kupper (1967) obtained from the Bradley–Terry model along the same lines as above:

$$P(i|i, j) = \Psi(\ln\pi_i - \ln\pi_j - \ln\xi) = \pi_i/(\pi_i + \xi\pi_j)$$

$$P(j|i, j) = \Psi(\ln\pi_j - \ln\pi_i - \ln\xi) = \pi_j/(\pi_j + \xi\pi_i) \qquad (4)$$

$$P(0|i, j) = \Psi(\ln\pi_i - \ln\pi_j + \ln\xi) - \Psi(\ln\pi_i - \ln\pi_j - \ln\xi)$$

$$= \pi_i \pi_j (\xi^2 - 1)/(\pi_i + \xi\pi_j)(\pi_j + \xi\pi_i),$$

with ξ denoting the threshold or tie parameter.

The original Bradley–Terry model, Equation (2) has the property that the odds ratio $P(i|i, j)/P(j|i, j) = \pi_i/\pi_j$, by which it satisfies Luce's (1959) choice axiom.

Davidson (1970) gives an extension of the Bradley–Terry model that retains this property but allows for ties:

$$P(i|i, j) = \pi_i/(\pi_i + \pi_j + \nu\sqrt{\pi_i\pi_j})$$

$$P(j|i, j) = \pi_j/(\pi_i + \pi_j + \nu\sqrt{\pi_i\pi_j}) \qquad (5)$$

$$P(0|i, j) = \nu\sqrt{\pi_i\pi_j}/(\pi_i + \pi_j + \nu\sqrt{\pi_i\pi_j}),$$

where ν is the tie parameter. In the model the probability of a tie is proportional to $\sqrt{\pi_i\pi_j}$, which is the mean $\frac{1}{2}(\ln\pi_i + \ln\pi_j)$ of the object parameters on a logarithmic scale.

The models discussed so far have the common property that one tie parameter is introduced for all judges. This is a drawback if judges differ in ability to discriminate between objects, which they obviously will do for some sets of objects. In such cases there is a wish for an *individual* tie parameter. Kousgaard (1976) presents two models with individual tie parameters, one of which will be ignored here because it contains no separate object parameters. The other one can be shown to be identical to Davidson's model in Equation (5) with ν

replaced by a tie parameter v_k whose value is dependent on respondent k. As will be clear from the remaining part of the chapter this model has many attractive properties.

7.3 COMPARISON OF THE MODELS

All models above are generalisations of either the Thurstone or the Bradley–Terry model since one of the two follows upon specifying an appropriate value of the tie parameter (viz. $\tau = 0$, $\xi = 1$, $\nu = 0$ and $v_k = 0$ for all judges, respectively). Also, all models behave in a fashion that does not go against our intuition. For example, in all models the probability of a preference is decreasing in the tie parameter, but increasing in the distance between the object parameters. To the authors of the chapter this means that statistical considerations ought to be decisive in the choice of one of these models.

For Glenn and David's model (weighted) least-squares estimation procedures for the parameters are available, but not much is known about the properties of the estimators. This is different for the Rao–Kupper and the Davidson models for which maximum-likelihood procedures have been studied extensively for a wide variety of designs. Of these two, Davidson's model is to be preferred for several reasons. First, numerical simplifications in the estimation procedure are possible due to the fact that the model still satisfies Luce's choice axiom. Second, unlike Davidson's model, for Rao–Kupper's model the uniqueness of the maximum-likelihood estimates is not established (cf. Davidson and Beaver, 1977). Third, Davidson's model has, as opposed to Rao–Kupper's, the attractive property that for balanced designs the maximum-likelihood estimator of the object parameter is a monotone increasing function of the number of preferences of the object over all other objects. Four, and most importantly, Davidson's model can be reparameterised into an exponential family of probability distributions, which opens the attractive possibility of conditional inference (Andersen, 1980, ch. 3).

In contrast with Davidson's original model, Kousgaard's version allows for individual difference between judges. As was argued before, this is a most favorable provision since for most sets of objects judges obviously differ in their abilities to discriminate between pairs of them. Therefore, our conclusion is that from the existing models Kousgaard's is to be preferred, in particular because of its possibility of parameter estimation along the lines of conditional inference. This will be outlined in the following section.

7.4 ESTIMATION IN THE MODEL WITH INDIVIDUAL TIE PARAMETERS

Kousgaard's model can be brought on exponential form by the following reparameterisation of (5):

$$\sqrt{\pi_i} = \exp(\theta_i)$$

$$v_k = \exp(\zeta_k)$$

Formally, we then have random variables X_{ijk} representing the outcome of a comparison between object i and j ($i, j = 1, \ldots, n$) by judge k ($k = 1, \ldots, m$) with possible values -1, 0, and 1 for the events 'j is preferred', 'a tie', and 'i is preferred', respectively, which are distributed as

$$P(X_{ijk} = x) = \frac{\exp\{(\theta_i - \theta_j)x + \zeta_k(1 + x)(1 - x)\}}{\exp(\theta_i - \theta_j) + \exp(\theta_j - \theta_i) + \exp(\zeta_k)} \quad (6)$$

with parameter space

$$\{(\zeta_1, \ldots, \zeta_m, \theta_1, \ldots, \theta_n) \in R^{m+n}, \sum_{i=1}^{n} \theta_i = 0\}$$ (Kousgaard, 1976).

This model, which is easily verified to belong to the exponential family of distributions, is a model with so-called 'structural parameters' $\{\theta_i; i = 1, \ldots, n\}$ and incidental parameters $\{\zeta_k, k = 1, \ldots, m\}$. Hence, we have no guarantee that the joint maximum-likelihood estimators of the structural parameters are consistent, for if the number of persons tends to infinity, the same holds for the number of unknown parameters ζ_k (Neyman and Scott, 1948).

If in cases like this sufficient statistics for the incidental parameters are present, *conditional* maximum-likelihood procedures are suitable. For the distributions in Equation (6) it can be shown that $u_k = \sum_{i<j} (1 + X_{ijk})(1 - X_{ijk}) n_{ijk}$, where n_{ijk} is the number of comparison of objects i and j by judge k with $n_{ijk} = 0$ or 1, is sufficient for ζ_k.

This statistic is simply the number of ties stated by judge k. By a standard argument it follows that the likelihood function associated with the conditional distribution of $\{x_{ijk}; i \; j = 1, \ldots, n, k = 1, \ldots, m\}$ given $(U_1 = u_1, \ldots, U_m = u_m)$ is equal to

$$L_c = \frac{\exp\left(\sum_{i=1}^{n} \theta_i s_i\right)}{\prod_{k=1}^{m} h_{(u_k)}(\theta)}, \tag{7}$$

with

$$h_{(u_k)}(\theta) = \sum_{(u_k)} \exp \sum_{i=1}^{n} \theta_i s_i \tag{8}$$

where s_i is equal to the number of comparisons in which i is preferred minus the number in which another object is preferred to i and $\sum_{(u_k)}$ denotes summation over all possible outcomes with u_k ties.

The attractive thing about Equation (7) is that it does not contain any tie parameters and thus allows maximum-likelihood estimation of $\{\theta_i\}$ without any contamination by characteristics of the individual judges. As Kousgaard (1976) has demonstrated, the conditional estimators of $\{\theta_i\}$ given by Equation (7) consequently have desired asymptotic properties.

The foregoing nicely illustrates the logic of conditional inference but still has a practical disadvantage: the computational burden and possible numerical inaccurateness in determining Equation (8). For larger sets of objects the number of terms in Equation (8) and the propagation of errors arising in their iterative numerical evaluation may even become prohibitive.

An alternative to Equations (7)–(8), noted as an aside by Kousgaard, is not to condition $\{X_{ijk}\}$ on $(U_1 = u_1, \ldots, U_m = u_m)$, but to condition each individual random variable X_{ijk} on $U_{ijk} = 0$, i.e. in the event of no tie in the comparison between i and j by judge k. In practical terms this means that instead of aggregating our data and then conditioning on the number of ties per judge, we now first remove the ties and only then aggregate our data to estimate the object parameters. Again, it is a standard derivation to show that the resulting conditional likelihood equation yielded by this procedure is of the product-binomial form with the Bradley-Terry model as success parameter:

$$L'_c = \prod_{i<j} \left(\frac{\pi_i}{\pi_i + \pi_j}\right)^{s_{ij}} \left(\frac{\pi_j}{\pi_i + \pi_j}\right)^{n_{ij} - s_{ij}} \qquad (9)$$

in which n_{ij} is the number of comparisons between i and j in which no tie occurred and s_{ij} is the number of comparisons in which i was preferred to j. This surprising result, which has brought us back to the Bradley-Terry model, again shows us how conditioning on relevant statistics yields estimates of the object parameters that are independent of the incidental tie parameters. To solve the likelihood equations following from Equation (9), a simple algorithm with known properties given by Ford (1957) can be used.

It is this conditioning at the level of the individual events of ties that brought us to another application in the following section.

7.5 THE RASCH MODEL AS A MODEL FOR PAIRED COMPARISONS WITH TIES

Suppose an individual k with ability α_k responds to a dichotomous test item i with difficulty δ_i. The Rasch model assumes that the probability of a successful response is governed by

$$P(X_{ki} = 1) = \frac{\alpha_k}{\alpha_k + \delta_i} \qquad (10)$$

with $X_{ki} = 1$ denoting a successful response and $X_{ki} = 0$ a failure. The usual estimation procedures for the difficulty parameters in Equation (10) are of the conditional maximum-likelihood type with conditioning on the number of successes per individual to remove the incidental ability parameters from the model (e.g. Fischer, 1974, ch. 14). This approach, however, runs into numerical problems comparable to those for Kousgaard's likelihood Equations (7)–(8) mentioned earlier. For this reason standard programs for Rasch analysis do not accept more then 60 items.

The formal resemblance between these two problems as well as between the Rasch model and the Bradley–Terry model inspired the authors to overcome the numerical difficulties for the Rasch model in the same fashion as illustrated above, namely by conditioning on a sufficient statistic for the incidental ability parameter *at the level of the individual response variables*. An important difference between the present problem and the one by Kousgaard is that for the response variable in Equation (10) reduction of its sample space results in a degenerate statistic; hence, (non-trivial) sufficient statistics for the ability parameter α_k are not available. However, the response process described by Equation (10) can be conceived of as inducing a paired-comparisons experiment at the level of a single individual responding to a *pair* of items. As this turns out to be an experiment with ties, an analysis of this experiment instead of the original Rasch experiment has the advantage that conditioning as in Kousgaard's model is possible. How this can be done is indicated in the following. Only an outline of the procedure and some results from the first runs of a new computer program are given. For details and more results we refer to a forthcoming paper by the same authors (van der Linden and Eggen, forthcoming).

Suppose an individual k responds to two dichotomous items, i and j. The possible outcomes of this experiment can be conceived of emanating from a paired comparison between the difficulties of the two items. The outcome $\{X_{ik} = 1, X_{jk} = 0\}$ indicates that according to 'judge' k item j is more difficult than i, $\{X_{ik} = 0, X_{jk} = 1\}$ indicates the reverse, whereas the outcomes with both items right or wrong indicate that k is indifferent with respect to i and j and that a tie has occurred. From Equation (10) the probabilities of these three events are given by:

$$P_k(1, 0) = \alpha_k \delta_j / \{(\alpha_k + \delta_i)(\alpha_k + \delta_j)\}$$

$$P_k(0, 1) = \alpha_k \delta_i / \{(\alpha_k + \delta_i)(\alpha_k + \delta_j)\} \qquad (11)$$

$$P_k(\text{tie}) = (\alpha_k^2 + \delta_i \delta_j) / \{(\alpha_k + \delta_i)(\alpha_k + \delta_j)\}.$$

It should be noted that among the set of comparisons between all possible pairs from a test of n items, some of the outcomes are dependent. Van der Linden and Eggen (forthcoming) show that the number of dependencies is a simple function of the individual's number-right score and present several algorithms for removing dependencies from the data.

Conditioning the response variable for individual k defined in Equation (11) on the event of 'no tie' yields the result that

T. J. H. M. Eggen and W. J. van der Linden

$$P[(1,0)|(0,1),(1,0)] = \delta_j/(\delta_i + \delta_j). \quad (12)$$

So a Rasch experiment at the level of an individual responding to a series of n items can be conceived of as a Bradley–Terry experiment between pairs of them, provided we are willing to condition on the outcome of a non-tie and to remove dependencies from the data. The parameters in Equation (12) can then be estimated using, for example, Ford's (1957) iterative algorithm.

To demonstrate the feasibility of the above procedure for estimating larger sets of items, a provisional computer program PAIRCOM was written that made use of the Ford algorithm and removed the dependencies between comparisons of items on the basis of random selection. The program, for which no attempts have been made yet to speed up numerical procedures, was run against PML, one of the standard programs available for the Rasch model (Gustafsson, 1979). Simulated data for 1000 individuals with ability parameter values sampled from $N(2, 1)$ and items with difficulty parameters also sampled from $N(2, 1)$ were used. Table 7.1 shows the results in CPU-seconds. The maximum number of items

Table 7.1 CPU-seconds needed for comparable runs with PML and PAIRCOM on simulated data for 1000 individuals

No. of items	PML	PAIRCOM Parameter estimation	Data editing
20	5.6	1.3	9.8
40	12.6	3.6	13.9
60	31.7	9.8	18.5
100	–	19.7	28.6
200	–	145.0	64.0

accepted by PML is equal to 60. It appears that PAIRCOM is able to cope with larger sets of items and needs fewer CPU-seconds for the estimation of sets for which comparison with PML is possible. More extensive comparisons and studies with larger sets of items are planned. Table 7.1 also gives the time needed to edit the data (removal of ties and dependencies). This editing was based on an algorithm with random selection. Attempts to speed up this algorithm and to study possible alternatives are undertaken in van der Linden and Eggen (forthcoming).

7.6 DISCUSSION

The methodology used in the above reformulation of the Rasch model can be summarised as follows. The attention was focused at an individual responding to a pair of items. On the sample space of this compound experiment a statistic with a range of three possible values was defined, one value indicating dominance of item i over j, another of item j over i and the remaining one a tie. The probability distribution of this statistic was derived from the original model governing the response of the individual to a single item. Conditioning on the event of a non-tie not only enabled us to get rid of the ties, but also freed the model from the characteristics of the individual relevant with respect to the items and permitted independent comparisons between the items. This was made possible because the original model, and hence the model for the pair of items, belonged to the exponential family and the partitioning of the sample space for the pair of items into ties and non-ties was sufficient for the person parameter in the model.

Another possible application of this procedure that comes into mind is the problem of unfolding. Coombs's (1976) observation that preferential-choice data are contaminated by the presence of ideal points is basically what in this chapter was called the 'problem of individual' or, following Neyman and Scott's terminology, the 'problem of incidental parameters'. Conditioning on sufficient statistics for individual parameters is therefore a possible stochastic alternative to the deterministic technique of unfolding. The experiment is then reduced to one that yields data belonging to Coombs's quadrant of stimulus-comparison data and is described adequately by the conditional model. A critical step in this procedure is the selection of the model that describes the response of the individual to a single item. The case of the Rasch model dealt with in this chapter suggests a choice from the exponential family of distributions.

Acknowledgments

The authors are indebted to Rien Steen for writing a provisional version of the computer program for the analysis of Rasch test items with the paired-comparisons algorithm, and to Anita Burchartz-Huls for typing the manuscript.

REFERENCES

ANDERSEN, E. B., *Discrete Statistical Models with Social Science Applications* (Amsterdam: North-Holland, 1980).
BEAVER, R. J. and GOKHALE, D. V., 'A Model to Incorporate Within-pair Order Effects in Paired Comparisons', *Communications in Statistics*, 4 (1975) 923–39.
BRADLEY, R. A., 'Science, Statistics and Paired Comparisons', *Biometrics*, 32 (1976) 213–32.
⎯⎯ and TERRY, M. E., 'Rank Analysis of Incomplete Block Design: I. The Method of Paired Comparisons', *Biometrika*, 39 (1952) 324–45.
COOMBS, C. H., *A Theory of Data* (Ann Arbor, Mich.: Mathesis Press, 1976).
DAVID, H. A., *The Method of Paired Comparisons* (London: Griffin, 1963).
DAVIDSON, R. R., 'On Extending the Bradley–Terry Model to Accommodate Ties in Paired Comparison Experiments', *Journal of the American Statistical Association*, 65 (1970) 317–28.
⎯⎯ and BEAVER, R. J., 'On Extending the Bradley–Terry Model to Incorporate Within-pair Order Effects', *Biometrics*, 33 (1977) 693–702.
⎯⎯ and FARQUHAR, P. H., 'A Bibliography on the Method of Paired Comparisons', *Biometrics*, 32 (1976) 241–52.
DIJKSTRA, O., 'Rank Analysis of Incomplete Block Designs: A Method of Paired Comparisons Employing Unequal Repetitions on Pairs', *Biometrics*, 16 (1960) 176–88.
FECHNER, G. T., *Elemente der Psychophysik* (Leipzig: Breitkopf und Härtel, 1860).
FISCHER, G. H., *Einführung in die Theorie psychologischer Tests* (Bern, Stuttgart, Wien: Verlag Hans Huber, 1974).
FORD, L. R. J., 'Solution of a Ranking Problem from Binary Comparisons', *American Mathematical Monthly*, 64 (1957) 241–52.
GLENN, W. A. and DAVID, H. A., 'Ties in Paired Comparisons Experiments using a Modified Thurstone – Mosteller Method', *Biometrics*, 16 (1960) 86–109.
GRIDGEMAN, N. T., 'Pair Comparison, With and Without Ties', *Biometrics*, 15 (1959) 382–8.
GUSTAFSSON, J. E., *PML: A Computer Program for Conditional Estimation and Testing in the Rasch Model for Dichotomous Items*, Reports from the Institute of Education University of Göteborg, no. 85 (1979).
KOUSGAARD, N., 'Models for Paired Comparisons With Ties', *Scandinavian Journal of Statistics*, 3 (1976) 1–14.
⎯⎯ 'A Conditional Approach to the Analysis of Data from Paired Comparisons Experiments Incorporating Within-pair Order Effects', *Scandinavian Journal of Statistics*, 6 (1979) 154–60.
LINDEN, W. J. van der and EGGEN, T. J. H. M., 'The Rasch Model as a Model for Paired Comparisons with an Individual Tie Parameter', (forthcoming).
LUCE, R. D., *Individual Choice Behavior* (New York: Wiley & Sons, 1959).

MOLENAAR, W., 'Paired Comparisons: Some Models and Tests', *Bulletin of the International Statistical Institute*, **15** (1973) 212–18.
MOSTELLER, F., 'Remarks on the Method of Paired Comparisons: I. The Least Squares Solution assuming Equal Standard Deviations and Equal Correlations', *Psychometrika*, **16** (1951) 3–9.
NEYMAN, J. and SCOTT, E. L., 'Consistent Estimates Based on Partially Consistent Observations', *Econometrica*, **16** (1948) 1–5.
RAO, P. V. and KUPPER, L. L., 'Ties in Paired-comparison Experiments: A Generalization of the Bradley–Terry Model', *Journal of the American Statistical Association*, **62** (1967) 194–204 (corrigenda **63**, 1550).
RASCH, G., *Probability Models for Some Intelligence and Attainment Test* (Copenhagen: Danmarks Paedagogiske Institut, 1960).
THOMSON, W. A. and SINGH, J., 'The Use of Limit Theorems in Paired Comparison Model Building', *Psychometrika*, **32** (1967) 255–64.
THURSTONE, L. L., 'Psychophysical Analysis', *American Journal of Psychology*, **38** (1927) 368–89.
ZERMELO, E., 'Die Berechnung der Turnier-Ergebnisse als ein Maximumproblem der Warscheinlichkeitsrechnung', *Mathematisch Zeitschrift*, **29** (1929) 436–60.

8 Unidimensional Unfolding Complemented by Feigin and Cohen's Error Model

A. W. van Blokland-Vogelesang

8.1 INTRODUCTION

We shall first introduce the unfolding model as outlined in Coombs (1964). Coombs's unfolding model (Coombs, 1964) is based on the analysis of complete orderings of preference. Each judge reports his ordering of preference for a number of objects: I-scale ('*I*ndividual'). It is the aim of unidimensional unfolding to find the underlying dimension (if there is one) on which objects as well as individuals find a place: J-scale ('Joint').

Figure 8.1 J-scale ABCD, with one I-scale BCAD for judge V

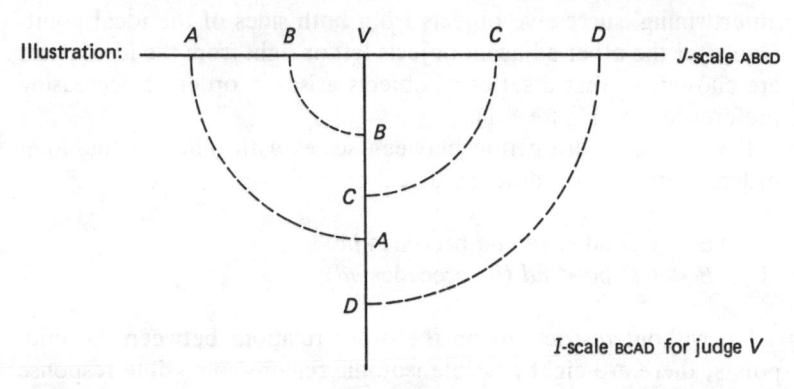

Illustration:

I-scale BCAD for judge V

If the J-scale ABCD is folded at point V, the I-scale BCAD for judge V arises. The general rule is: from the positions of a set of objects A, B, C, D . . . and a set of judges U, V, W, . . . on J-scale ABCD . . . we can determine the I-scales for all judges by 'folding' the J-scale at the appropriate point.

'Unfolding' is the inverse problem: on the basis of orders of preference of judges (*I*-scales) co-ordinates of judges and objects on a joint scale (*J*-scale) must be determined:

pp 1: A B C D
    2: B A C D   'UNFOLDING'   A   B   C   D   *J*-scale *ABCD*
    3: B C A D   •ₓ •   •   ₓ •
        : : : : :   U   V
        : : : : :
pp m: D A B C

In the unidimensional unfolding model possible orders of preference correspond to segments of the *J*-scale ('isotonic regions'):

The isotonic region *AB* is the set of ideal points (judges' points of highest preference) which are nearer to *A* than to *B*. In terms of unfolding: *AB* corresponds to the pattern of preference *AB* (*A* is preferred to *B*); *BA* to the pattern of preference *BA* (*B* is preferred to *A*).

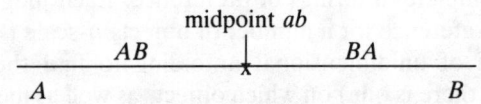

```
                    midpoint ab
            AB           |           BA
    _____x_____
    A                                                B
```

The *J*-scale for four stimuli *A*, *B*, *C* and *D* contains eight isotonic regions ('admissible regions'): *ABCD*, *BACD*, *BCAD*, *BCDA*, *CBAD*, *CBDA*, *CDBA* and *DCBA*. An isotonic region arises by 'intertwining' successive objects from both sides of the ideal point. One after the other adjacent objects left or right from the ideal point are chosen, so that a series of objects arises in order of decreasing preference (see Figure 8.1).

If we make a distinction between scales with different midpoint orders there are two different *J*-scales:

I. *AB* > *CD* ad < *bc* (*ad* precedes *bc*)
II. *AB* < *CD* *bc* < *ad* (*bc* precedes *ad*)

So, without restrictions on the order relations between the midpoints, there are eight possible isotonic regions/admissible response patterns in four-scale *ABCD*. The scale is called the *qualitative J-scale*. With restrictions on the order relations of midpoints one of the isotonic regions of the fourth *I*-scale (see Table 8.1) is excluded (only one order of *ad* and *bc* is possible), this scale is called the *quantitative J-scale*. A qualitative *J*-scale contains 2^{k-1} patterns, a

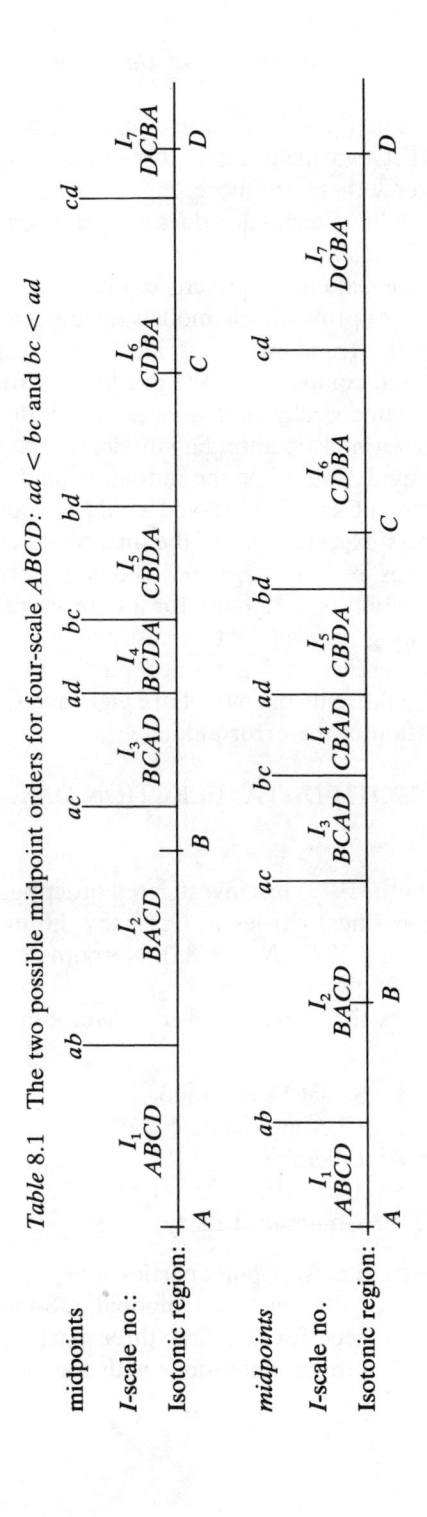

Table 8.1 The two possible midpoint orders for four-scale $ABCD$: $ad < bc$ and $bc < ad$

midpoints		ab		ac	ad	bc	bd		cd	
I-scale no.:	I_1 $ABCD$		I_2 $BACD$	I_3 $BCAD$	I_4 $BCDA$	I_5 $CBDA$		I_6 $CDBA$		I_7 $DCBA$
Isotonic region:	A		B					C			D

midpoints		ab		ac	bc	ad	bd		cd	
I-scale no.	I_1 $ABCD$		I_2 $BACD$	I_3 $BCAD$	I_4 $CBAD$	I_5 $CBDA$		I_6 $CDBA$		I_7 $DCBA$
Isotonic region:	A		B					C			D

quantitative J-scale $\binom{k}{2} + 1$ (k is the number of objects). So for $k=4$ we can construct two quantitative J-scales for every qualitative J-scale. For larger k there are more.

Coombs's unfolding technique does not provide for an error model or a criterion of scalability and hence is not applicable in a situation in which inadmissible patterns of preference occur ('deterministic model'). Some (parametric) probabilistic models have been developed which are rather specific (randomness of ideal points or randomness of object points) and complicated. We are looking for a simple model which adds (nonmetrically and nonparametrically) a probabilistic aspect to the deterministic unfolding model. By means of Feigin and Cohen's error model we made the unfolding model probabilistic, so that the number of errors observed could be compared with the number of errors expected. From the analysis of errors we can also determine a measure of concordance (homogeneity) among judges. From this a criterion of scalability for a data set can be derived.

In the following we will first discuss the data sets of Norpoth: orderings of preference of five political parties in Germany (Section 8.2). Section 8.3 presents the model of Feigin and Cohen and Section 8.4 the application of the error model.

8.2 THE NORPOTH-DATA: ELECTION DATA FROM 1969 AND 1972

Norpoth (Norpoth, 1979) has investigated orderings of preference of voters for five political parties in Germany during the elections of 1969 ($N = 907$) and 1972 ($N = 1785$). Norpoth determined qualitative J-scales for the two data sets.

The five parties that were involved in Norpoth's election investigation are:

1. SPD   ('S': Social Democrats)
2. CDU/CSU   ('C': Christian Democrats)
3. FDP   ('F': Liberals)
4. NPD   ('N': Ultra-Right Party)
5. DKP   ('K': Communist Party)

The three oldest and most popular parties are S, C and F. The extreme parties K and N are rather new and impopular. So we shall first try to unfold the preferences for the first three parties. Norpoth in his article distinguishes three dimensions with the three possible scales for F, S and C:

I. F S C : secular – clerical dimension
II. S C F : social – free enterprise dimension
III. S F C : left – right dimension

Each of these three-scales has two patterns in common with each of the other scales. In the samples of 1969 and 1972 respectively, we obtained the following frequencies per preference ordering:

Table 8.2 Three-scales for Norpoth's data sets

patterns	1969-scales F S C	S C F	S F C	1972-scales F S C	S C F	S F C
F S C	32	–	32	76	–	76
S F C	126	–	126	639	–	639
S C F	283	283	–	307	307	–
C S F	294	294	–	468	468	–
C F S	–	146	146	–	252	252
F C S	–	26	26	–	43	43
totally	735	749	330	1490	1070	1010
% perfect fit	81	83	36	83	60	57

Each J-scale for three items contains four patterns of preference. The 'best' J-scale can be defined as that combination of four preference patterns having maximal frequence. For the 1972 dataset the scale FSC contains 83 per cent of voters' preferences without error. For the 1969 dataset two scales are almost equally good: scale FSC contains 81 per cent of the voters' preferences without error, scale SCF 83 per cent. The F party occupies in most cases the lowest ranks, in fact it is 'dominated' by S and C.

Also for the five-tuples qualitative as well as quantitative J-scales have been determined. Table 8.2 contains the percentages of people that fit into qualitative/quantitative scales without errors: the results have been compared with those of Norpoth (Norpoth only gives the qualitative scales).

The qualitative J-scales obtained have a kernel $S\ C\ F$ (orderings (1) and (2)) or $F\ S\ C$ (orderings (3) and (4)). Left or right to this kernel the extreme parties, K and N, are placed. Actually there is hardly any difference in the results for the 1969 qualitative scales. For the 1972 data sets the results for scales (3) and (4) are superior to those for scales (1) and (2). The quantitative five-scales are more different. Scale *KFSCN* (3) is clearly the best one for both data sets.

Table 8.3 Five-scales for Norpoth's data sets

Norpoth data	1969				1972			
	qualitative		quantitative		qualitative		quantitative	
party ordering	Norpoth	author	Norpoth	author	Norpoth	author	Norpoth	author
(1) K S C F N	78	77		56		57	57	47
(2) N S C F K	78	77		52		57	57	44
(3) K F S C N	77	77		59		75	79	63
(4) N F S C K	75	75		48		76	76	56
N=	907				1785			

Finding the Best J-scale

The notion of a most likely ordering (J-scale) in a nonparametric model for unfolding is treated in Section 8.4. The 'best' qualitative J-scale can be defined as that order of k objects that makes a maximum number of judges fit the scale perfectly. This best qualitative J-scale can be found by backtracking all k! rankings. Most rankings will be rejected, because of bad fit, a minority can be selected for closer examination. If k is large, however, heuristic methods are required. An example of a heuristic method is the following: the best qualitative J-scale is constructed with the help of the mean order of preference. The two objects with highest mean preference are given adjacent positions along the J-scale. Remaining objects get positions (in decreasing order of mean preference) to the left or to the right of already-placed objects. This is possible in 2^{k-2} ways. In this way the mean number of inversions between judges' orders of preference and the patterns in the J-scale will be minimised in most of the cases. In fact this method will work if the stimuli form an 'efficient set' (Coombs and Avrunin, 1977; Coombs, 1975) and will not work if the density of ideal points over the J-scale is not unimodal.

All possible quantitative J-scales that can be derived from one qualitative J-scale can be represented as the possible paths through a lattice of qualitative patterns. On the basis of this representation of objects in the qualitative scale an algorithm has been developed to recover the best quantitative J-scale.

8.3 FEIGIN AND COHEN'S ERROR MODEL

Two important models for the analysis of ranking data have been proposed (Cohen and Mallows, 1983). In the first it is assumed that there is an underlying k-dimensional normal distribution. The ordering of a judge is assumed to be the result of ranking a random vector X from the underlying distribution. For each of the k items a score X_i can be associated, which is a random normal variable with mean u_i and variance σ_i^2 ($i = 1, \ldots, k$). There is a number of variations of this model. One particular case is when the scores X_i are assumed to be independent. This is the Thurstone–Mosteller–Daniels model (Daniels, 1950) and is characterised by 2k parameters $\mu_1, \ldots, \mu_k$, $\sigma_1^2, \ldots, \sigma_k^2$).

Another family of distributions for ranking data is a nonparametric one: it does not depend on parametric assumptions (linearity, normality). This family of distributions has been derived by Mallows (1957). The basis for his derivation was the Bradley–Terry model (1952) for paired comparisons. A particular case of this family is the model which has been proposed by Feigin and Cohen (1977, 1978). The distribution in this model depends on two parameters, which we denote in the notation of Feigin and Cohen (1977) by ω_0 and θ. The first is an ordering that acts as a location parameter ($\omega_0 = \omega_{01}, \ldots, \omega_{0k}$, 'basic ordering'). The second parameter is a nonnegative dispersion parameter. According to the model of Feigin and Cohen the probability of a ranking ω, $\omega = (\omega_1, \ldots, \omega_k)$ is:

$$P(\omega|\omega_0, \theta) = K\, \theta^{X(\omega_0, \omega)}$$

where K is a normalising constant so that the probabilities sum to 1, and $X(\omega_0, \omega)$ is the number of discordant pairs between the ranking ω and the location parameter ω_0. When $\theta = 0$ there is perfect concordance and all judges select the same ranking ω_0 (no dispersion around ω_0), while $\theta = 1$ corresponds to the uniform permutation distribution, when all $k!$ permutations are equally likely (no structure in the data). The model implies that all rankings with the same number of discordant pairs with respect to the basic ranking ω_0 will be equally likely, or equivalently, that rankings having the same Kendall's τ (Kendall, 1975) with ω_0 will be equally likely. This implies that the probability of interchanging objects is constant for each pair of objects.

The model of Feigin and Cohen can be interpreted as stating that judges have the same latent ordering ω_0 and make errors in reporting it. A low value of θ corresponds to judges making few errors. The larger the value of θ the more errors and the more improbable the existence of one underlying (preference) ordering will be. In the Feigin and Cohen model one basic ordering is sought which has minimal number of inversions from individual preference orderings. In the unfolding model a J-scale consists of $\binom{k}{2} + 1$ 'basic orderings' ω_{0i} ($i = 1, \ldots, \binom{k}{2} + 1$) corresponding to the admissible patterns of the J-scale. So, analogously to the Feigin and Cohen situation, the most likely J-scale is that ordered set of $\binom{k}{2} + 1$ admissible patterns which has minimal number of inversions from the individual response patterns. In Feigin and Cohen's model the maximum likelihood estimate for θ is that value of θ for which $\bar{X} = E_\theta(X)$. In the unfolding situation θ can be estimated in the same way, averaging over admissible patterns. Having obtained θ we are able to assess

$$E_\theta(\tau) = 1 - 2 \binom{k}{2}^{-1} \cdot \bar{X},$$

$E_\theta(\tau)$ being a linear transformation of a sufficient statistic for θ (Feigin and Cohen, 1978, p. 206). The advantage of using $E_\theta(\tau)$, rather than θ, is that it is a well-known estimate of the concordance between the judges and their underlying rankings, for which we know that $0 \leq E_\theta(\tau) \leq 1$, values nearer 1 corresponding to greater concordance.

The model assumptions for the extension of Feigin and Cohen's model in the unfolding situation can be formulated as follows:

(1) The quantitative *J*-scale is known.
(2) Each individual has a latent pattern of preference identical to one of the $\binom{k}{2} + 1$ admissible patterns of the *J*-scale.
(3) The ranking actually given by the judge has, according to Feigin and Cohen's model, this person's latent ordering as basic ordering. We can think of this as follows: when judging objects according to their individual pattern of preference people can make mistakes: adjacent objects (neighbours) can be interchanged.
(4) Every pair of neighbours has the same probability to be interchanged (no system in the errors).
(5) Most judges make no errors, some make one error and only very few make two or more errors. To simplify matters it will sometimes be assumed that nobody makes more than two errors.

8.4 ESTIMATION OF θ

When observing an inadmissible pattern we can determine how many inversions on our part are necessary to change an inadmissible pattern into an admissible one. With

X = number of inversions made by the judge when stating his pattern of preference;
Y = minimum number of inversions the researcher has to apply to an inadmissible pattern in order to change it into an admissible one;

we can investigate the relationship between X and Y. Feigin and Cohen's model in principle allows any number of errors. We assume

Table 8.4 $P_\theta (X)$ for selected values of θ and X

X \ θ	0.1	0.2	0.25	0.3
0	0.66	0.43	0.34	0.27
1	0.27	0.34	0.34	0.33
2	0.06	0.16	0.19	0.22
⩾3	0.01	0.07	0.13	0.18
$E_\theta(X)$	0.42	0.88	1.13	1.39

that every person has an admissible pattern in his head, but that he makes 'random' errors on it. To this assumption corresponds a low dispersion parameter θ, making the probability of many inversions (X) very small or even negligible. That means that a priori judgments about the value of θ can directly be translated into corresponding assertions about the distribution of X and about $E_\theta(\tau)$.

The relationship between X and Y is not quite straightforward. Observing an admissible pattern does not mean that the person in question has not made any errors. In the same way the number of inversions Y that we apply to an inadmissible pattern can be too low: the judge may have had another admissible pattern in his head than the nearest one. In any case $Y \leqslant X$. For $Y > 0$ the relationship between Y and θ can be determined from the relationship between X and Y and the relationship between X and θ. Hence θ can be estimated from the sample value of Y. Assuming equal probability for admissible patterns it is possible to determine the number of patterns which, at X inversions from an admissible pattern, can be changed into an admissible pattern with Y inversions (in the appendix $P(Y, X)$ for a five-scale is presented). From the appendix, the first scheme (admissible pattern $ABCDE$), we see that $P(Y = 1 | X = 2) = 2/9$. Summing over patterns we find $P(Y = 1 | X = 2) = 43/99$. Having obtained $P(Y|X)$ (which is independent of θ) we are able to assess the probability distribution of Y given θ: $P_\theta(Y) = \Sigma P(Y = y|x) \cdot P_\theta(X = x)$ $(x \geqslant y)$. We want to consider scales with a low value of θ only, i.e. with a high probability that $Y < 3$. So, all $Y \geqslant 3$ are lumped together:

$$P_\theta(Y = 0) \approx P(Y = 0 | X = 0) \cdot P(X = 0) + \ldots$$
$$+ P(Y = 0 | X = 3) \cdot P_\theta(X \geqslant 3).$$

In general: $P_\theta(Y = y) = \Sigma P(Y = y|x) \cdot P_\theta(X = x), (x \geqslant y).$

Table 8.5 $P_\theta(Y)$ for selected values of θ and Y

Y \ θ	0.1	0.2	0.25	0.30
0	0.80	0.63	0.57	0.51
1	0.17	0.27	0.30	0.32
2	0.03	0.08	0.11	0.14
⩾3	0.00	0.01	0.02	0.03
$E_\theta(Y)$	0.23	0.48	0.59	0.69

Again, we estimate θ as that value of θ for which $\bar{Y} = E_\theta(Y)$. In Tables 8.4 and 8.5 $P_\theta(X)$ and $P_\theta(Y)$ respectively, are presented for selected values of θ.

8.5 A CRITERION OF SCALABILITY: HOMOGENEITY OF JUDGES

With Y = minimal number of inversions necessary to make patterns of preference admissible, it is possible to compare observed values of Y with expected values of Y given certain values of θ. A low value of θ indicates a greater homogeneity among judges. A criterion of scalability could then be an upper bound for $\theta(\theta_c)$ or a lower bound for $E_\theta(\tau): \tau_c$. With a χ^2-test for goodness of fit it can be tested whether the observed distribution of Y-values corresponds with the expected distribution of Y-values for a certain $\theta \leq \theta_c$.

8.6 FEIGIN AND COHEN'S ERROR MODEL APPLIED TO NORPOTH'S DATA SETS

In Section 8.2 we have already obtained the 'best' quantitative scale. Now the quality control of the scale remains to be considered.

The unfolding model gave us the scale, Feigin and Cohen's error model gives numbers/percentages of errors that correspond with a certain value of the error parameter θ. Starting from the observed numbers of inversions Y it is possible to estimate θ. Subsequently it can be tested whether the observed Y values 'fit' into Feigin and Cohen's error model with that value of θ. The calculated values of Y for the best J-scale for Norpoth's data sets are presented below.

For the 1969 data $\bar{Y} = 0.50$, so $\hat{\theta} = 0.2$ (see Table 8.5). For the goodness-of-fit test all $Y \geq 3$ are lumped together. If $\hat{\theta} = .2$ the

Table 8.6 Observed values of y for found quantitative scales for Norpoth's 1969 and 1972 data sets

Y	data set 1969 number with Y	%	data set 1972 number with Y	%
0	534	58.88	1139	63.81
1	312	34.40	496	27.79
2	47	5.18	135	7.56
3	7	0.77	10	0.56
4	7	0.77	5	0.28
>4	–	–	–	–
N	907		1785	
$\bar{Y}$	0.50		0.47	

goodness-of-fit test yields $\chi^2 = 31.89$, $df = 3$, $p < 0.005$. For the 1972 data $\bar{Y} = 0.47$, so $\hat{\theta} = 0.2$ ($\chi^2 = 3.88$, $df = 3$, $0.25 < p < 0.50$). The 1972 data seem to fit Feigin and Cohen's model, the 1969 data don't. So for this data set we should reject the unfolding model. Having obtained $\hat{\theta}$ from $P_\theta(Y)$ we can switch to $P_\theta(X)$ to assess $E_\theta(\tau)$ (see Section 8.3):

$$E_{0.2}(\tau) = 1 - 2 \binom{5}{2}^{-1} \cdot E_\theta(X) = 0.82.$$

The estimated value of $\hat{\theta}$ of θ can be used to assess the degree of homogeneity of the judges: $E_\theta(\tau) = 0.82$ ($\hat{\theta} = 0.2$). So, the allocation of judges to admissible patterns of a most likely J-scale resulted in relatively little variation of judges' orderings around these patterns (low θ), thus relatively high concordance between judge's manifest and latent orderings ($E_\theta(\tau) = 0.82$). As scalability coefficients θ_c and τ_c can be used. For each $\tau_c \leq 0.82$ the 1972 data set would have been scalable.

REFERENCES

BLOKLAND-VOGELESANG, A. W. van, 'Unfolding of Preferences' (forthcoming thesis, 1987).
BRADLEY, R. A. and TERRY, M. E., 'Rank Analysis of Incomplete Block Designs I', *Biometrika*, **39** (1952) 324–45.

COHEN, A. and MALLOWS, C. L., 'Assessing Goodness of Fit of Ranking Models to Data', *The Statistician*, **32** (1983) 361–73.
COOMBS, C. H., 'A Theory of Data', (New York: Wiley, 1964).
____ 'A Note on the Relation between the Vector Model and the Unfolding Model for Preferences', *Psychometrika*, **40** (1975) 115–16.
____ and AVRUNIN, G. S., 'Single Peaked Functions and the Theory of Preference', *Psychological Review*, **84** (1977) 216–30.
DANIELS, H. E., 'Rank Correlation and Population Models', *Journal of Royal Statistical Society (B)*, **12** (1950) 171–81.
FEIGIN, P. D. and COHEN, A., *A Model for Concordance Between Judges*', Operations Research, Statistics and Economics, Mimeograph Series no. 189 (1977).
____ and ____ 'On a Model for Concordance between Judges', *Journal of Royal Statistical Society (B)*, **40** (1978) 203–13.
KENDALL, M. G., *Rank Correlation Methods* (London: Griffin, 1975).
MALLOWS, C. L., 'Non-null Ranking Models I'. *Biometrika*, **44** (1957) 114–30.
NORPOTH, H., 'The Parties Come to Order! Dimensions of Preferential Choice in the West German Electorate, 1961–1976', *American Political Science Revue* **73**(1979) 724–36.
VEN, A. H. G. S. van der, *Inleiding in de Schaaltheorie* (Deventer: Van Loghum Slaterus, 1977).

APPENDIX

$P(Y,X)$ for a quantitative five-scale ABCDE.

1. ABCDE

X \ Y	0	1	2	3	
1	1	3	0	0	4
2	1	2	6	0	9
3	1	2	4	8	15
	3	7	10	8	

2. BACDE

X \ Y	0	1	2	3	
1	2	2	0	0	4
2	1	5	3	0	9
3	1	2	8	4	15
	4	9	11	4	

3. BCADE

X \ Y	0	1	2	3	
1	2	2	0	0	4
2	2	4	3	0	9
3	1	4	7	3	15
	5	10	10	3	

4. BCDAE

X \ Y	0	1	2	3	
1	2	2	0	0	4
2	2	3	4	0	9
3	2	4	5	4	15
	6	9	9	4	

5. CBDAE

X \ Y	0	1	2	3	
1	2	2	0	0	4
2	2	4	3	0	9
3	2	3	8	2	15
	6	9	11	2	

6. CDBAE

X \ Y	0	1	2	3	
1	2	2	0	0	4
2	2	3	4	0	9
3	2	4	6	3	15
	6	9	10	3	

7. CDBEA

X \ Y	0	1	2	3	
1	2	2	0	0	4
2	2	5	2	0	9
3	2	3	9	1	15
	6	10	11	1	

8. CDEBA

X \ Y	0	1	2	3	
1	2	2	0	0	4
2	2	4	3	0	9
3	2	5	5	3	15
	6	11	8	3	

9. DCEBA

X \ Y	0	1	2	3	
1	2	2	0	0	4
2	2	5	2	0	9
3	1	4	9	1	15
	5	11	11	1	

10. DECBA

X \ Y	0	1	2	3	
1	2	2	0	0	4
2	1	5	3	0	9
3	1	3	7	4	15
	4	10	10	4	

11. EDCBA

X \ Y	0	1	2	3	
1	1	3	0	0	4
2	1	3	5	0	9
3	1	2	5	7	15
	3	8	10	7	

9 Stochastic Unfolding
W. H. van Schuur

9.1 INTRODUCTION

In survey research we regularly encounter the following type of question: 'Which of these stimuli do you prefer most?, which of the remaining ones do you now prefer most?' etcetera. Sometimes a full rank order of preferences is asked in this way, more often only a partial rank order is obtained. Sometimes even only the question is asked: 'Which k of these n stimuli do you prefer most?', or, even more generally, 'Which of these n stimuli do you prefer?' These questions can be referred to as 'rank n/n', 'rank k/n', 'pick k/n', and 'pick any/n' data, respectively. Stimuli may be political parties, candidates, career possibilities or brand names of some consumer good. Rather than asking about 'preference' the questions may also be phrased in terms of other evaluative concepts like 'sympathy' or 'importance'. In this chapter I will be concerned with analysing such data of the form 'pick k/n' or 'pick any/n' data.

Generally these data types are difficult to analyse. Often responses to such data are only reported in the form of frequency distributions of the number of times a stimulus is mentioned as most preferred, as second most preferred, etc. Trying to find structure in these responses, for instance with the help of standard techniques like factor analysis or cumulative scaling is not possible, either because no full set of responses to all stimuli are available, or because the responses given are not independent. It is then difficult to answer the question whether all responses given were based on the same underlying criterion, for instance. In this chapter an analysis technique is presented that allows 'pick k/n' or 'pick any/n' data to look for structure in the responses to these questions. Since complete or partial rank orders can always be recoded to the 'pick k/n' form, and since independently responded survey questions, like five-point Likert items, can be recoded to the 'pick any/n' form, the type of data analysis presented here is very general.

The data-analysis technique presented here is a dichotomous version of the unfolding model, proposed by Coombs (1950, 1964), as 'parallelogram analysis'. It differs from Coombs's original proposal in the following ways: the technique proposed here allows for some error (i.e. it conforms to a stochastic model), and it is an exploratory technique to search for maximal subsets of stimuli that are representable in a unidimensional unfolding scale. In both these aspects the 'parallelogram analysis' model proposed here resembles the stochastic unidimensional cumulative scaling technique, developed by Mokken (1971). The reader should be warned that the technique presented here is not an all-purpose technique for analysing 'pick k/n' or 'pick any/n' data, but only for such types of data that can be expected to conform to the unfolding model!

9.2 THE PERFECT UNIDIMENSIONAL UNFOLDING MODEL FOR FULL RANK ORDERS OF PREFERENCE

In this section I will first summarise some basic ideas behind unfolding analysis, by using an example from Meerling (1981). In an investigation by Ritzema and van der Kloot preference rank orders were collected for the following statements:

O: People can be changed in any conceivable direction, provided that the environment is manipulated in the proper way (O = *omgeving*, environment);
I: The major condition for people to change is for them to have a clear understanding of their situation (I = *inzicht*, understanding);
E: Behavior is determined much more strongly by emotions than by rational considerations (E = *emoties*, emotions);
A: Inborn characteristics determine to a large extent what kind of person someone becomes (A = *aangeboren*, inborn).

These four statements were shown to colleague psychologists, and the following six types of preference rank orders were found: *OIEA, IOEA, IEOA, EIOA, EAIO* and *AEIO*.

In applying the unfolding model we assume that there is a latent dimension on which each of these statements can be represented. Meerling suggests for these statements and these preference rank orders that a 'nurture – nature' dimension may be appropriate, in which the statements are arranged in the order $O\ I\ E\ A$.

When the location of each of the statements on this dimension is

Figure 9.1 Midpoint m (OI) divides the dimension into two areas

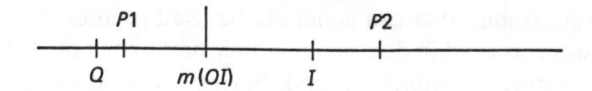

```
         P1           |         P2
  ───────┼─┼──────────┼──────────┼────────
         Q   m(OI)              I
```

established, the dimension can be divided into two areas for each pair of statements (O, I): the first area, in which the first statement is preferred to the second, and the second area, in which the second statement is preferred to the first. The boundary between these two areas lies in the middle between these two stimuli, and is called the 'midpoint of the pair of stimuli', $m(OI)$. This midpoint allows us to locate individuals who give their preference rank order along this dimension. An individual, *P1*, who prefers statement O to statement I will be located to the left of midpoint $m(OI)$, whereas another individual, *P2*, who prefers statement I to statement O, will be located to the right of that midpoint. (see Figure 9.1)

All four statements together give rise to the six midpoints. These divide the dimension up into seven areas, namely the areas that are separated by the midpoints. Each of these areas is characterised by a special preference rank order, and is called an 'isotonic region' (see Figure 9.2):

Figure 9.2 4 stimuli, 6 midpoints, and 7 isotonic areas or subject types

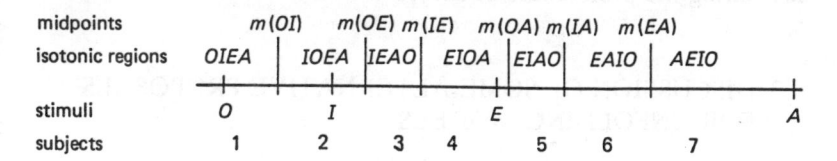

midpoints		$m(OI)$	$m(OE)$	$m(IE)$	$m(OA)$	$m(IA)$	$m(EA)$	
isotonic regions	OIEA	IOEA	IEAO	EIOA	EIAO	EAIO	AEIO	
stimuli	O		I		E			A
subjects	1	2	3	4	5	6	7	

A subject is usually represented along the scale by a single point, called his 'ideal point'. The preference order of the subject is called his '*I*ndividual scale', or '*I*-scale' for short. The representation of all subjects and all stimuli jointly on the same dimension is called the '*J*oint-scale', or '*J*-scale' for short. The *I*-scale gives the order of the stimuli in terms of their distance from the ideal point of the individual. In other words: the *I*-scale has to be 'unfolded' at the ideal point to give the *J*-scale.

Unfolding analysis is designed to find a joint representation of stimuli and subjects in one dimension, that is, to find a unidimensional

J-scale on the basis of the preference rank orders of the individuals' I-scales. Finding a J-scale brings us two things: First, an unfoldable order of the stimuli that can generally be used to infer the criterion that the subjects used in determining their preference order (e.g. the nurture – nature criterion). Second, having a J-scale means that we can combine a subject's answers to the n survey questions in a single rank order, that can be used to measure the preference of the subject, in terms of his ideal point on the criterion-dimension. By measuring a subject's preference in this way we create a new variable that can be related to other characteristics of the subject. The purpose of creating such a new variable is to try to explain why people differ in their preferences, or to explain other attitudes or behaviours on the basis of subjects' scale values on the J-scale.

If we have perfect data, such as we usually find in textbooks on scaling (and by perfect data I mean I-scales that can be perfectly represented in a unidimensional unfolding scale), it is no problem to find the J-scale that represents the I-scales. Problems only begin when the data are not perfect, which is almost immediately. The major reason why the unfolding technique has so far been relatively unpopular and why it has as yet not been incorporated into most standard statistical packages, is that up to now we have not been able to unfold imperfect data in a satisfactory way. If we could find a usable unfolding technique the interest for it should be great, since the model is plausible, and there is a great deal of interest in measuring the preferences of subjects.

9.3 DISCUSSION OF SOME ALTERNATIVE PROPOSALS FOR UNFOLDING MODELS

Before introducing my own model I will first consider five strategies that have been developed in the literature and that attempt to find useful and interpretable unfolding results. These strategies are all derived from a description of the ideal type of unfolding analysis, namely the perfect representation of a complete rank order of preferences in a unidimensional space, in which all stimuli and all individuals can be represented. These five strategies are:

1. Analyse the I-scales after they have been dichotomised into the k most-preferred and the $n-k$ least-preferred stimuli.

2. Relax the criterion of perfect representation to allow stochastic representation.
3. Find a representation in more than one dimension.
4. Find a representation for a maximal subset of the stimuli.
5. Find a representation of a maximal subset of the subjects.

The first strategy is dichotomising full or partial rank orders of stimuli into the k most-preferred and the $n-k$ least-preferred stimuli. The unfolding analysis of such data, parallelogram analysis, can be defended by pointing out that the stimuli a subject prefers most will be the most salient ones for him, and a subject will therefore be able to single them out more reliably than the remaining ones. Moreover, although the unfolding model assumes that successively chosen stimuli are in a sense substitutes for the subjects' most-preferred stimulus to a decreasing degree, gradually, in the course of giving a full rank order of preference, a subject may begin to use other criteria. Coombs (1964) talked about the 'portfolio model' in this respect, and Tversky (1972) suggested an 'Elimination by Aspects' model, in which different criteria for preference are hierarchically ordered. If we are interested in finding the dominant criterion that is used first by all respondents, then we should restrict ourselves to analysing only the first few most-preferred stimuli, lest we run the risk of introducing idiosyncratic noise.

Two more practical advantages of this strategy can be mentioned. First, if applying an unfolding model in which the distinction between the k most-preferred and the $n-k$ least-preferred stimuli does not lead to a good-fitting representation, than it is no use trying more sophisticated models that require the full rank order, or that may even require metric preference information. Second, the unfolding of dichotomous data implies that essentially all types of data can be used in doing a preference analysis, as long as the most-preferred responses can be distinguished from the others.

The second criterion is to relax the criterion of perfect representation to allow stochastic representation. I regard it as obvious that preference judgements reflect so many idiosyncratic influences, that we should be happy to find that a rather heterogeneous group of subjects agrees on at least a dominant criterion. Stochastic models have been proposed before (Sixtl, 1973; Zinnes and Griggs, 1974; Bechtel, 1976; Jansen, 1983). I regard these proposals as inferior to the model I propose for at least the following two reasons. First, many of the probabilistic unfolding models assume that the order of the stimuli along the *J*-scale is already known, and the only thing needed is parameter estimation of subjects and stimuli on the basis of the known order. In many cases such an approach is begging the question, since often this order of the stimuli is not known in advance. Second, other stochastic unfolding models require that for each subject we need his probability of preferring one stimulus to the other. In many practical applications this information will be impossible to obtain: it is expensive and time-consuming enough to ask respondents one single time to compare all pairs of stimuli with respect to preference.

A third strategy to analyse data that are not unfoldable in one dimension is to try to represent them in more than one dimension. It is possible that subjects did not use a single criterion in making their preference judgements; they may instead have used two or three criteria simultaneously. Multidimensional models have been proposed by Bennett and Hays (1960); Roskam (1968); Schönemann, 1970; Carroll, 1972; Young, 1972; Gold, 1973; Kruskal *et al.*, 1973; and Heiser, 1981, among others. They are appealing, because the use of more than one dimension implies the possibility of using a number of additional models that differ in the way in which these different dimensions are combined: the vector model, the weighted distance model, or the compensatory distance model, to mention only a few.

There are at least four possible problems with the multidimensional unfolding model. First, in applying a nonmetric multidimensional unfolding model, we may find an almost degenerate solution, in which most subjects are close together in the centroid of the space, and most stimuli lie in a circle around it. Second, also with respect to nonmetric multidimensional unfolding, there is a fundamental difference between the nonmetric analysis of similarities data and the nonmetric analysis of preference data, even though both models are based on the same principle. In the multidimensional analysis of similarities the isotonic region in which a stimulus falls becomes so small that for a sufficient number of stimuli each stimulus can only be represented by a point in the space, rather than by a region. But in multidimensional unfolding the representation of some respondents in the form of such isotonic regions is different: some isotonic regions do not shrink to points, but remain open. Such respondents cannot be uniquely represented by one point in the space. Third, multidimensional unfolding assumes that all dimensions are used simultaneously, rather than in an hierarchical order. This is an empirical question, rather than an untestable assumption. Fourth, the assumption that all dimensions are appropriate for all stimuli is equally an empirical question, rather than an untestable assumption.

We are told that reality is not unidimensional. Indeed, a chair has a colour, a weight and a number of sizes. A person has an age, a sex and a preference for certain drinks. And a political party may be large, religious and right-wing. Still, we never analyse reality. We analyse *aspects of* reality! We do not compare chairs, subjects or political parties, but sizes of chairs, ages of subjects and ideological positions of political parties. The fact that objects or subjects have more aspects than the ones we are interested in, does not at all imply that our analyses need to be multidimensional. That may be so, but that is an empirical question, and not an untestable assumption from the outset. I do not fundamentally object to a multidimensional representation of preferences of a group of subjects. There may be instances in which that is indeed the best model. But the use of different models will have to show in their practical applicability.

With respect to the last two strategies for salvaging the unfolding model, selecting a maximal subset of stimuli and selecting a maximal subset of subjects, it is established practice in multidimensional unfolding analysis to assign stress values to subjects. This implies that any difficulties in finding a representation can be explained by pointing at subjects who used different criteria, or who perhaps even behaved completely at random. A possible procedure, given this assumption, is to delete respondents whose stress values are too high.

However, it may be the case that large stress values occur because one or more stimuli cannot be represented since they do not belong in the same universe of content with the other stimuli. Subjects are allowed to differ in their evaluation of the stimuli, but for unfolding to apply, they have to agree about the cognitive aspects of the stimuli: whether gentlemen prefer blondes or brunettes is a different matter from establishing whether Marilyn is blonde or brown. If there is no agreement among the subjects about the characteristics of a stimulus, differences in preference will be difficult to represent.

Often, subjects are selected as representatives of a larger population. Deleting subjects lowers the possibility of generalising from a sample to a population. Stimuli, on the other hand, are often not so much a random sample of a population of stimuli, but are more often intended to serve as the best and most prototypical indicators of a latent trait: we are often not so much interested in the actual stimuli, but only in their implications for measuring subjects along this latent trait. This means that we generally can delete stimuli with less harm, compared to deleting subjects.

The discussion of these strategies is intended to justify the strategy adopted in the technique to be described below, of finding a stochastic representation of a maximal subset of stimuli and all subjects in one dimension, using the first few preferences of each subject.

9.4 UNFOLDING DICHOTOMOUS DATA: THE CONCEPT OF 'ERROR'

We generally do not know in advance which stimuli are representable in an unfolding scale, let alone in which order they are representable. The approach used here is a form of hierarchical cluster analysis, in which first the best smallest unfolding scale is found, which then is extended by more stimuli, as long as they continue to fulfil the criteria of an unfolding scale. The smallest unfolding scale consists of three stimuli, since it takes at least three stimuli to falsify the unfolding model. If stimuli A, B and C form a perfect unfolding scale in this order, then subjects who prefer A and C, but not B, do not exist. For the unfolding scale ABC the response patterns in which A and C are preferred but B is not, is defined as the 'error pattern' of that triple of stimuli. But since we do not know in advance in what order the stimuli form an unfolding scale, we must take all three permutations into account, in which each of the three stimuli is the middle one: BAC, ABC and ACB. If a subject prefers A and B, but not C, he makes an error according to the unfolding scale ACB, for instance.

For each triple of stimuli and a dichotomous response to each stimulus, eight response patterns are possible: *111*, *110*, *101*, *011*, *100*, *010*, *001* and *000*. If these stimuli form part of an unfolding scale, then one of these eight patterns cannot occur: the pattern '*101*' (see Table 9.1). This pattern is called the 'error response'.

For each triple of stimuli, in each of its three possible permutations, the frequency of occurrence of the error pattern can be counted. This idea of counting frequencies of error-response patterns can be extended to larger response pattern, in which each subject evaluates more stimuli. Table 9.2 gives five response patterns in which two or three stimuli are preferred from a set of four. In the first two response patterns only one triple is in error. In the last three response patterns two triples are in error. The amount of error in a

Table 9.1 Parallelogram analysis of perfect 'pick 3/11' data
1: subject prefers stimulus
0: subject does not prefer stimulus

subjects:	1	2	3	4	5	6	7	8	9		
stimuli:	A	B	C	D	E	F	G	H	I	J	K
subject nr.	response pattern:										
1	1	1	1	0	0	0	0	0	0	0	0
2	0	1	1	1	0	0	0	0	0	0	0
3			1	1	1						
4				1	1	1					
5					1	1	1				
6						1	1	1			
7							1	1	1		
8	0	0	0	0	0	0	0	1	1	1	0
9	0	0	0	0	0	0	0	0	1	1	1

response pattern will be defined as the number of triples in that response pattern that are in error. The last three response patterns therefore contain twice a much error as the first two.

In the second example there are four subjects who prefer six out of seven stimuli. For the amount of error in their response pattern it makes an enormous difference whether the stimulus not preferred is D, C, B or A. In the case of D the amount of error is maximal, whereas in the case of A there are no errors at all.

9.5 STOCHASTIC UNFOLDING

The stochastic aspect of the unfolding strategy proposed here lies in comparing the amount of error observed with the amount of error expected under statistical independence. In the deterministic unfolding model the k stimuli that are preferred by a subject are found within the symmetric closed interval around the subject's ideal point. The probability of preferring a set of stimuli (e.g. two, three or more) will be one if all stimuli fall within the subject's preference interval, and 0 if at least one stimulus falls outside this interval.

The null model differs from the deterministic model in two ways. First, local independence is assumed among preference responses for different stimuli. This means that for each subject the probability of a

Table 9.2 Two examples of response patterns that contain error

Example 1:

A	B	C	D	Error in triples
1	0	1	0	ABC
0	1	0	1	BCD
1	0	0	1	ABD ACD
1	1	0	1	ACD BCD
1	0	1	1	ABC ABD

Example 2:

A	B	C	D	E	F	G	Error in triples
1	1	1	0	1	1	1	ADE ADF ADG BDE BDF BDG CDE CDF CDG
1	1	0	1	1	1	1	ACD ACE ACF ACG BCD BCE BCF BCG
1	0	1	1	1	1	1	ABC ABD ABE ABF ABG
0	1	1	1	1	1	1	none

preference-response pattern to a set of stimuli is the product of the positive (preference) response to each of the stimuli. Second, the null model assumes that there are no individual differences in the probabilities of giving a positive-preference response to the stimuli. The expected frequency with which a set of stimuli is preferred will therefore be the product of the relative frequencies with which each stimulus is preferred times the number of cases in the case that subjects are free to select as many stimuli as they wish as most preferred:

$$\text{Exp.Freq.}(ijk, 101) = p(i) \cdot (1 - p(j)) \cdot p(k) \cdot N$$

where $p(i)$ is the relative frequency with which stimulus i is preferred, and

N is the number of cases.

The expected number of errors responses under the null model for 'pick k/n' data is first explained for 'pick $3/n$' data. It consists of two steps:

1. determine the expected frequency of the '*111*' response pattern by applying the n-way simple quasi-independence model (e.g. Bishop et al., 1975);
2. from the '*111*' responses to each triple, other response pattern – like *110*, *101*, or *011* – can be deduced.

In a data matrix, in which each of the N subjects picks exactly three out of n stimuli as most preferred, the relative frequency $p(i)$ with which each stimulus is picked can be found. Under the null model these $p(i)$s arise from the addition of the expected frequency of triples (i, j, k) for all combinations of j and k with a fixed i. This expected frequency of triple $i, j, k, a(ijk)$, is the product of the item parameters $f(i), f(j), f(k)$ times a general scaling factor f, without interaction effects: $a(ijk) = f \cdot f(i) \cdot f(j) \cdot f(k)$.

The values for f, and each $f(i)$ are found iteratively. The details of this procedure are given in van Schuur (1984).

Once the expected frequency of the '*111*' pattern of all triples is known the expected frequency of the other response patterns can be found, given that each subject picked exactly three stimuli as most preferred. For example, consider the situation in which there are five stimuli A, B, C, D and E, and each subject chooses three stimuli as most preferred. For the unfolding scale ABC the error-response

148   Stochastic Unfolding

Table 9.3 Observed data matrix and matrix with expected frequencies

Observed data matrix:

	stimuli:									SUM
subjects:	A	B	C	D	...	i	j	k	... n	
1	1	1	1	0		0	0	0	0	3
2	1	1	0	1		0	0	0	0	3
⋮										
v	0	0	0	0		1	1	1	0	3
⋮										
N	0	1	0	0		0	1	0	1	3
	$p(A)$	$p(B)$	$p(C)$	$p(D)$		$p(i)$	$p(j)$	$p(k)$	$p(n)$	

Matrix with expected frequencies:

	stimuli:									
triples:	A	B	C	D	...	i	j	k	... n	
(ABC)	a_{ABC}	a_{ABC}	a_{ABC}	0		0	0	0	0	a_{ABC}
(ABD)	a_{ABD}	a_{ABD}	0	a_{ABD}		0	0	0	0	a_{ABD}
⋮										
(ijk)	0	0	0	0		a_{ijk}	a_{ijk}	a_{ijk}	0	a_{ijk}
⋮										
$\binom{n}{3}$										
	$p(A)$	$p(B)$	$p(C)$	$p(D)$		$p(i)$	$p(j)$	$p(k)$	$p(n)$	

a_{ijk}: expected frequency of triple (ijk)
a_{ijk}: $= f \cdot f(i) \cdot f(j) \cdot f(k)$ (i.e. no interaction).
The values for f and $f(i)$ are found iteratively.

pattern is the pattern *101*, in which stimuli A and C are picked, but stimulus B is not. If B was not one of the subject's choices, then D or E must have been. We can therefore calculate the expected frequency across all respondents of the response pattern *101* for the triple ABC by summing the expected '*111*' responses of the triples ACD and ACE. In general:

$$\text{Exp.Freq.}(ijk, 101) = f \cdot f(i) \cdot f(k) \cdot \sum_{s \neq i,j,k} f(s)$$

This procedure can easily be generalised to the 'pick k/n' case, where $k = 2$, or where $k > 3$. First the expected frequency of each k-tuple, ranging between 1 and $\binom{n}{k}$ is found. Second, the expected frequency of the error-response pattern of an unfolding scale of three stimuli is found by calculating:

Exp.Freq.$(ijk, 101) = f \cdot f(i) \cdot f(k) \cdot Q$

where Q is the sum over all $\binom{n-3}{k-2}$ $k-2$ tuples of the product of their $f(s)s$, where s is not equal to i, j or k.

Once we know the frequency of the error response observed, Obs.Freq.$(ijk, 101)$, as well as the frequency expected under the null model, Exp.Freq.$(ijk, 101)$, for each triple of stimuli in each of its three essentially different permutations, we can compare the two by using a scalability coefficient, analogous to Loevinger's H (Loevinger, 1948; Mokken, 1971):

$$H_{ijk} = 1 - \frac{\text{Obs.Freq.}(ijk, 101)}{\text{Exp.Freq.}(ijk, 101)}$$

For each triple of stimuli $(i, j$ and $k)$ three coefficients of scalability can be found: $H(ijk)$, $H(ikj)$ and $H(jik)$. Perfect scalability is defined as $H = 1$. This means that no error is observed. When $H = 0$ the amount of error observed is equal to the amount of error expected under statistical independence.

The scalability of an unfolding scale of more than three stimuli can also be evaluated. In this case we can simply calculate the sum of the error responses to all relevant triples of the scale, for both the observed and expected error frequency, and then compare them, using the coefficient of scalability H:

$$H = 1 - \frac{\sum_{(ijk)=1}^{\binom{p}{3}} \text{Obs.Freq.}(ijk, 101)}{\sum_{(ijk)=1}^{\binom{p}{3}} \text{Exp.Freq.}(ijk, 101)}$$

The scalability of single stimuli in the scale are equally evaluated. This is done by adding up the frequencies of the error patterns observed and expected, respectively, in only those triples that contain the stimulus under consideration, and then compare these frequencies by using the scalability coefficient for each stimulus separately.

9.6 MUDFOLD: MULTIPLE UNIDIMENSIONAL UNFOLDING, THE SEARCH PROCEDURE

After having obtained all relevant information about each triple of stimuli in each of its three different permutations (e.g. Obs.Freq.(ijk, 101), Exp.Freq.(ijk, 101) and $H(ijk)$), we can begin to construct an unfolding scale. This is a two-step procedure. First, the best elementary scale is found, and second, new stimuli are added, one by one, to the existing scale.

The best triple of stimuli that conforms to the following criteria is the best elementary scale:

1. its scalability value should be positive in only one of its three permutations, and negative in the other two. This guarantees that the best triple has a unique order of representation;
2. its scalability value has to be higher than some user specified lower boundary. This guarantees that if the scalability value is positive, it can be given a substantively relevant interpretation.
3. the absolute frequencies of the perfect patterns with at least two of the three stimuli (i.e. 111, 110 and 011) is highest among all triples fulfilling the first two criteria. This guarantees the representability of the largest group of respondents.

Once the best elementary scale is found, each of the remaining $n-3$ stimuli is investigated to see whether it might make the best fourth stimulus. The fourth stimulus (e.g. D) may be added to the three stimuli of the best triple (e.g. ABC) in any of four places: $DABC$, $ADBC$, $ABDC$ and $ABCD$, denoted as place 1 to place 4, respectively. The best fourth – or, more general, $p + 1$-st – stimulus has to fulfil the following criteria:

1. All new ($\binom{p}{2}$) triples, including the $p + 1$-st stimulus and two stimuli from the existing p-stimulus scale, have to have a positive $H(ijk)$-value. This guarantees that all stimuli are homogeneous with respect to the latent dimension.
2. The $p + 1$-st stimulus should be uniquely representable, in only one of the p possible places in the p-stimulus scale. This guarantees the later usefulness and interpretability of the order of the stimuli in the scale.
3. The $H(i)$-value of the new stimulus, as well a the H-value of the scale as a whole, has to be higher than some user-specified lower

boundary (see second criterion for the best elementary scale).
4. If more than one stimulus conforms to the criteria mentioned above, that stimulus will be selected that leads to the highest overall scalability value for the scale as a whole.

This procedure of extending a scale with another stimulus can continue as long as the criteria mentioned above are met. If, however, no stimulus conforms to these criteria, the p-stimulus scale is a maximal subset of unfoldable stimuli. A new procedure then starts which begins by selecting the best triple among the remaining $n-p$ stimuli. This procedure, in which for a given pool of stimuli more than one maximal subset of unidimensionally unfoldable stimuli can be found, is called 'multiple scaling'.

9.7 THE DOMINANCE AND ADJACENCY MATRICES: VISUAL INSPECTION OF MODEL CONFORMITY

Once a maximal subset of unfoldable stimuli is found, a final visual check of model conformity can be applied by inspecting the dominance matrix and the adjacency matrix. The dominance matrix is a square asymmetric matrix that contains in its cells (i, j) the proportion of respondents who preferred stimulus i but not stimulus j. If the stimuli are ordered in their ordering along the J-scale, then for each stimulus i the proportions $p(i, j)$ should decrease from the first column toward the diagonal and increase from the diagonal to the last column. The adjacency matrix is a lower triangle that contains in its cells (i, j) the proportion of respondents who preferred both i and j. If the stimuli are ordered in their ordering along the J-scale, then for each stimulus i the proportions $p(i, j)$ should increase from the first column to the diagonal and decrease from the diagonal to the last row. This pattern is called a 'simplex pattern'. Stimuli that disturb these expected characteristic monotonicity patterns should be considered for deletion from the scale.

9.8 SCALE VALUES

Once an unfolding scale of a maximal subset of stimuli has been found, scale values for stimuli and subjects must be found. The scale value of a stimulus is defined as its rank number in the unfolding

Table 9.4 Dominance and adjacency matrix for a perfect four-stimulus unfolding scale

Data matrix:

A	B	C	D
1	0	0	0
0	1	0	0
0	0	1	0
0	0	0	1
1	1	0	0
0	0	1	1
0	1	1	0
1	1	1	0
0	1	1	1

frequency: $p, q, r, s, t, u, v, w, x$

Dominance matrix:

	A	B	C	D
A	–	p	$p+t$	$p+t+w$
B	$q+u+x$	–	$q+t$	$q+t+u+w$
C	$r+u+v+x$	$r+v$	–	$r+u+w$
D	$s+v+x$	$s+v$	s	–

Adjacency matrix:

	A	B	C	D
A	–	p	–	–
B	$t+w$	–	$u+w+x$	–
C	w	–	–	–
D	O	x	$v+x$	–

Table 9.5 Assignment of scale values to stimuli and subjects

stimuli rank number subject nr.	A 1	B 2	C 3	D 4	E 5	F 6	G 7	scale value of subject
1	0	1	1	1	0	0	0	3
2	0	0	1	0	0	0	0	3
3	1	0	1	0	1	0	0	3
4	0	1	1	0	0	0	0	2.5
5	0	0	0	1	0	1	1	5.67
6	1	1	1	0	1	1	1	4
7	0	0	0	0	0	0	0	– (missing datum)

scale. The scale value of a subject is defined as the mean of the scale values of the stimuli that the subject chose as most preferred. Subjects who did not pick any stimulus from the scale cannot be given a scale value, and have to be treated as missing data. Some examples of the assignment of scale values are given in Table 9.5.

Respondents may have different response patterns, but still be assigned, the same scale value. This can be seen by comparing subjects 1, 2 and 3. Subjects 4 and 5 show that a scale value for a subject does not need to be an integer value. Respondent 6 shows that a scale value is assigned to a subject regardless of the amount of error in his response pattern, which in his case is maximal. Subject 7 does not pick any of the seven stimuli and therefore cannot be represented on this scale.

9.9 AN EXAMPLE: PICK THE TWO MOST SYMPATHETIC OUT OF SIX EUROPEAN PARTY GROUPS

As part of the Middle Level Elite Project (e.g. van Schuur, 1984), sympathy scores to six European party groups in the European Parliament of 1979 were elicited from party activists from fifty political parties in the European Community. The response of 1786 subjects about their two most sympathetic party group are analysed. The six party groups are given with the letter by which they will be denoted, and by the frequency with which they were mentioned as sympathetic between brackets:

A: Communists (359); B: Social Democrats (747); C: European Democrats for Progress (366); D: European Liberals and

Table 9.6 Labelled *H*-matrix for 'pick 2/6' European party groups, $N = 1786$

	Scale jik E(o)	E(e)	H(ijk)	Scale ijk E(o)	E(e)	H(ijk)	Scale jik E(o)	E(e)	H(ijk)
ABC	106	88	−0.21	9	36	0.75	341	86	−2.97
ABD	202	177	−0.14	3	73	0.96	341	86	−2.97
ABE	86	226	0.62	2	93	0.98	341	86	−2.97
ABF	12	171	0.93	4	71	0.94	341	86	−2.97
ACD	124	75	−0.66	3	73	0.96	9	36	0.75
ACE	50	95	0.47	2	93	0.98	9	36	0.75
ACF	77	72	−0.07	4	71	0.94	9	36	0.75
ADE	217	192	−0.13	2	93	0.98	3	73	0.96
ADF	116	146	0.20	4	71	0.94	3	73	0.96
AEF	437	186	−1.35	4	71	0.94	2	93	0.98
BCD	124	75	−0.66	202	177	−0.14	106	88	−0.21
BCE	50	95	0.47	86	226	0.62	106	88	−0.21
BCF	77	72	−0.07	12	171	0.93	106	88	−0.21
BDE	217	192	−0.13	86	226	0.62	202	177	−0.14
BDF	116	146	0.20	12	171	0.93	202	177	−0.14
BEF	437	186	−1.35	12	171	0.93	86	226	0.62
CDE	217	192	−0.13	50	95	0.47	124	75	−0.66
CDF	116	146	0.20	77	72	−0.07	124	75	−0.66
CEF	437	186	−1.35	77	72	−0.07	50	95	0.47
DEF	437	186	−1.35	116	146	0.20	217	192	−0.13

Democrats (662); *E*: Christian Democrats (792); and *F*: Conservatives (646).

The frequency with which each pair of parties is mentioned as most sympathetic is:

AB(341) *AC*(9) *AD*(3) *AE*(2) *AF*(4) *BC*(106) *BD*(202) *BE*(86) *BF*(12) *CD*(124) *CE*(50) *CF*(77) *DE*(217) *DF*(116) *EF*(437).

On the basis of this information a labelled matrix can be constructed that contains for each triple of stimuli in each of its three essentially different permutations the values Obs.Freq.(*ijk*, *101*), or *E*(*o*), Exp.Freq.(*ijk*, *101*), or *E*(*e*), and *H*(*ijk*). This information is given in Table 9.6.

Table 9.6 provides all the necessary information to construct an unfolding scale. First the best elementary unfolding scale is found among those triples that have a positive scalability value in only one of its three permutations. This leaves the ordered triples *ABC, ABD, BCF, BDE, CDE, DCF, CFE* and *DEF*. Triple *ABD* is the best triple, since the sums of the pairs (*A, B*) and (*B, D*) is highest. The *H*-value of triple *ABD* is 0.96, which is well above the recommended default user specification of 0.30.

On the basis of scale *ABD*, stimulus *C* cannot be represented in this scale in any position, since the triple *B, C, D* has negative *H*-values in all three permutations. Stimulus *E* is uniquely representable in place 4, forming scale *ABDE*, whereas stimulus *F* is representable in either place 1 (scale *FABD*) or place 4 (scale *ABDF*). Stimulus *E* is selected because it is the only one uniquely representable. The four-stimulus scale is *ABDE*, its *H*-value is 1–93/485 = 0.81, which is acceptably high. For the best fifth stimulus we only need to consider stimulus *F*. This is now only representable in place 5, which gives the final scale *ABDEF*. Its *H*-value is 1–245/1185 = 0.79.

In the process of scale construction the *H*-values of individual stimuli are also calculated. For the triple *ABD* these values are the same: $H(A) = H(B) = H(D) = H(ABD) = 0.96$. For the four- and five-stimulus scale these values have to be computed separately. The resulting *H*-values for the final scale are given in Table 9.7,.along with the dominance matrix and the adjacency matrix for the stimuli in the order of the final scale. Both matrices do not show any violation of the expected characteristic monotonicity pattern.

Five of the six European party groups can be included in an unfolding scale based on party activists' sympathy scores for these

Table 9.7 Final unfolding scale for 'pick 2/6' European party groups

	$p(i)$	$H(i)$
A Communists	0.20	0.96
B Social Democrats	0.42	0.85
D European Liberals and Democrats	0.37	0.71
E Christian Democrats	0.44	0.72
F Conservatives	0.36	0.78

$N = 1786\ H = .79$

Dominance matrix

	A	*B*	*D*	*E*	*F*
A	–	1	20	20	20
B	23	–	31	37	41
D	37	26	–	25	31
E	44	40	32	–	20
F	36	35	30	12	–

Adjacency matrix

	A	*B*	*D*	*E*	*F*
A	–	–	–	–	–
B	19	–	–	–	–
D	0	11	–	–	–
E	0	5	12	–	–
F	0	1	6	24	–

party groups. The scale can be interpreted as a left–right dimension, with the Communists represented in the left-most place and the Conservatives in the right-most place. To corroborate this interpretation I have correlated subjects' scale scores for this unfolding scale with their scores on a left–right self-placement scale. This correlation was 0.66.

The European Democrats for Progress (EDP, stimulus C) was not incorporated in the scale. This party group consists of the French Gaullists (RPR), the largest Irish party Fianna Fail (FF) and the Danish Progress Party (FRP). This party group is not represented in many EC countries, so it is probably less well known than other party groups, and did therefore not receive high sympathy scores from respondents who might have been expected to do so on the basis of their positions on the scale.

9.10 CONCLUDING REMARKS

The procedure described above for the analysis of 'pick k/n' data can be extended to apply to 'rank k/n' data. Such procedures have been independently proposed by Davison (1979) and by van Schuur and Molenaar (1982). Using partial rank-order information might provide more precise measurements for both the stimuli and the subjects. However, since in this procedure all six permutations of a triple of stimuli have their own observed and expected error patterns, the accuracy of estimation with the same data set decreases sixfold. As Table 9.7 already shows, the $H(ijk)$-value of some triples is based on the comparison of rather small numbers, and such comparison will therefore be even more difficult in the 'rank'-case. Moreover, for small k the increase in measurement precision is minimal, and I have already expressed some doubts about the reliability of the kth preference judgement when k gets large.

A computer program (MUDFOLD) has been devised to perform a multiple unidimensional unfolding analysis on complete or partial rank-order data, 'pick k/n' or 'pick any/n' data, or on the usual attitude data like Likert items or thermometer scores. The program is interactive, self-explanatory and very user-friendly. The user may define a startset rather than use the best elementary scale to find a larger unfolding scale, or test the unfoldability of a given set of stimuli in a given order. In either case, if a triple of stimuli in the user-defined order has a negative $H(ijk)$-value, this triple will be flagged, along with its $E(o)$-, $E(e)$- and $H(ijk)$-value. The output not only consists of the H- and $H(i)$-value of the final scale, but also gives an overview of which stimuli at which places were candidates for selection at what step of enlargement, and the H- and $H(i)$-values of the stimuli in the scale at each step of enlargement. Moreover, the output contains a variety of additional information that may help the researcher either to find a better scale, or explain why certain stimuli did not fit in the unfolding scale. The computer program is available from the University of Groningen. The development of the unfolding model presented above, together with more than twenty applications, is described in more detail in van Schuur, (1984).

REFERENCES

BECHTEL, G. G., *Multidimensional Preference Scaling* (The Hague: Mouton, 1976).
BENNETT, J. F. and HAYS W. L., 'Multidimensional Unfolding: Determining the Dimensionality of Ranked Preference Data', *Psychometrika*, 25 (1960) 27–43.
BISHOP, Y. M. M., FIENBERG, S. E. and HOLLAND, P. W., *Discrete Multivariate Analysis: Theory and Practice* (Cambridge, Mass.: MIT Press, 1975).
CARROLL, J. D., 'Individual Differences and Multidimensional Scaling', in SHEPARD, R. N. et al. (eds) *Multidimensional Scaling: Theory and Applications in the Behavioral Sciences, vol. I: Theory* (New York: Seminar Press, 1972).
COOMBS, C. H., 'Psychological Scaling Without a Unit of Measurement', *Psychological Review*, 57 (1950) 148–58.
———, *A Theory of Data* (New York: Wiley & Son, 1964).
DAVISON, M. L., 'Testing a Unidimensional, Qualitative Unfolding Model for Attitudinal or Developmental Data', *Psychometrika*, 44 (1979) 179–94.
GOLD, E. M., 'Metric Unfolding: Data Requirements for Unique Solutions and Clarifications of Schönemann's Algorithm', *Psychometrika*, 38 (1973) 555–69.
HEISER, W. J., 'Unfolding Analysis of Proximity Data, University of Leiden: unpublished dissertion, 1981.
JANSEN, P. G. W. (1983). 'Rasch Analysis of Attitudinal Data', Catholic University of Nijmegen – Rijks Psychologische Dienst, Den Haag: unpublished dissertation.
KRUSKAL, J. B., YOUNG, F. W. and SEERY, J. B., 'How to Use KYST: A Very Flexible Program to do Multidimensional Scaling and Unfolding' (Murray Hill: Bell Labs, mimeo, 1973).

LOEVINGER, J., 'The Technique of Homogeneous Tests composed with Some Aspects of 'Scale Analysis' and Factors Analysis; *Psychological Bulletin*, **45** (1948) 507–29.

MEERLING, F., *Methoden en Technieken van Psychologisch Onderzoek, deel 2: Data-analyse en Psychometrie* (Meppel: Boom, 1981).

MOKKEN, R. J., *A Theory and Procedure of Scale Analysis, with Application in Political Research* (The Hague: Mouton, 1971).

ROSKAM, E. E., *Metric Analysis of Ordinal Data* (Voorschoten: VAM, 1968).

SCHÖNEMANN, P. H., 'On Metric Multidimensional Unfolding', *Psychometrika*, **35** (1970) 349–66.

VAN SCHUUR, H., *Structure in Political Beliefs: A New Model for Stochastic Unfolding with Application to European Party Activists* (Amsterdam: CT Press, 1984).

——, and MOLENAAR, I. W., 'MUDFOLD, Multiple Stochastic Unidimensional Unfolding', in CAUSSINUS, H., ETTINGER, P. and THOMASSONE, R. (eds) *COMPSTAT 1982*, part I: *Proceedings in Computational Statistics* (Vienna: Physica-Verlag, 1982) 419–24.

SIXTL, F., 'Probabilistic Unfolding', *Psychometrika*, **38** (1973) 235–48.

TVERSKY, A., 'Elimination by Aspects: A Theory of Choice, *Psychological Review*, **79** (1972) 281–99.

YOUNG, F. W., 'A Model for Polynomial Conjoint Analysis Algorithms', in SHEPARD, R. N. *et al.* (eds) *Multidimensional Scaling: Theory and Applications in the Behavioral Sciences*, vol. I: *Theory* (New York: Seminar Press, 1972).

ZINNES, J. L. and GRIGGS, R. A., 'Probabilistic Multidimensional Unfolding Analysis', *Psychometrika*, **39** (1974) 327–50.

10 Reliability Estimation in Mokken's Nonparametric Item Response Model

K. Sijtsma

10.1 INTRODUCTION

In this chapter we will investigate and improve two methods of estimating reliability that were originally proposed by Mokken (1971). Based on these methods, a third way of estimating reliability is proposed. The three methods are estimates of the classical reliability concept, which is the ratio of true score variance to observed score variance (see, for example, Lord and Novick, 1968), in the context of nonparametric item response theory (Mokken, 1971; Henning, 1976; Stokman and van Schuur, 1980; Mokken and Lewis, 1982). Apart from new theoretical developments, results from a Monte Carlo study will also be reported and discussed. In this study the three methods already mentioned are compared with four 'classical' methods of estimating the reliability of psychological measures. These four methods are the well-known lower bounds *alpha* (Cronbach, 1951) and *lambda*-2 (Guttman, 1945), and the lower bounds *mu*-2 and *mu*-3 (ten Berge and Zegers, 1978). Finally, some remarks will be made concerning the use of the estimation methods.

10.2 THE DOUBLY MONOTONIC MODEL

Mokken (1971) has presented an item response model that may be called 'nonparametric' for two reasons: no mathematical form of the item characteristic functions is specified and no assumptions are made concerning the distribution of the latent subject parameters. The consequence is that in the case of an empirically fitting model items and subjects can only be (partially) ordered. In this respect this item response model has weaker measurement properties than the well-known Rasch and Birnbaum models, which have mathematically specified item characteristic functions.

Underlying Mokken's model are four assumptions concerning a test consisting of dichotomously scored items:

1. Unidimensionality of the items from which the measurement device is composed.
2. Local stochastic independence of the item responses of a fixed subject.
3. Non-decreasing item characteristic functions, implying monotonicity of the success probabilities on an item in the latent trait, ξ.
4. Identical ordering of success probabilities on a set of items for all values of ξ, i.e. monotonicity in the item difficulties.

Because of the two kinds of monotonicity that are distinguished, the model is called 'doubly monotone' (Mokken, 1971). In this model, item characteristic functions do not intersect, but they may touch with an extreme instance of coinciding curves. Mokken (1971) and Molenaar (1982a, b) have proposed methods for empirically checking and testing the doubly monotonic model. Further research in this area is currently being conducted by the present author.

Mokken (1971) has proposed two global measures for assessing the quality of measurement within the context of the doubly monotonic model. The first one is the scalability coefficient H, that was originally proposed by Loevinger (1948). This coefficient evaluates the degree of Guttman homogeneity (Guttman, 1950; see also Molenaar and Sijtsma, 1984) or, equivalently, the degree of reproducibility of subjects' item response patterns given their raw scores. Although in the doubly monotonic model only the raw score is used for assessing subjects, a large positive value of H means that much confidence may be placed in subjects' item responses, thereby obtaining additional information besides their raw scores. Recently the role of H in the doubly monotonic model proposed by Mokken has become the subject of a debate in several media (Jansen, 1982a, b; 1983; Jansen et. al., 1982; Molenaar, 1982b, c; Sijtsma, 1984).

The second measure of measurement quality is the classical reliability coefficient. Mokken (1971, pp. 142-7) has proposed two methods for estimating the reliability of measures within the context of the doubly monotonic model. These methods make use of the item characteristic functions and seem especially suited for nonparametric item response theory. Furthermore, indications exist that in most instances Mokken's methods of reliability estimation are less biased than classical methods (Molenaar and Sijtsma, 1984). In this chapter we will further concentrate on reliability estimation in the context of nonparametric item response theory as proposed by Mokken.

10.3 RELIABILITY OF MEASUREMENTS IN ITEM RESPONSE THEORY

In general there seems to be little appreciation for the classical reliability concept in the context of item response theory (see, for example, Fischer, 1974; Lumsden, 1976; Weiss and Davison, 1981). There are several reasons why abandonment of the reliability concept would be unwise. Here, we will only mention them briefly. For further details see Sijtsma and Molenaar (in press).

First, items complying with the general monotonely homogeneous model – nondecreasing trace lines which are allowed to intersect – correlate nonnegatively (Mokken, 1971, p. 131; see also Wood, 1978). As an extreme case, items complying with some item response model may measure (almost) nothing in common. This situation may be avoided by demanding a high reliability for a test of a manageable length.

Second, the population-dependent reliability coefficient gives information with respect to the degree to which differences between scores are affected by measurement error. Application of the test in another population than the original one requires a re-evaluation of the reliability of measurements.

Third, the information function approach which is popular in parametric item response theory (see, for example, Birnbaum, 1968; Lord, 1977; 1980; Hambleton and Cook, 1977), cannot be applied in nonparametric item response theory. The reason is that the latent subject and item parameters of the doubly monotonic model cannot be estimated, and consequently the information function cannot be estimated either. Even if the information function were available, the classical reliability coefficient would not be superfluous since it summarises the information of the test for the population of interest. A comparison of the information function for the maximum-likelihood estimate $\hat{\xi}$ of the latent subject parameter ξ in parametric item response theory, and the reliability coefficient for $\hat{\xi}$, shows that there is a positive relationship between them. The more accurately ξ is estimated, the larger the information obtained by means of its estimate will be. In that case differences between scores on the latent scale become more meaningful too, which is reflected in an increase of the reliability of $\hat{\xi}$. Therefore, one may use the reliability coefficient for ξ on a global level in addition to the information function, which is conditional upon ξ.

10.4 RELIABILITY ESTIMATES IN THE DOUBLY MONOTONIC MODEL

Mokken's approach to reliability is based on the classical concept which is written in terms of the latent trait, ξ. To accomplish this we must consider two stochastic processes that are assumed to underlie testing behaviour. The first one is the random selection of a subject from a population and the second one is the consecutive random selection of an item score from a subject's propensity distribution (see, for example, Lord and Novick, 1968, p. 30) conditional on his/her latent trait parameter. We may then decompose the variance of the observed scores, $\sigma^2(X)$, as follows:

$$\sigma^2(X) = \sigma^2_\xi [E(X|\xi)] + E_\xi [\sigma^2(X|\xi)] \tag{1}$$

where the first part on the right-hand side denotes the 'true-score' variance across subjects and the second part denotes the average error variation. We may now define the reliability coefficient as

$$\varrho_{xx'} = \frac{\sigma^2_\xi [E(X|\xi)]}{\sigma^2(X)} = 1 - \frac{E_\xi [\sigma^2(X|\xi)]}{\sigma^2(X)} \tag{2}$$

In the sequel we will use the right-hand-side expression for the reliability.

Mokken's approach to reliability estimation avoids the assumptions of equivalence that are usual in classical approaches. We will give a short exposition of his methods and then propose some improvements and an alternative method.

Let $\pi_i(\xi)$ denote the success probability of a subject with latent trait value ξ on item i, then the conditional variance of item i equals $\pi_i(\xi)[1 - \pi_i(\xi)]$, and the variance of the raw test score, X, equals

$$\sigma^2(X|\xi) = \sum_i \pi_i(\xi)[1 - \pi_i(\xi)] =$$
$$= \sum_i [\pi_i(\xi) - \pi_i^2(\xi)] \tag{3}$$

The expectation of Equation (3) across subjects yields

$$E_\xi [\sigma^2(X|\xi)] = \int \sum_i [\pi_i(\xi) - \pi_i^2(\xi)]dG(\xi) =$$
$$= \sum_i (\pi_i - \pi_{ii}) \qquad (4)$$

where $G(\xi)$ is the cumulative distribution function of the continuous latent trait, ξ. In Equation (4) π_i denotes the proportion of subjects that respond positively to item i and π_{ii} denotes the proportion responding positively on two hypothetical independent replications of item i. Substitution of Equation (4) in the reliability formula Equation (2) yields

$$\varrho_{xx'} = 1 - \frac{\sum_i (\pi_i - \pi_{ii})}{\sigma^2(X)} \qquad (5)$$

In this formula, π_i can be estimated by means of the unbiased and consistent estimator $\hat{\pi}_i = n_i/n$, where n_i denotes the number of positive responses to item i and n the total number of responses to item i. The same properties hold for the proportion of subjects answering positively to both item i and j ($i \neq j$), where $\hat{\pi}_{ij} = n_{ij}/n$ is an estimator of π_{ij}.

Mokken has presented two methods for approximating π_{ii} that make use of the π_i ($i = 1, \ldots, k$) and the π_{ij} ($i, j = 1, \ldots, k; i < j$). The rationale on which these methods are based, is extensively discussed by Molenaar and Sijtsma (1984) and Sijtsma and Molenaar (in press). Here, a brief exposition of the rationale will be given.

First, it may be noted that

$$\pi_{ii} = \int \pi_i(\xi)\pi_i(\xi)dG(\xi) \qquad (6)$$

Approximation of π_{ii} takes place by replacing one of the terms, $\pi_i(\xi)$, in the integrand by a linear function of one (Mokken's method 1) or two (Mokken's method 2) $\pi_j(\xi)$, where $j \neq i$.

Second, double monotonicity of item characteristic functions implies, when items are ordered from difficult to easy,

$$\pi_{i-1}(\xi) \leqq \pi_i(\xi) \leqq \pi_{i+1}(\xi) \qquad (7)$$

In Mokken's method 1

$$\tilde{\pi}_i(\xi) = \pi_{i-1}(\xi) \frac{\pi_i}{\pi_{i-1}}, \text{ implying } \tilde{\pi}_{ii} = \pi_{i-1,i} \frac{\pi_i}{\pi_{i-1}} \qquad (8)$$

where $\tilde{\pi}_i(\xi)$ and $\tilde{\pi}_{ii}$ denote approximations to $\pi_i(\xi)$ and π_{ii}, respectively, and

$$\tilde{\pi}_i(\xi) = \pi_{i+1}(\xi)\frac{\pi_i}{\pi_{i+1}}, \text{ implying } \tilde{\pi}_{ii} = \pi_{i,\,i+1}\frac{\pi_i}{\pi_{i+1}} \qquad (9)$$

According to Mokken (1971, p. 147) one should choose Equation (8) if π_i is closer to π_{i-1} than to π_{i+1} and Equation (9) otherwise. For $i = 1$ and $i = k$ only one possible choice exists.

In Mokken's method 2 $\tilde{\pi}_i(\xi)$ is an interpolation of $\pi_{i-1}(\xi)$ and $\pi_{i+1}(\xi)$:

$$\tilde{\pi}_i(\xi) = \pi_{i-1}(\xi) + [\pi_{i+1}(\xi) - \pi_{i-1}(\xi)]\frac{\pi_i - \pi_{i-1}}{\pi_{i+1} - \pi_{i-1}} \qquad (10)$$

implying

$$\tilde{\pi}_{ii} = \pi_{i-1,\,i} + (\pi_{i,\,i+1} - \pi_{i-1,\,i})\frac{\pi_i - \pi_{i-1}}{\pi_{i+1} - \pi_{i-1}} \qquad (11)$$

Mokken recommends resorting to method 1 for $i = 1$ and $i = k$.

Two additional approximation methods to π_{ii} apply when the scale direction is reversed: negative and positive item scores are interchanged. The proportion of 'ones' now equals $1 - \pi$. Substitution in formulas (10) and (11) of method 2 yields the same results, but substitution in formulas (8) and (9) of method 1 yields (Molenaar and Sijtsma, 1984)

$$\tilde{\pi}_{ii} = \pi_{i-1,\,i}\frac{1-\pi_i}{1-\pi_{i-1}} + \pi_i\frac{\pi_i - \pi_{i-1}}{1-\pi_{i-1}} \qquad (12)$$

and

$$\tilde{\pi}_{ii} = \pi_{i,\,i+1}\frac{1-\pi_i}{1-\pi_{i+1}} - \pi_i\frac{\pi_{i+1} - \pi_i}{1-\pi_{i+1}} \qquad (13)$$

respectively. This result looks perhaps somewhat surprising since reversal of the scale does not influence the population reliability; Mokken's method 1 leads to different results however, when it is applied to the original and reversed scales. We will need Equations (12) and (13) in order to define a third way of estimating reliability.

Molenaar and Sijtsma (1984) have compared reliability estimates based on method 1 and method 2 and the classical coefficient *alpha* (Cronbach, 1951) in an analytical study. In this study all relevant parameters were calculated directly from two-parameter logistic functions for $\pi_i(\xi)$, $i = 1, \ldots, k$, and a standard normal density of ξ. Since the parameter values obtained by the three methods, as well as the true reliability were known, it was possible to assess the bias of the methods. Mokken's methods mostly led to only slightly biased approximations and their bias was always smaller than the bias of coefficient *alpha*. Thus it seems worth while to study the sampling behaviour of Mokken's reliability estimates and compare them with some classical lower bounds to the reliability.

In the same simulation study, Molenaar and Sijtsma (1984) obtained indications that π_{ii}, when estimated by means of Equations (8) and (13), tends to be negatively biased, while the estimates obtained by means of Equations (9) and (12) tend to be positively biased. When averaged the biases more or less cancel each other, implying that a less-biased estimate of π_{ii} can be obtained by simply taking the mean of the four estimates mentioned. This suggestion comprises the third method of estimating π_{ii} and the reliability, respectively. The population results of the analytical study mentioned above mostly favour this third method in terms of bias compared to Mokken's methods (without the proposals made in Section 10.5 however).

10.5 NEW PROPOSALS CONCERNING THE RELIABILITY ESTIMATES

Methods 1 and 2 of Mokken and the method proposed by Molenaar and Sijtsma (MS-method in the sequel) are not always applicable to empirical data. An example is the case where three or more item difficulties (proportions correct) are equal, e.g. $\pi_{i-1} = \pi_i = \pi_{i+1}$. Now it is impossible to approximate $\pi_{i-1, i-1}$, π_{ii} and $\pi_{i+1, i+1}$ by means of method 2, see formula (11), since the items cannot be ordered. Consequently, for a specific item it cannot be decided which items are its neighbours in the ordering of item difficulties. We propose solutions for this and other problems in the sequel. In this section only theoretical results are presented. For an extensive treatment of this topic the reader is referred to Sijtsma and Molenaar (in press).

Table 10.1 A 'plus' sign means that a problem (horizontal) is valid for a method for estimating π_{ii} (vertical), while a 'minus' sign either denotes the contrary or means that a problem is irrelevant to the method under consideration.

		lower bound to π_{ii}: $\hat{\pi}_{ii} < \pi_i^2$	upper bound to π_{ii}: $\hat{\pi}_{ii} > \pi_i$	equal proportions correct: $m \geq 2$	equal proportions correct: $m \geq 3$	equidistance of proportions correct: $\hat{\pi}_{i+1} - \hat{\pi}_i = \hat{\pi}_i - \hat{\pi}_{i-1}$
	(8)	+	−	+	−	−
	(9)	+	−	+	−	−
method 2:	(11)	+	−	−	+	−
	(12)	+	−	+	−	−
	(13)	+	−	+	−	−
method 1:		+	−	−	+	+

10.5.1 Upper and Lower Bounds to π_{ii}

Approximations to π_{ii} may sometimes become unreasonably low or high. Therefore we propose bounds to π_{ii}. We propose basing a lower bound on the case of global independence among replications of item i, in which case $\pi_{ii}(L) = \pi_i^2$. Values of π_{ii} below this bound are regarded as unreasonable, since they would imply a negative correlation between replications, which is not allowed in the doubly monotonic model (Mokken, 1971, pp. 120, 130). With the exception of approximation (11) it can be proved that $\tilde{\pi}_{ii} < \pi_{ii}(L)$ if and only if the items involved in the approximation are correlated negatively. In practice there is no serious problem since one usually starts the item analysis by removing items which correlate negatively with many other items. As an upper bound to π_{ii} we propose $\pi_{ii}(U) = \pi_i$, which seems to be a rather evident choice.

So, whenever the $\tilde{\pi}_{ii}$ are estimated empirically it should be checked afterwards if $\hat{\pi}_i^2 \leq \hat{\pi}_{ii} \leq \hat{\pi}_i$ holds true. If not, $\tilde{\pi}_{ii}$ should be replaced by the appropriate bound. (In the sequel we write $\hat{\pi}_{ii}$ instead of $\hat{\tilde{\pi}}_{ii}$ for notational convenience.) The first two columns in Table 10.1 indicate cases in which approximations to π_{ii} may cross the bounds.

10.5.2 Equality of Univariate Proportions Correct

Equality of univariate proportions of correct answers poses problems to the application of all methods that are vertically depicted in Table

10.1. Before considering these problems we present two theorems with respect to equal proportions correct in the doubly monotonic model and then go on with the presentation of a solution for the estimation problems.

It can be shown that in the doubly monotonic model the following two theorems hold true (Sijtsma and Molenaar, in press):

THEOREM 1:

$$\pi_{i+1}(\xi) = \ldots = \pi_{i+m}(\xi) \text{ iff } \pi_{i+1} = \ldots = \pi_{i+m} \qquad (14)$$

THEOREM 2:

$$\pi_{i,i+1} = \ldots = \pi_{i,i+m} = \pi_{i+1,i+2} = \ldots = \pi_{i+m-1,i+m} \text{ iff}$$

$$\pi_i = \ldots = \pi_{i+m}. \qquad (15)$$

Two important results follow from our theorems. Combining theorem 1 and formula (6) for the arbitrary case of three items i, j and h, leads to the conclusion that $\pi_{ii} = \pi_{jj} = \pi_{hh}$. Also $\pi_{ij} = \pi_{ih} = \pi_{jh}$ and it can easily be inferred that $\pi_{ii} = \pi_{ij}$, etc.

So far we have only considered population results. In the sample we will assume a set, C, consisting of m items having equal univariate proportions correct. From our theory derived thus far we may estimate π_{ii} by means of $\hat{\pi}_{ij}$, where i and j belong to C. But actually π_{ii} can be estimated by any bivariate proportion $\hat{\pi}_{jh}$, where $j \neq h$ and j and h belong to C. Then we can improve the estimation of π_{ii} by using all bivariate proportions of the m items belonging to C:

$$\hat{\pi}_{ii} = \frac{2}{m(m-1)} \sum_{\substack{j<h \\ j,h \in C}} \hat{\pi}_{jh} \qquad (16)$$

This estimate can be used for all items belonging to C. The third and fourth column of Table 10.1 indicate that in some approximation methods $m \geq 2$ poses problems, while in other methods the same is true for $m \geq 3$.

10.5.3 Equal Distances Between Univariate Proportions Correct

The third problem occurs only in method 1 when $\hat{\pi}_i - \hat{\pi}_{i-1} = \hat{\pi}_{i+1} - \hat{\pi}_i$, since no choice can be made whether to use formula (8) or (9). A solution to this problem might be based on the sampling variability of proportions: this variability equals $\sigma^2(\hat{\pi}) = \pi(1 - \pi)/n$ and is at its maximum when $\pi = 0.5$ and decreases towards the extremes. When we take, for example, $\hat{\pi}_{i-1} = 0.5$, $\hat{\pi}_i = 0.6$ and $\hat{\pi}_{i+1} = 0.7$, we may argue that since the confidence interval concerning π_{i-1} is larger than the one concerning π_{i+1}, the difference $\pi_i - \pi_{i-1}$ is likely to be smaller than $\pi_{i+1} - \pi_i$ when one is willing to take the confidence bounds into consideration. The decision would then be to choose formula (8). For the example $\hat{\pi}_{i-1} = 0.10$, $\hat{\pi}_i = 0.35$ and $\hat{\pi}_{i+1} = 0.60$ we would choose formula (9) following the same rationale. So in general one should always approximate the item characteristic function with item proportion correct that is closest to 0.5.

When $\hat{\pi}_i = 0.5$ no clearcut decision follows from our rule, and we will resort to method 2, which in that case is adapted to

$$\tilde{\pi}_i(\xi) = \pi_{i-1}(\xi) + \frac{1}{2}[\pi_{i+1}(\xi) - \pi_{i-1}(\xi)] \qquad (17)$$

where the multiplication constant equals one-half so that equal use of both item characteristic functions is being made. The approximation to π_{ii} now becomes

$$\tilde{\pi}_{ii} = \frac{1}{2}(\pi_{i-1,i} + \pi_{i,i+1}) \qquad (18)$$

10.6 SAMPLING BEHAVIOUR OF THE RELIABILITY ESTIMATES

As a first step in studying the sampling behaviour of the three reliability approximations discussed thus far, a Monte Carlo study was carried out. Besides Mokken's methods 1 and 2 and the MS-method, four classical reliability coefficients were studied. They are coefficient *alpha* (Cronbach, 1951), *lambda*-2 (Guttman, 1945; Jackson and Agunwamba, 1977) and *mu*-2 and *mu*-3 (ten Berge and Zegers, 1978). Ten Berge and Zegers (1978) have shown that these coefficients belong to an infinite series of coefficients, which they denote μ_0 (*alpha*), μ_1 (*lambda*-2), $\mu_2, \mu_3, \ldots$. Furthermore

$$\mu_0 \leq \mu_1 \leq \mu_2 \leq \mu_3 \leq \ldots \leq \varrho_{xx'}$$

holds, with equality when all items or test parts, on which the coefficients are based, are essentially *tau*-equivalent (see, for example, Lord and Novick, 1968, p. 90). Thus, coefficient *alpha* is the smallest lower bound of the series, though it is the lower bound most commonly used in practice. One may further note that its sampling theory has been derived analytically (Kristof, 1963; Feldt, 1965), though under rather restrictive conditions. Therefore, we will not use it in the present study, but its robustness properties deserve attention, see, for example, Sedere and Feldt (1977).

Finally the reason for studying only the first four coefficients of the series is that the increase of the coefficient levels off very fast (ten Berge and Zegers, 1978).

10.6.1 Method

We are especially interested in two dependent variables as a result from our Monte Carlo study. They are the standard deviation and the average bias of statistics across random samples from a known population. Denoting reliability statistics by t and the true reliability by $\varrho_{xx'}$, the standard deviation and the average bias of t with respect to $\varrho_{xx'}$ can be combined in the mean squared error (MSE):

$$\text{MSE} = \frac{1}{N} \sum_{r=1}^{N} (t_r - \varrho_{xx'})^2 =$$

$$= (\bar{t} - \varrho_{xx'})^2 + \frac{1}{N} \sum_{r=1}^{N} (t_r - \bar{t})^2$$

where N denotes the number of random samples. The first expression on the right-hand side denotes the squared average bias of t with respect to $\varrho_{xx'}$, and the second expression denotes the variance of t across replications. The mean squared error is a measure of the overall error in the statistic t, and its square root is also reported in this study.

Four independent variables are manipulated in this study. They are:

(i) The difficulty parameters. We consider equal distances between the difficulty parameters in each cell of the design. Two levels are distinguished: relatively small and large distances. The difficulty parameters are chosen symmetrically with respect to the density of ξ.

(ii) The discrimination parameters. These are held constant for each item and they vary across cells in the design. Two levels are distinguished: relatively small and large discrimination.
(iii) The number of subjects. It is well known that the sampling variability of useful statistics decreases when the number of observations is increased. Therefore, we consider both relatively small and relatively large samples.
(iv) The number of items. The reliability of a measure often increases when the number of items in the measurement device is increased (see, for example, Lord and Novick, 1968, p. 103). Thus, we consider tests composed of relatively small and large numbers of items.

Taking all combinations of the factors into consideration leads to a $2 \times 2 \times 2 \times 2$ design.

Finally, random samples of item responses were drawn from a population in which ξ was standard normal distributed and $\pi_i(\xi)$ was chosen to be a two-parameter logistic trace line. In each cell of the design, 200 data matrices were constructed ($N = 200$), where a matrix is of the order n (subjects) by k (items) and the elements are dichotomously scored item responses. Further technical details can be found in Sijtsma and Molenaar (in press).

10.6.2 Results

Since the results of the Monte Carlo study are too numerous to discuss in this chapter, we will only present some main conclusions.

The results in Table 10.2 are quite characteristic for other results of our study.

The entries in the table are averages across 200 replications, where each replication consists of a 100 (subjects) by 7 (items) data matrix. The table shows results for two levels of item discrimination ($D\alpha$) and two levels of distance between the item difficulties ($d(\delta)$).

First, it may be noted that the stability of the three methods discussed in this chapter, is mostly less than the stability of the classical estimates, though the differences are rather small.

Second, the bias of the three methods is mostly smaller than the bias of the classical methods, which is especially true for method 1 and the MS-method. In cell 4 the differences are very pronounced: both methods are almost unbiased, while the bias of the classical methods is considerable. Also, Mokken's method 2 performs rather

Table 10.2 Standard deviation (SD), bias and square root of the mean squared error (RMSE) of seven reliability estimates (Mokken's methods 1 and 2, method of Molenaar and Sijtsma, *alpha*, *lambda-2*, *mu-2* and *mu-3*), where $N = 200$, $n = 100$ and $k = 7$. The entries in the table should be multiplied by 0.001; e.g. an entry '69' means 0.069.

		$d(\delta) = 0.20$						$d(\delta) = 0.67$					
		Mok-1	Mok-2	MS	alpha	1am-2	mu-2	mu-3	Mok-1	Mok-2	MS	alpha	1am-2	mu-2	mu-3
		1							2						
$D\alpha = 1.00$	SD	62	62	62	58	54	54	54	81	80	80	77	70	70	70
	BIAS	-5	-6	-6	-6	6	8	8	-13	-16	-11	-22	-3	1	1
	RMSE	62	62	62	59	55	55	55	82	81	81	80	71	70	70
		3							4						
$D\alpha = 3.00$	SD	21	20	19	19	19	18	18	40	35	31	33	31	31	30
	BIAS	-1	-3	-1	-13	-11	-11	-10	0	-35	1	-87	-53	-45	-44
	RMSE	21	20	20	23	22	21	21	40	49	31	93	61	55	53

Note: the true reliability ($\varrho_{xx'}$) equals 0.589, 0.534, 0.882, and 0.812 in the cells 1, 2, 3 and 4 respectively.

poorly. The reason why the classical estimates perform badly with respect to bias is that the items in cell 4 strongly deviate from essential *tau*-equivalence. When this equivalence condition holds true, the classical parameters equal the reliability (see also Molenaar and Sijtsma, 1984), which however does not imply that their sample counterparts are unbiased.

Generally, we may conclude that the bias of method 1 and the MS-method is negligible, while the stability of the latter method is always a little bit better compared to the former method.

The same conclusions hold when the number of subjects is raised from 100 to 300 in each replication, while keeping constant the other characteristics that apply to Table 10.2. Roughly speaking the bias is of the same magnitude, but the standard deviation is smaller by a factor $\frac{1}{2}$ to $\frac{3}{4}$.

Raising the number of items from 7 to 15, where the difficulty parameters again are equidistant, but intervals between them are rather small, leads to comparable conclusions, though the bias as well as the standard deviation are of a smaller magnitude.

The square root of the mean squared error (RMSE) is considerably smaller for the methods of Mokken and the MS-method than for the classical methods, when the items deviate strongly from essential *tau*-equivalence. In the other cases no large differences are found.

Cross-validation of some cells in the design has left the conclusions unchanged.

10.7 DISCUSSION

On a general level we may conclude that the stability of all reliability estimates does not differ very much, although there is a definite trend in favour of the classical estimates. Mokken's method 1 and the MS-method show negligible bias in all situations under consideration in this study. The classical estimates perform rather poorly when the items strongly deviate from essential *tau*-equivalence, which is to be expected in most practical applications. The two estimates mentioned before, and to a lesser degree Mokken's method 2, are insensitive to such deviations since they are not based on any equivalence assumptions. Theoretically the assumption of double monotonicity may pose a serious restriction on the usefulness of the estimates presented here. Results on the stability and the bias of the estimates under violation of double monotonicity have not been collected yet. Consequently, for the time being applications of the methods should be restricted to the case of double monotonicity.

REFERENCES

BERGE, J. M. F. ten and ZEGERS, F. E., 'A Series of Lower Bounds to the Reliability of a Test', *Psychometrika*, **43** (1978) 575–9.
BIRNBAUM, A., Part v in LORD, F. M. and NOVICK, M. R., *Statistical Theories of Mental Test Scores* (Reading, Mass.: Addison-Wesley, 1968).
CRONBACH, L. J., 'Coefficient Alpha and the Internal Structure of Tests', *Psychometrika*, **16** (1951) 297–334.
FELDT, L. S., 'The Approximate Sampling Distribution of Kuder–Richardson Reliability Coefficient Twenty', *Psychometrika*, **30** (1965) 357–70.
FISCHER, G. H., *Einführung in die Theorie psychologischer Tests* (Bern: Huber, 1974).
GUTTMAN, L., 'A Basis for Analyzing Test–Retest Reliability', *Psychometrika*, **10** (1945) 255–82.
—— 'The Basis for Scalogram Analysis', in STOUFFER, S. A., GUTTMAN, L., SUCHMAN, E. A., LAZARSFELD, P. F., STAR, S. A. and CLAUSEN, J. A. (eds), *Measurement and Prediction* (Princeton, N.J.: Princeton University Press, 1950).
HAMBLETON, R. K. and COOK, L. L., 'Latent Trait Models and Their Use in the Analysis of Educational Test Data', *Journal of Educational Measurement*, **14** (1977) 75–96.
HENNING, H. J., 'Die Technik der Mokken-Skalenanalyse', *Psychologische Beiträge*, **18** (1976) 410–30.
JACKSON, P. H. and AGUNWAMBA, C. C., 'Lower Bounds for the Reliability of the Total Score on a Test Composed of Non-homogeneous Items: I. Algebraic Lower Bounds', *Psychometrika*, **42** (1977) 567–78.
JANSEN, P. G. W., 'Homogenitätsmessung mit Hilfe des Koeffizienten H von Loevinger: Eine Kritische Diskussion', *Psychologische Beiträge*, **24** (1982a) 96–105.
—— 'De Onbruikbaarheid van Mokkenschaal-analyse', *Tijdschrift voor Onderwijsresearch*, **7** (1982b) 11–24.
—— *Rasch Analysis of Attitudinal Data* (Den Haag: Rijks Psychologische Dienst, 1983) (dissertation).
—— ROSKAM, E. E. Ch. I. and WOLLENBERG, A. L. van den, 'De Mokkenschaal gewogen', *Tijdschrift voor Onderwijsresearch*, **7** (1982) 31–42.
KRISTOF, W., 'The Statistical Theory of Stepped-up Reliability Coefficients When a Test has been Divided into Several Equivalent Parts', *Psychometrika*, **28** (1963) 221–38.
LOEVINGER, J., 'The Technique of Homogeneous Tests Compared with

Some Aspects of "Scale Analysis" and Factor Analysis', *Psychological Bulletin*, **45** (1948) 507–30.

LORD, F. M., 'Practical Applications of Item Characteristic Curve Theory', *Journal of Educational Measurement*, **14** (1977) 117–38.

―― *Applications of Item Response Theory to Practical Testing Problems* (Hillsdale, N.J.: Lawrence Erlbaum, 1980).

―― and NOVICK, M. R., *Statistical Theories of Mental Test Scores* (Reading, Mass.: Addison-Wesley, 1968).

LUMSDEN, J., 'Test Theory', *Annual Review of Psychology*, **27** (1976) 251–80.

MOKKEN, R. J., *A Theory and Procedure of Scale Analysis* (The Hague: Mouton, 1971).

―― and LEWIS, C., 'A Nonparametric Approach to the Analysis of Dichotomous Item Responses', *Applied Psychological Measurement*, **6** (1982) 417–30.

MOLENAAR, I. W., 'Mokken Scaling Revisited', *Kwantitatieve Methoden*, vol. 3, **8** (1982a) 145–64.

―― 'Een Tweede Weging van de Mokken-Schaal', *Tijdschrift voor Onderwijsresearch*, **7** (1982b) 172–81.

―― 'De Beperkte Bruikbaarheid van Jansen's Kritiek', *Tijdschrift voor Onderwijsresearch*, **7** (1982c) 25–30.

―― and SIJTSMA, K., 'Internal Consistency and Reliability in Mokken's Nonparametric Item Response Model', *Tijdschrift voor Onderwijsresearch*, **9** (1984) 257–68.

SEDERE, M. U. and FELDT, L. S., 'The Sampling Distributions of the Kristof Reliability Coefficient, the Feldt Coefficient, and Guttman's lambda-2', *Journal of Educational Measurement*, **14** (1977) 53–62.

SIJTSMA, K., 'Useful Nonparametric Scaling: A Reply to Jansen', *Psychologische Beiträge*, **26** (1984) 423–37.

―― and MOLENAAR, I. W., 'Reliability of Test Scores in Nonparametric Item Response Theory, *Psychometrika*, (in press).

STOKMAN, F. N. and SCHUUR, W. H. van, 'Basic Scaling', *Quality and Quantity*, **14** (1980) 5–30.

WEISS, D. J. and DAVISON, M. L., 'Test Theory and Methods', *Annual Review of Psychology*, **32** (1981) 629–58.

WOOD, R., 'Fitting the Rasch Model – A Heady Tale', *British Journal of Mathematical and Statistical Psychology*, **31** (1978) 27–32.

Part IV
Scaling Continuous Data

11 Some Empirical Tests of the Predictive Strength of Three Multi-attribute Preference Models

K. J. Veldhuisen

11.1 INTRODUCTION

The research, for which the empirical tests have been carried out, is directed at the design of residential situations for which the utility of the user(s) is optimal. The ultimate objective is to produce residential situations by CAD, optimising the user's utilities measured through interactive Computer Assisted Data Collection. As residential situations usually are judged on a considerable number of properties, we have to establish the utilities that people (may) derive from those properties and the way they integrate these utilities into judgements of residential situations as a whole.

The judgement and choice of residential situations by an individual decision-maker are usually the results of a process in which that individual has made a number of trade-offs between positive and negative aspects associated with the various properties of possible choices. The judgement of a residential situation can thus be conceptualised as the result of a mental process by which an individual cognitively integrates the part-worth utilities defined on the levels of the various attributes of that situation according to some mathematical function. The application of this model implies the choice of some measurement procedure to measure the part-worth utilities and secondly the identification of the functional form which describes the way in which an individual arrives at an overall utility.

In order to establish the part-worth utilities of subjects two general approaches may be followed, the compositional and the decompositional approach.

In the compositional approach the attribute levels of the choice alternatives are separately and explicitly evaluated by individuals and subsequently combined into an overall judgement using some prespecified mathematical function. The contribution of the part-worth utilities to the overall utility is usually weighted by either directly measured relative importance weights or weights based on regression coefficients. A disadvantage of the use of the regression coefficients in the context of evaluation of residential situations is that subjects have to judge objects with more than six or seven attributes. Several authors have concluded that, given this number of attributes, these methods probably lead to less reliable results (e.g. Meehl, 1954; Goldberg, 1968; Lathrop and Peters, 1969; Slovic and Lichtenstein, 1971; Veldhuisen and Kapoen, 1979).

In the decompositional approach some overall utility measure is decomposed into part-worth utilities given some type of composition or combination rule.

The two approaches evidently differ in two main aspects. First, in the compositional approach a researcher must *a priori* specify a mathematical function to combine the separate evaluations and cannot test the appropriateness of this function unless an external criterium is available in the form of an overall utility measure. Second, the compositional approach necessitates the direct measurement of relative importance weights as regression analysis may be unreliable. In contrast the decompositional approach renders it possible to test the appropriateness of the form of the utility function either by statistical goodness-of-fit tests or by comparing measures which indicate the fit between the predictions from the derived scale values and the measurements.

In the past decades a number of measurement procedures have been developed to measure and analyse the judgements and evaluations that people may attach to various objects. Three of these procedures which have attracted wide attention are those concerning Magnitude Estimation or Psychophysical Scaling (Stevens, 1957 and 1966), Conjoint Measurement (Luce and Tukey, 1964) and Information Integration Theory or Functional Measurement (Anderson, 1974; Shanteau, 1975). Magnitude estimation has been used in various situations where measurement of social phenomena is necessary (Rainwater, 1974; Saris, Bruinsma, Schoots and Vermeulen, 1977); Conjoint and Functional Measurement have been used to measure the evaluations of elements of residential situations, the way that subjects integrate these evaluations into one judgement and the choice they (might) make on the basis of their judgement (Lieber, 1976; Louviere, 1976 and 1978; Knight and Menchick, 1976). Using Magnitude Estimation involves the application of the compositional approach while the Conjoint and Functional Measurement involve the decompositional approach.

From tests comparing the three procedures three main conclusions could be drawn (Veldhuisen and Timmermans, 1981a, 1981b, 1984): First, there are only minor differences in results obtained by the Conjoint and Functional Measurement. Second, to a rather high degree it is possible to reproduce the results obtained by applying decompositional methods from the results obtained by the direct measurements. This implies that simple direct measurements of evaluations of attributes of residential situations may be included validly into survey questionnaires, which may subsequently be combined according to some prespecified mathematical function to compute overall evaluations of residential situations as a whole. The problem which remains in this case is that the chosen functional form has to be specified in advance and may thus be wrong. Third, subjective importance weights derived from overall judgements are generally not linearly related to the importance weights obtained directly by asking subjects to indicate the importance they attach to various attributes of a residential choice alternative. This point is of especial importance if these weights differ greatly and should be used in the calculation of the overall judgement.

The experiment at hand is directed at testing the appropriateness of the three measurement procedures to predict residential choice from dweller's evaluations of residential attributes. The remainder of this chapter concerns

- a short review of the three measurement procedures
- a description of the experiment
- the conclusions.

11.2 A SHORT REVIEW OF THE PRINCIPLES OF THE THREE MEASUREMENT PROCEDURES

Magnitude Estimation
Originally magnitude estimation has been developed in the context of psychophysics, but more recently some evidence has accumulated

that this measurement procedure can also be used successfully to measure attitudes and judgements (e.g. Hamblin, 1973; Rainwater, 1974; Saris et al., 1977). Magnitude estimation is based on the following assumptions and experimental and analytical procedures.

First, it is assumed that a sensation is functionally related to the quantity of a stimulus raised to the power n that is, the relationship between a sensation (Y) and a stimulus (S) may be expressed as (e.g. Stevens, 1957; Stevens and Galanter, 1957).

$$Y = k \cdot S^n \qquad (1)$$

where k is a constant and n denotes the power.

Second, it is assumed that subject's sensations can be measured directly by asking a subject to express his/her sensations either in terms of a ratio of a given scale (ratio-estimation) or most commonly as an absolute number which reflects the absolute magnitude of the sensation. Third, Equation (1) may be applied also to attitudes and associated social stimuli to give (Stevens, 1966; Hamblin, 1973).

$$A = a \cdot (S - b)^c \qquad (2)$$

where A is an attitude score or judgement, S is the social stimulus and a, b and c are parameters to be estimated. The parameter b is used to scale S from its natural zero (Stevens, 1966; Hamblin, 1973). Fourth, an overall attitude (A^*) or judgement may be obtained by combining separate attitudes, for instance according:

$$A^* = a \cdot S_1^{c1} \cdot S_2^{c2} \ldots S_n^{cn} \qquad (3)$$

were A^* denotes a composite-judgement and S^c the judgements concerning the separate social stimuli.

It will be evident that this procedure assumes for cases of multi-attribute alternatives that the following requirements are satisfied. The attributes of the choice alternatives should be utility-independent. In addition, a mathematical function as a representational model of the way in which subjects combine their separate judgements to arrive at an overall judgement should be specified *a priori* and, finally, the relative importance weights for the various attributes should be determined separately, either by measuring them directly or by estimating them by linear regression procedures. It should be stressed that the procedure does not entail any inherent mechanisms to identify the form of the composition rules on the basis of the psychophysical measurements nor to test the other assumptions.

Conjoint Measurement

Assume that a subject has provided some ordinal measure of preference for a set of multi-attribute choice alternatives. The problem is to identify the composition rule which has been applied in this task to arrive at the overall preference measure and infer part-worth utilities of the attribute levels. This measurement problem is known as the 'conjoint measurement problem' (Luce and Tukey, 1964; Krantz, 1964). Thus, conjoint measurement is concerned with simultaneously scaling the joint effect of two or more independent variables on the ordering of a dependent variable.

Conjoint measurement involves first that the attributes of the choice alternatives are categorised into a number of categories (levels). Next, these categories are combined according to the principles of factorial or fractional factorial designs to yield a set of hypothetical stimulus combinations. Alternatively, the attributes may be combined in pairs. Subjects are then requested to rank all possible stimulus combinations. In the non-metric case the part-worth utilities defined on the attribute levels are derived by iteratively adjusting trial scale values such that the ordering of the stimulus combinations predicted by a specific composition rule is as nearly monotonic as possible with the manifest rank ordering of the stimulus combinations. Several models may be used to define the way in which the part-worth utilities are combined (see Timmermans, 1980). The goodness-of-fit of the scaling solution is usually provided by a measure called 'stress', which is for the three attributes case defined as:

$$S = \frac{\sum_j \sum_k \sum_l (\hat{Z}_{jkl} - Z_{jkl})^2}{\sum_j \sum_k \sum_l n_{jkl} \cdot (Z_{jkl} - \bar{Z})^2} \qquad (4)$$

where $\hat{Z}_{jkl}$ is the monotone regression value which predicts Z_{jkl} most accurately from the rank orders;
Z_{jkl} is the corresponding value derived from the specified measurement model;
n_{jkl} is the number of observations for combination j, k, l; and

$$\bar{Z} = (\sum_j \sum_k \sum_l n_{jkl} \cdot Z_{jkl}) / (\sum_j \sum_k \sum_l n_{jkl})$$

The most appropriate model may be identified by comparing stress values for alternative measurement models, the lowest value indicating the best model.

Although the procedure sketched above represents a frequently employed procedure, different experimental procedures and estimation techniques exist. The reader is referred to Timmermans (1984) for a detailed account of these developments.

It will be evident that conjoint measurement constitutes a straightforward approach to derive part-worth utilities from an overall preference ordering of stimulus combination. Nevertheless, this measurement procedure is characterised by some restrictions. First, the procedure assumes that subjects respond on a unidimensional scale which might not be a realistic assumption for every decision-making task (Green and Rao, 1971). Second, since one is concerned with essentially ordinal data a multitude of measurement models and part-worth utilities might account almost equally well for the manifest rank ordering of the dependent variable. Third, it is not always possible to identify the most appropriate combination rule, especially with relatively high stress values (Green, Carmone and Wind, 1972). Fourth, the identification of the test model is dependent upon the number and spacing of the attribute levels (see Lieber, 1976).

Functional Measurement

Functional measurement is closely associated with the development of information integration theory which assumes that individuals give some response by combining or integrating judgements about different attributes according to simple algebraic rules. Like conjoint measurement, functional measurement also involves presenting a set of stimulus combinations defined according to the principles of factorial or fractional factorial designs to subjects and asking them to provide some measure of overall preference. Unlike conjoint measurement, however, a subject is usually requested to rate the stimulus combinations on some interval scale. Consequently, a battery of statistical tests may be used to identify the form of the utility function.

Consider, for instance, a simple averaging model for two attributes of the following form:

$$R_{ij} = \frac{w_0 s_0 + w_{r_i} s_{r_i} + w_{c_j} s_{c_j}}{w_0 + w_{r_i} + w_{c_j}} + e_{ij} \tag{5}$$

where R_{ij} is the response on stimulus combination i, j;
w_{r_i}, w_{c_j} are the weights of the stimulus in row i and column j respectively;
s_{r_i}, s_{c_j} are the values of the stimulus in row i and column j respectively;
e_{ij} is an additive random variable with zero mean.

If it is assumed that the weights are independent from the attribute levels it follows that

$$R_{ij} = C + w_r s_{r_i} + w_c s_{c_j} + e_{ij} \tag{6}$$

It follows from Equation (6) that

$$R_{1j} - R_{2j} = w_r (s_{r_1} - s_{r_2}) \tag{7}$$

Hence, Equation (7) implies that rows 1 and 2 differ by the same amount in each column if error is ignored and that consequently these rows should plot as parallel lines.

Actually, testing the form of the model in functional measurement is either based on an inspection of such data plots or on an analysis of variance test. In particular an additive model is supported by the data if the marginal means of the rows or columns of the factorial design plotted against their corresponding attribute levels plot as a series of parallel lines. This implies that an analysis of variance should indicate that none of the interaction terms are statistically different from zero. Likewise, a multiplicative model is supported by the data if the plots show a series of diverging/converging lines and by statistically significant interaction terms with all of the variance in the interaction effects localised in the multilinear components. If the model passes the fit, functional scales of the stimuli can be obtained as the marginal means of the factorial design. Separate weight and value parameters for each stimulus generally require additional assumptions, but several solutions for this case have been developed (Anderson, 1971; Leon, Oden and Anderson, 1973; Himmelfarb and Anderson, 1974; Norman, 1976). The reader is referred to Anderson (1974) and Louviere (1976, 1978, 1981) for further details on experimental and analytical procedures associated with functional measurement.

Comparing these three alternative measurement procedures it seems, in theory at least, that they all can be applied to specify and measure residential utility functions; although each with its own restrictions. Magnitude estimation seems to be a straightforward measurement procedure. Its main restrictions concern the validity of the applied measurement scales and the lack of an inherent mechanism to test the form of the combination rule. In contrast, conjoint measurement is less demanding in terms of a subject's ability to express his/her preferences because it only requires ordinal responses. On the other hand, functional measurement has an associated error theory to test the form of the model statistically whereas the identification of the best model in the context of conjoint measurement rests on comparing stress measures, an evidently rigorous procedure. Hence it seems worth while to study the usefulness of these three measurement procedures in empirical applications in order to check these expectations. The next sections describe the experimental procedures and analytical results of applications of these measurement procedures in the context of measuring residential utility functions and the prediction of residential choice.

11.3 THE EXPERIMENT

Introduction

Utility has been conceived as 'that property in any object, whereby it tends to produce benefit, advantage, pleasure, good or happiness . . . or . . . to prevent the happening of mischief, pain, evil, or unhappiness to the party whose interest is considered' (Bentham, cited by Crombag, 1979). One may suppose a strong correlation between the utility people derive from certain properties of objects and their explicit evaluation of those properties because in most cases not the (existence of the) property is being evaluated but the utility itself. There exists, however, a possibility that two different properties are evaluated on the same level but differ in salience or importance for a particular subject. In that case the subject would derive more pleasure from one of the properties than from the other. In theory at least, the utility of a certain property of an object may be thus approximated with a function of the evaluation and the relative importance weight of that property.

The Application of Magnitude Estimation

The application of magnitude estimation is in the context of the experiment at hand, restricted to the use of category-scales because of the ease of the measurements (see also Shinn, 1973) and the interpretation of the results of the analysis. In order to transform the scores on the category scales into interval values the outcomes of large-scale surveys in which the relationship between verbal category and graphic evaluation scales have been used (Veldhuisen and Hacfoort, 1983). The verbal categories of the scale and the mean graphic scale values (between 0 and 100) are:

Verbal categories	Scale value	Class
1. Extremely bad	12.1	–14
2. Very bad	16.4	15–20
3. Bad	24.9	21–32
4. Neither bad nor good	40.6	33–48
5. Fair	57.4	49–67
6. Good	76.6	68–81
7. Very good	86.3	82–89
8. Excellent	92.1	90–

The verbal categories are so formulated as to keep respondents from scoring in or close to the centre of the scale. Consequently the distances at the extremes of the graphic scale are definitely smaller than those in the centre of the scale.

The measurements are further described as 'direct measurements', the results form the 'evaluation' component in the utilities.

The Application of the Conjoint Measurement

In principle conjoint measurement is based on the rank-ordering of objects defined as a combination of all the possible attribute-levels (full factorial design). As we plan to describe our residential situations with at least 10 attributes, each to be divided into 2 to 4 levels, this would lead approximately 170,000 different situations to be ordered. In order to reduce these numbers a fractional design, based on the trade-off model (see Westwood, Lunn and Beazly, 1974), combined with a balanced design, is used to generate the hypothetical residential situations. A trade-off matrix consists of the combinations of two attributes describing the choice alternatives. If for instance residential situations are differentiated according to 'number of rooms' and 'dwelling type' this may result in the following trade-off matrix with the rank-order given by a particular subject (where 1 relates to the least- and 6 to the most-preferred):

	number of rooms		
	3	4	5
Single family house	2	5	6
Multiple family house	1	3	4

In this case the subject trades off the difference between 4 and 5 rooms against the difference between the types.

It may be noted that under the condition of independence between the attributes a monotonic ordering within the rows and columns may be expected. A reversed order is considered to form an inconsistency. This particular trade-off matrix contains 15 two-by-two rank-orders.

As the 10 planned attributes would lead to 45 of these trade-off matrices and consequently to too large a task for the subjects, a balanced design is used to reduce that number. In that balanced design each attribute is only three times combined with another to produce the hypothetical residential situations, therefore reducing the task to the rank-ordering of 15 trade-off matrices.

Attribute	1	2	3	4	5
6	*	*	*		
7	*			*	*
8	*	*			*
9		*	*	*	
10			*	*	*

The values of the utilities (implicitly the weighted evaluations) are calculated so that they reproduce the rank-orders by either addition or multiplication of the utilities of the pairs involved. The values are derived through a gradient search algorithm so that the percentage of two-by-two rank-orders is at maximum for all the (15) trade-off matrices.

The Application of the Functional Measurement

The functional measurement is accomplished by scoring on the same combinations, as used in the conjoint measurement, with the similar scales as in the direct measurements. The same transformation has been carried out.

The Research Design

The starting-point of the exercise is formed by a visualised description of the major part of the Dutch housing stock, approximately 80 per cent, by photographs of 13 typical residential situations, including the direct environment of the dwellings. These 13 situations were presented to 34 subjects after they had filled out a number of forms concerning the 10 major attributes of the residential situations. The latter attributes formed a more verbal description of the photographs. Attributes which could not be seen or inferred from the exterior of the situations were printed in a corner of the pictures. These attributes included amongst others the number of rooms, ownership and costs. The complete list is given in Table 11.1.

Table 11.1 The attributes and attribute-levels of the residential situations

1. Number of rooms	(4–3, 4, 5 or 6)
2. Location dwelling	(3–from city centre to small community)
3. Ownership	(2–rented or owned)
4. Monthly costs	(3–fl 700, 500, 350)
5. Amount of traffic in street	(3–from heavy to destination traffic)
6. Parking of car	(3–from centralised to own garage)
7. Common green area	(3–from no green area to extensive)
8. Type of dwelling	(4–from apartm. to single family house)
9. Exterior	(4–from bad to excellent)
10. Age of dwelling	(4–from old to new)

(the first number between the parentheses denotes the number of levels)

The balanced design for the experiment looked as follows:

Table 11.2 The pairwise combinations of attributes

Attribute	Owner-ship	Costs	Traffic	Parking	Green
Number of rooms	*	*			*
Location of dwelling	*		*	*	
Type of dwelling	*	*			*
Exterior		*	*	*	
Age of dwelling			*	*	*

The tasks were presented in the following form

1. The attribute-levels were to be rated on a 8-point scale from 'extremely negative' to 'extremely positive'.
2. The relative importance weights of the attribute-levels were to be rated on a 5-point scale from 'most important' to 'not at all important'.
3. Answers to the questions which of the attribute-levels were considered to be completely unacceptable and which ones should in any case be included in a preferred residential situation.
4. The rank-ordering of the 15 trade-off matrices.
5. The rating of all the pairwise combinations of attribute-levels (from the trade-off matrices) on the 8-point scale.
   (4 and 5 were presented in different order for half of the subjects)
6. The rank-ordering of a set of 13 photographs, describing approximately 80 per cent of the Dutch housing stock. In this rank-ordering the own residential situation of the subject had to be included.
7. A description of the own residential situation in terms of the available attribute-levels.

Analysis and Results

The Internal Inconsistency

The first tests concern the internal consistency of both the conjoint and the functional measurement. In Table 11.3 the subjects are divided over those who started with the rank-ordering and those who started with the direct measurements. In the left columns (R) the number of inconsistencies, counted over the 15 rank-ordered factor-combinations, are given; in the middle columns (D) the number of inconsistencies over the direct measurement for the same combinations. In both cases the minimum of inversions in rows and columns was counted, in the case of the direct measurements equal scores were not considered to be inconsistent. The right columns (C) contain the number of inconsistencies which are observed in the same rows and columns of the corresponding factor-combinations.

The direct measurements show far more inconsistencies than the rank-orderings (388 v. 208). This result is the more striking as the probability of inconsistent ranking is larger than inconsistent scoring because equal objects have to be ordered in any case while these

Table 11.3 The number of inconsistencies in the rank-orderings and the direct measurements

Measured as subject	R 1	D 2	C	Subject	R 2	D 1	C
1.	10	21	2	2.	2	13	1
3.	19	8	2	4.	8	2	0
5.	6	9	4	7.	4	8	0
6.	6	8	1	8.	0	7	0
9.	6	10	3	11.	15	26	5
10.	14	21	4	12.	3	11	1
13.	2	12	1	14.	12	14	3
16.	6	4	0	15.	2	2	0
18.	13	10	2	17.	5	11	1
19.	19	19	7	20.	0	5	0
21.	1	11	0	23.	3	25	2
22.	1	11	0	24.	11	17	3
26.	3	3	0	25.	0	13	0
28.	8	11	3	27.	4	23	3
29.	6	16	4	30.	3	9	0
33.	2	10	0	31.	4	8	1
34.	4	4	0	32.	6	15	4
Total	126	179			82	209	

objects can get the same score in the direct measurements. Moreover the learning effects are larger in the case of the rankings than in the case of the direct measurements. As the inconsistencies do hardly agree between the two measurement procedures they cannot be attributed to interaction-effects or the lack of unidimensionality. The conclusion has to be drawn that the numbers of inconsistencies reflect the unreliability of the measurement procedures and that the used form of direct measurements is less reliable than the used form of conjoint measurement.

The Prediction of the Residential Choice

The second step in the analysis concerns the comparison of the three procedures on the prediction of residential choice through the rank-ordering of the photographs. The columns consist of Spearman's Rank-order Correlations calculated over the observed and the predicted ordering of the presented photographs. The main distinction is made between additive and multiplicative combination rules. The three procedures are denoted as D(irect), F(unctional) and C(onjoint). As the relative importance weights have been applied, a distinction is made between the weighted (W) and unweighted (U) results of the direct measurements. The utilities have been estimated trough scaling (S) and in the case of the functional measurement also with regression analysis yielding least-squares estimators (LS).

The conclusion on the basis of previous research, e.g. that the procedures yield comparable results is sustained. The picture that is presented by Table 11.4, however, does not directly point to the procedure or model with the best results. Based on the highest correlations per row it may nevertheless be possible to compare the quality of the three procedures. For the additive and multiplicative models both the ratio between the highest correlations in the direct and those in the non-direct procedures is approximately 1 to 3. This means that the performance of the conjoint and the functional measurement is on average better than that of the direct measurement. This relation holds too when the columns are compared separately be it that the ratios are less prominent. In Table 11.5 the ratios of the highest correlations per pair of columns are presented. Under each column the percentage of highest correlations, totalised over all columns, is given.

From the order in the procedures it may be clear that the amount of information contained by functional measurements outweighs the unreliability they have shown in comparison with the conjoint measurements. That the direct unweighted measurements perform less than the functional and the conjoint measurements both is not surprising, the latter procedures produce utilities in which the weight is included. The fact that the weighted (direct) evaluations show the worst predictions is probably due to the difficulties subjects have with judging the relative importance they attach to the attribute-levels. For a number of subjects it has shown almost impossible to make a difference between the evaluation and the relative importance of those attribute-levels. In view of the fact that subjects tend to favour functional over conjoint measurement the former procedure seems to be the best choice.

The performance of the models shows a less clear picture, columns 3, 4 and 5 end almost *ex aquo*. If, however, the best predictive model or combination-rule for each individual could be derived comparing the values of the stress-values for both models the quality of the prediction for the sample could be raised. This possibility is examined in the following paragraph.

Table 11.4 The comparison of the three-measurement procedures on the prediction of the ranking of the residential situations with Spearman's Rank-order Correlations

	Additive					Multiplicative			
	Direct		Conj	Functional		Direct		Conj	Func
Subject	U	W	S	S	LS	U	W	S	S
1.	0.74	0.81	0.67	0.76	0.82	0.59	0.56	0.61	0.72
2.	0.91	0.79	0.89	0.93	0.93	0.80	0.75	0.80	0.92
3.	0.90	0.86	0.73	0.85	0.85	0.90	0.88	0.70	0.81
4.	0.78	0.83	0.85	0.82	0.80	0.73	0.77	0.85	0.83
5.	0.63	0.46	0.63	0.70	0.75	0.56	0.60	0.46	0.62
6.	0.66	0.77	0.86	0.90	0.89	0.67	0.75	0.85	0.89
7.	0.79	0.82	0.95	0.96	0.96	0.73	0.73	0.96	0.79
8.	0.82	0.75	0.96	0.93	0.96	0.83	0.77	0.97	0.78
9.	0.62	0.79	0.70	0.66	0.74	0.84	0.66	0.78	0.65
10.	0.18	0.26	0.52	0.26	0.52	0.03	0.29	0.54	0.20
11.	0.88	0.79	0.78	0.69	0.67	0.82	0.49	0.86	0.54
12.	0.87	0.73	0.84	0.68	0.69	0.60	0.53	0.87	0.71
13.	0.40	0.37	−0.10	0.41	0.39	0.49	0.46	−0.03	0.83
14.	0.82	0.82	0.86	0.80	0.82	0.84	0.84	0.87	0.86
15.	0.64	0.75	0.67	0.80	0.73	0.87	0.72	0.72	0.48
16.	0.80	0.75	0.82	0.85	0.81	0.67	0.41	0.80	0.74
17.	0.87	0.90	0.74	0.93	0.90	0.71	0.75	0.80	0.77
18.	0.86	0.82	0.87	0.83	0.84	0.85	0.85	0.89	0.85
19.	0.56	0.56	0.48	0.78	0.79	0.50	0.15	0.56	0.81
20.	0.81	0.75	0.80	0.48	0.54	0.82	0.50	0.81	0.76
21.	0.94	0.91	0.92	0.90	0.91	0.96	0.93	0.91	0.91
22.	0.88	0.71	0.85	0.92	0.92	0.86	0.81	0.86	0.90
23.	0.32	0.53	0.24	0.32	0.43	0.41	0.20	0.42	0.71
24.	0.85	0.89	0.83	0.87	0.86	0.83	0.80	0.80	0.87
25.	0.74	0.71	0.67	0.82	0.83	0.77	0.61	0.65	0.79
26.	0.73	0.54	0.83	0.79	0.81	0.76	0.59	0.78	0.84
27.	−0.02	0.06	0.29	0.62	0.51	0.15	0.17	0.20	0.52
28.	0.81	0.79	0.82	0.85	0.85	0.90	0.86	0.84	0.73
29.	0.92	0.90	0.89	0.91	0.86	0.83	0.82	0.90	0.87
30.	0.73	0.77	0.84	0.87	0.88	0.74	0.77	0.85	0.88
31.	0.81	0.77	0.88	0.87	0.86	0.81	0.77	0.80	0.90
32.	0.55	0.52	0.82	0.62	0.75	0.58	0.48	0.86	0.75
33.	0.79	0.78	0.85	0.85	0.90	0.87	0.90	0.80	0.82
34.	0.91	0.82	0.86	0.81	0.75	0.88	0.88	0.77	0.73

The Specification of the Combination Rule

The third step in the analysis concerns the comparison of the models on the fitting of the data and the prediction of the rank-ordering of

Table 11.5 The ratio of the highest correlations between the procedures and models

	Compared with columns								
	1	2	3	4	5	6	7	8	9
Column 1	–	20:12	16:17	9:24	9:24	16:16	24:10	14:16	15:18
2	–	–	12:22	12:21	11:20	13:21	18:14	10:19	14:18
3	–	–	–	14:19	13:19	19:14	26: 8	14:19	18:15
4	–	–	–	–	12:17	21:13	23:10	21:12	20:13
5	–	–	–	–	–	23:11	24: 9	20:12	17:13
6	–	–	–	–	–	–	22: 8	13:19	10:23
7	–	–	–	–	–	–	–	7:25	8:25
8	–	–	–	–	–	–	–	–	17:16
9	–	–	–	–	–	–	–	–	–
Percentage highest R	49	40	54	62	65	46	28	55	54

Ranking according to the totalised percentages leads to:

Measurement proc.	Model	Derivement utilities
1. Functional	Additive	Least squares
2. Functional	Additive	Scaling (linear)
3. Conjoint	Multiplicative	Scaling (linear)
4. Functional	Multiplicative	Scaling (linear)
5. Conjoint	Additive	Scaling (linear)
6. Direct	Additive	Transformation/unweighted
7. Direct	Multiplicative	Transformation/unweighted
8. Direct	Additive	Transformation/weighted
9. Direct	Multiplicative	Transformation/weighted

the photographs. This analysis is carried out for the functional and the conjoint measurements of the factor-combinations. In Table 11.6 the columns contain the following information. In the left columns for each of the data-collection methods the final function values are given for the additive and the multiplicative model respectively. For the functional measurements these values consist of the minimal average absolute differences between the observed and the predicted utilities for each presented object. For the conjoint measurements these values consist of the percentage of correctly predicted pairwise rank-orderings. The A and M denote respectively the best predictive performance of the additive or multiplicative model, the U means the models perform the same.

Table 11.6 The comparison of the additive and multiplicative model on fit and prediction

Subj.	Functional Add.	Mult.	Conjoint Add.	Mult.	Subj.	Functional Add.	Mult.	Conjoint Add.	Mult.
1.	0.077	0.077 A	90.7	91.5 A	18.	0.102	0.095 M	93.3	94.5 M
2.	0.106	0.081 A	97.3	98.4 A	19.	0.087	0.080 M	89.4	90.0 M
3.	0.062	0.066 A	86.7	85.1 A	20.	0.115	0.056 U	96.4	95.3 M
4.	0.058	0.059 M	93.4	93.5 U	21.	0.108	0.096 A	95.3	93.8 A
5.	0.087	0.085 A	86.7	86.4 A	22.	0.100	0.096 M	96.0	95.8 M
6.	0.071	0.075 A	88.2	88.9 A	23.	0.183	0.139 U	89.8	83.2 M
7.	0.094	0.060 A	94.0	94.0 M	24.	0.081	0.082 A	92.7	92.9 A
8.	0.073	0.066 A	99.4	97.3 M	25.	0.118	0.067 M	98.9	97.6 A
9.	0.070	0.066 A	90.7	94.4 M	26.	0.075	0.071 A	91.7	94.1 A
10.	0.101	0.104 A	94.4	92.0 M	27.	0.096	0.080 A	93.6	90.0 A
11.	0.115	0.100 A	88.8	86.8 M	28.	0.091	0.072 A	91.3	94.5 A
12.	0.082	0.085 M	87.5	94.9 M	29.	0.087	0.085 A	93.5	97.1 M
13.	0.132	0.114 M	96.3	95.4 M	30.	0.074	0.061 M	92.7	94.1 M
14.	0.078	0.068 M	93.5	90.3 M	31.	0.081	0.067 M	95.4	87.2 A
15.	0.076	0.072 A	92.4	94.8 M	32.	0.066	0.072 M	90.4	93.4 M
16.	0.074	0.076 A	94.8	95.0 A	33.	0.063	0.061 A	93.9	93.9 A
17.	0.084	0.065 A	97.3	96.4 M	34.	0.063	0.060 A	91.8	95.5 A

The results of Table 11.6 show that the form of the best-fitting model does not necessarily coincide with the best prediction model. The distribution of both models is

		Best prediction		
		M	A	
Best fit	M	21	22	43
	A	11	9	20
		32	31	63

not counting the equal results. The multiplicative model is in the majority in producing the best fit, the numbers of best predictions by both models are equal. The data-collection methods show a kind of inverse relationship, from out of the 29 multiplicative best fits in the case of the functional measurements 17 additive models for prediction ensue. From out of 14 additive best fits in the case of conjoint measurements 8 multiplicative models follow. The found discrepancy between fit and prediction confirms the results in an experiment directed at the design of dwellings (Veldhuisen, Thijssen and Timmermans, 1984a and 1984b).

The cause of the discrepancy between fit and prediction may be due to the possible stochastic character of the subject's scores which then accounts for variance in the stress-value. The dominance of the multiplicative best fits may be caused by the fact that this functional form can absorb erratic scores of subjects better than the additive model.

The consequence of the discrepancy necessitates the prespecification of the model of the combination-rule. As the additive model produces the best results but non-additive effects may be present, this model presents the best choice, be it that in that case the non-additivity has to be detected or at least be eliminated. The non-additive effects may be due to, for some of the individual subjects, extreme and therefore unacceptable attribute-levels. If such is the case these effects may be an artefact of the specification of the attribute-levels.

As far as the analysis is concerned, generally the best way to deal with the possible non-additivity is through analysis of variance. Interaction between the different attribute-levels is then determined by testing whether the increment in the proportion of variance of the dependent variable is significant. Unfortunately the balanced design, used to establish the factor-combinations, leads to a bias against the detection of interaction. The increments in variance do as a rule not account for significant F-ratios, as the increment in variance is calculated over only a small part of the matrix, but compared with the variance over the complete matrix. This means that other means to take care of the non-additive effects have to be employed.

The Elimination of the Non-Additive Effects

The main cause of the existence of non-additive effects may lie in the unacceptability of some attribute-levels. As a question to that effect was answered by the subjects, the prediction of the rank-ordering of the photographs could be adjusted, taking the unacceptability into account. This was done by dividing the calculated order into an acceptable and an unacceptable part, conserving the original order within the two parts. The results of that exercise, as shown in the second column of Table 11.7 are not very encouraging. In only 12 cases the prediction is improved. As a result of approaching 10 other

Table 11.7 The results of the elimination of the unacceptable attribute-levels on the quality of the prediction

Subj.	F–LS	1	2	3	Max.	Subj.	F–LS	1	2	3	Max.
1.	0.82	0.81	0.84	0.84	0.82	18.	0.84	0.85	0.87	0.84	0.89
2.	0.93	0.89	0.89	0.93	0.93	19.	0.79	0.60	0.85	0.89	0.81
3.	0.85	0.69	0.91	0.96	0.85	20.	0.54	0.56	0.78	0.61	0.76
4.	0.80	0.80	0.82	0.82	0.85	21.	0.91	0.60	0.92	0.94	0.92
5.	0.75	0.70	0.70	0.75	0.75	22.	0.92	0.93	0.93	0.93	0.92
6.	0.89	0.90	0.89	0.89	0.89	23.	0.43	0.44	0.64	0.60	0.71
7.	0.96	0.96	0.96	0.96	0.96	24.	0.86	0.80	0.87	0.87	0.87
8.	0.96	0.96	0.96	0.96	0.97	25.	0.83	0.65	0.85	0.86	0.83
9.	0.74	0.81	0.84	0.85	0.78	26.	0.81	0.43	0.82	0.81	0.84
10.	0.52	0.21	0.73	0.67	0.54	27.	0.51	0.51	0.63	0.60	0.62
11.	0.67	0.70	0.85	0.85	0.86	28.	0.85	0.75	0.94	0.92	0.85
12.	0.69	0.78	0.85	0.85	0.87	29.	0.86	0.86	0.93	0.93	0.91
13.	0.39	0.51	0.59	0.64	0.83	30.	0.88	0.91	0.92	0.89	0.88
14.	0.82	0.69	0.88	0.90	0.87	31.	0.86	0.86	0.91	0.88	0.90
15.	0.73	0.64	0.64	0.77	0.80	32.	0.75	0.46	0.82	0.81	0.86
16.	0.81	0.75	0.87	0.87	0.85	33.	0.90	0.86	0.91	0.91	0.90
17.	0.90	0.91	0.91	0.91	0.93	34.	0.75	0.85	0.84	0.89	0.86

subjects with the question to rank-order the photographs while protocols were made of their reasoning behind the ordering, another calculating procedure was developed. It seemed in general that the subjects used only one or two of the unacceptable attribute-levels to screen the photographs into manageable numbers. Therefore the recalculation of the rank-ordering is first based on the exclusion of the most important unacceptable attribute-level and second on the combination of the most and the second-most important attribute-level. The results of these adjustments are shown in the third and the fourth columns. In the fifth column the highest calculated correlations (Table 11.4) are shown.

In most cases the disadvantage of the application of the functional measurement-additive model is offset by the elimination of some of the unacceptable attribute-levels. In some of the cases excluding the second unacceptable attribute-level already leads to a lower correlation; apparently those subjects only use one attribute-level to make the first distinctions and further on disregard their rejection of the other attribute-levels while finishing the rank-ordering.

11.4 CONCLUSIONS

This experiment was directed at testing the appropriateness of the direct, the conjoint and the functional measurement procedures for the prediction of residential choice. It has been shown that the three measurement procedures yield comparable results in establishing the judgements of attributes of residential situations. These judgements can be considered as the expression of the utilities that people derive from those properties. It has also become clear that although the directly measured evaluations may be comparable to the (implicit) utilities they perform less well in predicting residential choice than utilities based on trade-offs people make when confronted with conflicting properties of residential situations. This applies more so when the directly measured importance weights of the attribute-levels are used. Apparently only when people have to choose between two or more different properties the relative-importance weights of the different properties may be established. Therefore the decompositional approaches have an advantage above the compositional approach. This means that direct measurement of evaluations, combined with a prespecified combination rule shows some disadvantage compared with the application of conjoint and functional measurement procedures.

The comparison between the two decompositional approaches shows the following:

- functional measurement procedures generate tasks which are considered easier by the subjects than the rank-ordering tasks in the context of conjoint measurement;
- rank-ordering tasks yield more reliable data than the direct measurements in the context of functional measurement procedures;
- the application of the functional measurements procedures, combined with regression analysis produces slightly better results when predicting choices of residential situations;
- non-additive effects of unacceptable attribute-levels can be successfully eliminated.

REFERENCES

ANDERSON, N. H., 'Integration Theory and Attitude Change', *Psychological Review*, **78** (1971) 171–206.

_____ 'Information Integration Theory: A Brief Survey', in *Contemporary Developments in Mathematical Psychology*, ed. D. H. KRANTZ et al. (San Francisco: Academic Press, 1974) 236–301.
CROMBAG, H. F. M., 'Recht als wetenschap', *Hollands Maandblad*, **21**, (1979) 29–39.
GOLDBERG, L. R., 'Simple Models of Simple Processes? Some Research on Clinical Judgements', *American Psychologists*, **23** (1968) 483–96.
GREEN, P. E., CARMONE, F. J. and WIND, Y., 'Subjective Evaluation Models and Conjoint Measurement', *Behavioral Science*, **17** (1972) 288–99.
_____ and RAO, V. R., 'Conjoint Measurement for Quantifying Judgmental Data', *Journal of Marketing Research*, **8** (1971) 355.
HAMBLIN, R. L., 'Social Attitudes: Magnitude Measurement and Theory', in BLALOCK, H. (ed.) *Measurement in the Social Sciences* (London: Macmillan, 1973).
HIMMELFARB, S. and ANDERSON, N. H., 'Integration Theory Applied to Opinion Attribution', *Journal of Personality and Social Psychology*, **31** (1974) 1064–72.
KNIGHT, R. L. and MENCHICK, M. D., 'Conjoint Preference Estimation for Residential Land Use Policy Evaluation', in GOLLEDGE, R. G. and RUSHTON, G. (eds) *Spatial Choice and Spatial Behavior* (Columbus: Ohio State University Press, 1976).
KRANTZ, D. H., 'Conjoint Measurement: the Luce–Tukey Axiomatization and Some Extensions', *Journal of Mathematical Psychology*, **1** (1964) 248–77.
LATHROP, R. G. and PETERS, B. E., 'Subjective Cue Weighting and Decisions in Familiar Task', *Proceedings of the 77th Annual Convention*, APA (1969).
LEON M., ODEN, G. C. and ANDERSON, N. H., 'Functional Measurement of Social Values', *Journal of Personality and Social Psychology*, (1973) 301–10.
LIEBER, S. R., 'A Comparison of Metric and Nonmetric Scaling Models in Preference Research', in GOLLEDGE, R. G. and RUSHTON, G. (eds) *Spatial Choice and Spatial Behavior* (Columbus: Ohio State University Press, 1976).
LOUVIERE, J. J., 'Information Processing Theory and Functional Measurement in Spatial Behavior', in GOLLEDGE, R. G. and RUSHTON, G. (eds) *Spatial Choice and Spatial Behavior* (Columbus: Ohio State University Press, 1976).
_____ 'Psychological Measurement of Travel Attributes', in HENSHER, D. A. and DALVI, U. (eds) *Determinants of Travel Choice* (London: Saxon House, 1978).
_____ 'On the Identification of the Functional Form of the Utility Expression and Its Relationship to Discrete Choice', in HENSHER, D. A. and JOHNSON, L. W. (eds) *Applied Discrete Choice Modelling* (London: Croom Helm, 1981) 385–415.
LUCE, R. D. and TUKEY, J. W., 'Simultaneous Conjoint Measurement: A New Type of Fundamental Measurement', *Journal of Mathematical Psychology*, **1** (1964) 1–27.

MEEHL, P. E., *Clinical vs. Statistical Prediction: A Theoretical Analysis and Review of the Evidence* (Minneapolis: University of Minnesota Press, 1954).
NORMAN, K. L., 'A Solution for Weights and Scale Values in Functional Measurement,' *Psychological Review*, **83** (1976) 80–4.
RAINWATER, L., *What Money Buys, Inequality and the Social Meanings of Income* (New York: Basic Books Inc., 1974).
ROSKAM, E. E., *Unidimensional Conjoint Measurement (UNICON) for Multi-faceted Designs* (Nijmegen: Psychologisch Laboratorium, 1974).
SARIS, W. E., BRUINSMA, C., SCHOOTS, W. and VERMEULEN, C., 'The Use of Magnitude Estimation in Large-Scale Survey Research', *Mens en Maatschappij*, **52** (1977) 369–95.
SHANTEAU, J., 'An Information-Integration Analysis of Risky Decision Making', in KAPLAN, M. F. and SCHWARTZ, S. (eds) *Human Judgement and Decision Processes* (New York: Lacademic Press, 1975).
SHINN, A. M., 'Relations between scales', in BLALOCK, H. (ed.) *Measurement in the Social Sciences* (London: Macmillan, 1973).
SLOVIC, P. and LICHTENSTEIN, S., 'A Comparison of Bayesian and Regression Approaches to the Information Processing in Judgement', *Organizational Behavior and Human Performance*, **6** (1971) 649–744.
STEVENS, S., 'On the Psychophysical Law', *Psychological Review*, **64** (1957) 153–81.
____ 'Ratio Scales of Opinion', in WHITLA, D. K. (ed.) *Handbook of Measurement and Assessment in Behavioral Sciences* (Mass.: Addison-Wesley Reading, 1966).
____ and GALANTER, E. H., 'Ratio Scales and Category Scales for a Dozen Perceptial Continua', *Journal of Experimental Psychology* **54** (1957) 377–411.
TIMMERMANS, H. J. P., 'Unidimensional conjoint measurement and consumer decision-making', *Area*, **12** (1980) 291–300.
____ 'Decompositional Multi-attribute Preference Models in Spatial Choice Analysis: A Review of Some Recent Developments', *Progress in Human Geography*, **8** (1984) 189–221.
VELDHUISEN, K. J. and HACFOORT, E. J. H., *Bewonerswaarderingen, verhuisgeneigdheid en woonvoorkeuren: Een onderzoek in de provincie Zuid-Holland* (P. P. D. Zuid-Holland, 1983).
____ and KAPOEN, L. L., *Een regionaal locatiemodel*, Stichting PVP (Eindhoven: 1979).
____ THIJSSEN, A. P. and TIMMERMANS, H. J. P., *Bewonersvoorkeuren en Drager-inbouw Systemen* Dept of Architecture, Building and Planning, University of Technology (Eindhoven: 1984a).
____ THIJSSEN, A. P. and TIMMERMANS, H. J. P., 'Conjoint Measurement Applied to the Judgement and Design of Dwellings', *Open House*, **9** (1984b) 27–33.
____ and TIMMERMANS, H. J. P., 'Voorkeuren en waarderingen 1: Een drietal meetsystemen', *Mens en Maatschappij*, **56** (1981a) 154–72.
____ and ____ 'Voorkeuren en waarderingen 2: De vergelijking van een drietal meetsystemen', *Mens en Maatschappij*, **56** (1981b) 275–93.

____ and ____ 'Specification of Residential Utility Functions', *Environment and Planning*, **A**, **16** (1984) 1573–583.

WESTWOOD, D., LUNN, T. and BEAZLY, D., 'The Trade-off Model and Its Extensions', *Journal of Market Research Society*, **16** (1974) 227–41.

12 Individual Response Functions and Correlations between Judgements

W. E. Saris

In survey research many variables are measured by the answers to single questions. This makes it impossible to study the way a respondent expresses his/her opinions.

In psychophysics this problem does not exist because in this discipline a standard experiment exists in which many stimuli of the same kind are presented to the respondent, who is asked to express his/her perception of these stimuli in his/her responses. This means that the relationship between the stimuli and the responses can be studied if the stimuli are metric. The responses can be expressed in different modalities. The most frequently used modalities are categories (category scales), numbers (magnitude estimation), line lengths (line production), loudness of sounds (sound production) and duration (time production). For an overview of relevant experiments done in psychophysics, we refer to Stevens (1975). For similar experiments in the social sciences we refer to Hamblin (1974) and Saris *et al.* (1977). More recent developments can be found in Lodge (1981) and Wegener (1982).

In order to detect whether people use different response functions when they give answers to questions, we will rely on the type of experiments done in the psychophysics and in the social sciences where several stimuli of the same kind are presented to the respondents and their 'opinions' are asked about these stimuli. This may seem somewhat strange within a survey context, but it can teach us how people answer normal questions which do not provide us with the possibility of studying the response behaviour of the respondents.

In psychopysics one assumes a two-stage process between the presentation of stimulus and the response given by the subject. First of all, it is expected that the stimulus presented leads to a perception

Figure 12.1 The model at the left represents judgement processes in psychophysics. The model at the right judgement processes in the social sciences

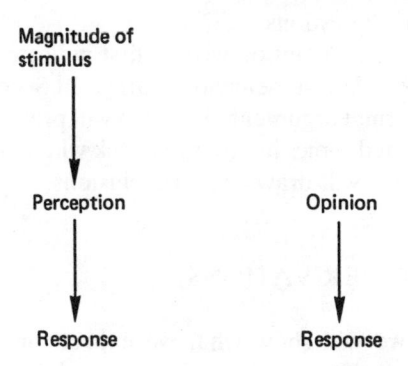

```
Magnitude of
stimulus
    │
    ▼
Perception          Opinion
    │                 │
    ▼                 ▼
Response          Response
```

by the subject and, second, that the subject expresses this perception in a response (Rule and Curtis, 1982).

In social science experiments we do not expect a relationship between the stimulus and the perception because the stimuli are of a different type than in psychophysics. The purpose of the stimuli in an interview or questionnaire is to elicit a response about an opinion which a respondent already has. This means that in opinion research the first part of the psychophysical process is not existing but the second part is quite similar. In both cases the subject or respondent is asked to express an internal state (perception or opinion) into a response. The similarities and differences between the two processes are indicated in Figure 12.1. Because of the similarity of the position of the perception and the opinion in this process we will use these terms interchangeably.

In this chapter we must introduce a simplification; we limit the study to topics for which the stimuli are metric and on which little doubt exists about the perception of the stimuli so that we can assume that the respondents probably have the same perception about them. Therefore, if their answers are nevertheless different this must be attributed to variation in the way they express their perceptions. These assumptions seem reasonable, for instance, in the evaluation of lengths of lines or the sizes of surfaces. We think it most likely that people can accurately judge the differences in sizes of surfaces and that they will agree on this point.

A less obvious topic which we will also use has to do with job evaluation. We have asked workers in a Dutch steel factory to evaluate how qualified a person is for his job if he works at it 2, 4, 5, 10 years and so on. In this case the equal opinion assumption is already less certain, but we guess that it is still more likely than in most social science questions.

Starting from this assumption we will first indicate intuitively what will happen if the response behaviour varies. In Section 12.1 we will provide a more formal argument. Than we will present some data for the above-mentioned topics in order to check whether the predictions hold, and finally we will draw some conclusions.

12.1 INTUITIVE DERIVATIONS

In Section 12.1 we will show what we expect for the correlations between judgements if people have the same opinion but vary in their response behaviour. But in order to do so we must first examine a situation in which all respondents have the same opinion and express them in more or less the same way. In that case for each individual we can expect approximately the relationship presented in Figure 12.2.

Figure 12.2 The relationship between opinions and responses in case no variation in response behaviour exists

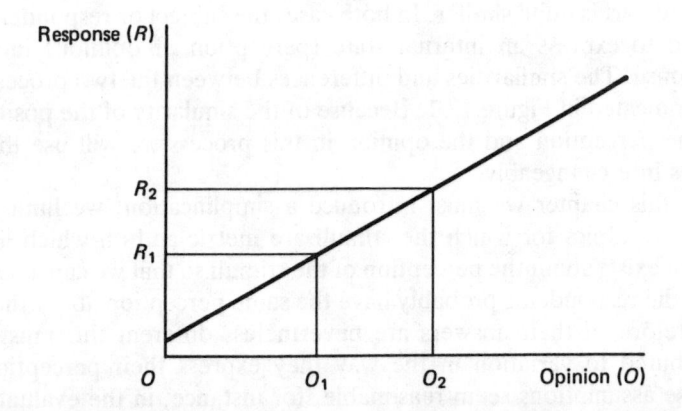

The choice of a linear relationship is arbitrary, also the parameters of the relationship are unimportant; what is important is that whatever the relationship is like, it is the same for all respondents, i.e. all respondents will answer R_1 and R_2 on stimulus 1 and 2. However this means that in a scattergram representing the responses on stimulus 1 and stimulus 2 for all respondents one would see only one point. Allowing for mistakes in the responses one would get a cloud around the point R_1 and R_2 and the correlation between these two judgements would be approximately zero.

Let us now assume that all respondents have the same opinion about the different stimuli, but that they have different ways of expressing themselves. This would mean that for each respondent a different response curve has to be drawn. This point is illustrated in Figure 12.3.

Figure 12.3 The relationship between opinions and responses in case variation in response behaviour exists

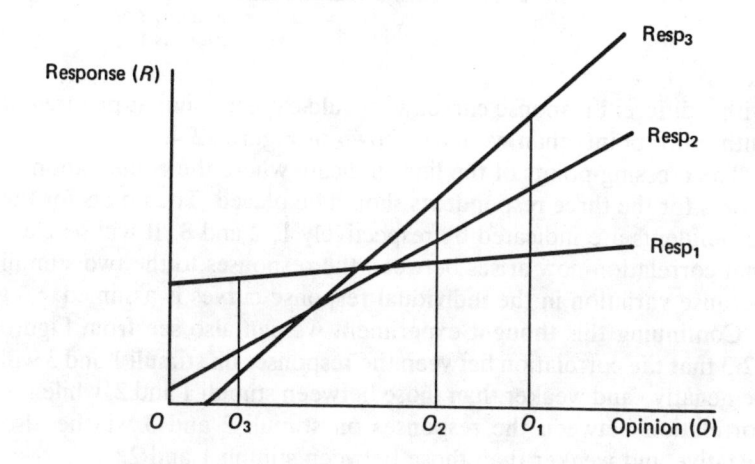

Figure 12.3 illustrates the use of different ways of expressing one's opinion. Respondent 1 makes hardly any variation in the responses (understatements). Respondent 3 makes a lot of variation (overstatements). Respondent 2 always gives responses which are approximately half-way between the responses of the other two. This figure shows that the responses of the respondents on each stimulus vary with the parameters of the response curve of the different respondents.

If such a situation exists and we make a scattergram for the responses on two different stimuli then we can see that correlation between the stimuli will arise. If we first look at stimuli 1 and 2, we can see that respondent 1 has the lowest response on both items, respondent 2 has a higher score on both and respondent 3 has the highest scores on both items. If there were more respondents, each

Figure 12.4 The relationship between two judgement variables in the case of variation in response behaviour

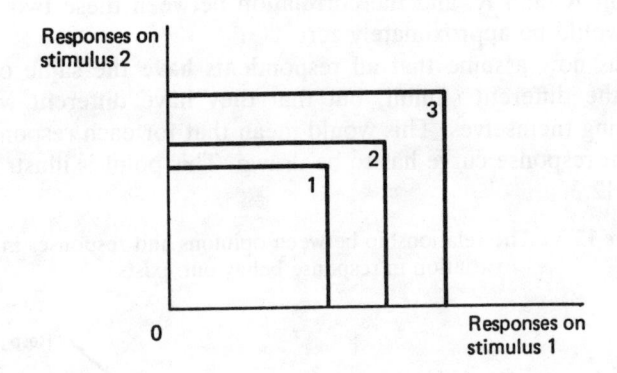

[Figure: A graph with "Responses on stimulus 2" on the vertical axis and "Responses on stimulus 1" on the horizontal axis, showing three nested right-angle lines labeled 1, 2, and 3, with origin 0.]

with a different response curve, we would expect a similar picture but with more points than we have shown in Figure 12.4.

The crossing-points of the lines indicate where the combination of scores for the three respondents should be placed. The points for the respondents are indicated by respectively 1, 2 and 3. It will be clear that correlation now arises between the responses to the two stimuli because variation in the individual response curves is assumed.

Continuing this thought experiment we can also see from Figure 12.3 that the correlation between the responses on stimuli 1 and 3 will be negative and weaker than those between stimuli 1 and 2, while the correlation between the responses on stimuli 2 and 3 will be also negative and weaker than those between stimuli 1 and 2.

In general we can expect that when respondents have the same opinions with respect to a number of stimuli of the same kind, but where they differ as to the way in which they express their opinions that:

(1) The variation in responses can be explained to a large extent by the values of the parameters of the response curve for the different respondents.
(2) The responses to stimuli which are close together on the high end or the low end of the scale will correlate higher with each other than with items in the middle of the scale.
(3) The correlation of the responses for stimuli at the same end will decrease as the distance between the stimuli increases.
(4) The responses to stimuli at different ends of the scales will correlate negatively with each other.

The same results can also be derived more formally. This is the topic of Section 12. If one is not interested in this formal derivation one can skip this section without losing track of the argument.

12.2 THE FORMAL DERIVATION

So far we have assumed that the relationship between the stimuli and the opinions was linear. This is, however, not in agreement with the available literature. But we will show that, after transformation, this assumption will hold in general. Let us start with the knowledge available in the literature. There has been a debate about the type of relationship which exists between the values of the stimuli and the perceptions of the respondents. The relationship assumed depends to some degree on the measurment procedure used. In the tradition of Fechner one would hypothesise a logarithmic relationship, while in the Stevens School (Stevens, 1975) a power function is assumed. Finally, Anderson's School suggests linear relationships (see, for example, Anderson, 1982). Wagenaar (1982) has shown that, on the basis of data, it is very hard to distinguish which function is the correct one. Whatever the form of the relationship is, it is always possible by means of a simple transformation to make the relationship linear.

In answering questions one can formulate the task of the respondent as a matching task where perceptions of stimuli – in this case the responses – are matched with opinions about which questions have been asked (Saris et al., 1980). Assuming an appropriate transformation, the relationship between the responses and the opinions can be represented in Equation (1) allowing for individual variation in response function:

$$R_i = \alpha + \beta . O_i + \varepsilon_i \qquad (1)$$

where R_i represents the transformed response on stimulus i
O_i represents the transformed opinion about stimulus i
ε_i represents the disturbance in the relationship,
while α and β represent the parameters in this equation.

It should be remarked here that α and β are constant across stimuli for each respondent, but these parameters are not constant across respondents. In fact if we study the relationship in (1) across respondents, O_i is a constant, because all respondents are assumed to have the same opinion about stimulus i, but the parameters α and β vary from person to person and are therefore random variables.

If we look at the relationships for all stimuli at the same time, analysing across respondents we can formulate the following matrix equation for these response variables:

$$R = \Lambda f + \varepsilon \tag{2}$$

where
$$R = (R_1 \ldots R_k)' \quad f = (\alpha\ \beta)' \quad \varepsilon = (\varepsilon_1 \ldots \varepsilon_k)'$$
and
$$\Lambda = \begin{bmatrix} 1 & O_1 \\ 1 & O_2 \\ \cdot & \cdot \\ 1 & O_k \end{bmatrix}$$

From this it will be clear that we have formulated a somewhat unusual factor analysis model. We call the model unusual because the two factors which we expect are the two parameters of Equation (1) which vary across persons, while the loadings are 1 and O_i. The last loading varies from equation to equation, but the value is the same for each respondent. The stimuli can be ordered in such a way that the loadings O_i are ordered according to size. Most of the time we can expect these loadings to vary from a large positive value to a large negative value.

A logical consequence of this formulation of the model is that the variation in the responses can be explained, except for the disturbance in the equation, by the variation in the individual response curve and therefore by the variation in α and β. This was one of the results we had derived intuitively in Section 12.1.

The results with respect to the correlations between the response variables can be obtained by the derivation of the covariances between the different response variables R_i and R_j denoted as σ_{RiRj} and the variance covariance matrix for all variables denoted as Σ_{RR}. If we assume that the errors are independent of the factors – a reasonable assumption – and that the errors for the different stimuli are independent of each other – an assumption which requires closer examination (Seip et al., forthcoming – then it follows that:

$$\Sigma_{RR} = \Lambda \Sigma_{ff} \Lambda' + \Sigma_{\varepsilon\varepsilon} \tag{3}$$

where Σ_{ff} represents the variance covariance matrix of the factors and $\Sigma_{\varepsilon\varepsilon}$ represents the variance covariance matrix for the errors.

For a specific element we can write:

$$\sigma_{RiRj} = \sigma_{\alpha\alpha} + O_i\sigma_{\alpha\beta} + O_j(\sigma_{\alpha\beta} + O_i\sigma_{\beta\beta}) \qquad (4)$$

Given Equation (4) a comparison can be made between the different covariances. Let us assume that stimulus i is any positive stimulus and stimulus 2 is smaller but still positive, while stimulus 3 is again smaller than 2 but also positive. The following result follows for the covariances:

$$\sigma_{RiR2} = \sigma_{\alpha\alpha} + O_i\sigma_{\alpha\beta} + O_2(\sigma_{\alpha\beta} + O_i\sigma_{\beta\beta}) \qquad (5)$$

$$\sigma_{RiR3} = \sigma_{\alpha\alpha} + O_i\sigma_{\alpha\beta} + O_3(\sigma_{\alpha\beta} + O_i\sigma_{\beta\beta}) \qquad (6)$$

We see that for both covariances (σ_{RiR2} and σ_{RiR3}) the first two terms of the right-hand side of Equations (5) and (6) are the same. Therefore, in a comparison of the covariances only the last term is significant. As we assume that $O_2 > O_3$, it follows that

$$\sigma_{RiR2} > \sigma_{RiR3} \text{ if } (O_i\sigma_{\beta\beta} + \sigma_{\alpha\beta}) > O \qquad (7)$$

Even though $\sigma_{\alpha\beta}$ is normally smaller than zero, condition (7) is certainly fulfilled if stimulus i is a large positive item since $\sigma_{\beta\beta} > O$.

The same result can be derived for stimuli at the other end of the scale as can easily be verified, taking into account that O_i and O_j are now smaller than zero and assuming that stimulus i is smaller than stimulus j.

These two results are the same as those described in Section 12.1 where it was said that the covariances between the stimuli at both ends of the scale will decrease as the distance between the stimuli increases.

An interesting case also arises if O_i is extremely positive and O_j is extremely negative. In that case the first term in Equation (4) will be positive, but the other two terms will be negative and it is quite likely that the covariance between such extremes is negative. This is a result which was also suggested in the last section.

Finally, we have to compare the two situations: one in which both stimuli are large and have the same sign and the other in which both stimuli are rather small but have the same sign. We have seen in Equation (7) that the covariance will be very positive if stimulus i is large. On the other hand we can see from Equation (4) that in the case of two small items the first term will be positive, the second negative while the sign of the third term cannot be predicted: this third term will, in any case, be much smaller than when both stimuli are large. From this argument the third consequence follows as described in Section 12.1: the covariation between large stimuli with the same sign will be much larger than the covariance between small stimuli with the same sign.

This last argument completes this more formal derivation. We have given here the derivation for the covariances instead of for the correlations, but, in general, the same pattern will hold after standardisation of the variables which is necessary for obtaining the correlations. Only under very exceptional conditions will these derivations not be true for correlations, but it would lead us too far to discuss these here.

12.3 METHODOLOGY

In 1975 a survey interview was held among the workers of a Dutch steel factory. The sample consisted of 505 people. In this survey a first test of magnitude estimation in The Netherlands was done. In order to become familiar with this measurement procedure, the respondents were given a training task. They were asked to determine the size of seven squares, presented on cards. They were asked to express their answers on a category scale and in numbers. Due to the fact that the sizes of the squares were known to us it was possible to study the relationship between the values of the stimuli and the responses for each person. In this study it was assumed that the relationship for the magnitude estimation data was a power function (Stevens, 1975) and therefore a logarithmic transformation was done on the data to obtain linear relationships (Saris et al., 1977). On the categorical data no transformation was performed, assuming that, in this case, the relationship was already linear. The regression coefficients obtained in this way for each person for both measurement procedures have been added to the file for each individual. In Section 12.4 we will report on the relationship between these coefficients and the responses for the different stimuli in order to test the first derivation made in the last two sections. Although these coefficients do not represent the parameters of the response functions, they can nevertheless be used for the test because the variation in these coefficients is due to the variation in the parameters of the response function if the opinions of the respondents are the same.

Furthermore the correlations between the responses on the different stimuli have been computed across persons. The data obtained by magnitude estimation were again transformed as before while no transformation was performed on the categorical data. The resulting correlations will be reported in Section 12.4 in order to test the derivations made with respect to the correlations between the response variables.

Besides this training task the respondents were asked to make several other judgements (Saris et al., 1977); the one we will report here is the evaluation of the qualification of workers if they have 2, 4, 6, 9 or 10 years' experience in a particular job. Also for these evaluations magnitude estimation and categorical judgements have been used and the transformation and analysis of the data is done in exactly the same way.

12.4 THE RESULTS

In this section the results of the experiment described above are reported. We will discuss mainly two points. The first point is whether the parameters of the individual response curves indeed correlate highly with the responses obtained. The second point that we will check is whether the correlation matrices are indeed in agreement with the predictions. We will begin with the relationship between the parameters of the individual curves and the responses for the different stimuli. This means that for a psychophysical task we have six correlations and for the experience evaluation seven correlations. We have in fact correlations for the α and β coefficient for magnitude estimation, while for the categorical data we have only presented the correlations with the β coefficient because the α coefficient was nearly perfectly related (-0.92) to the β coefficient. This means that this coefficient does not provide much more new information. Table 12.1 and 12.2 summarise the results.

In these tables the stimuli have been ordered according to their value. The first stimulus has the lowest value, the last stimulus has the highest value. These two tables indicate very clearly the relationship we expected. Even for the judgement of the sizes of squares – where it is very likely that people have the same perceptions of the stimuli – the correlations are quite high. In the social evaluations the correla-

Table 12.1 The correlations between the parameters of the individual response functions and the responses for the sizes of squares

Stimulus	Correlations between the responses for different stimuli and parameters from the individual response functions for		
	magnitude estimation		*category scaling*
	β	α	β
1	−0.64	0.70	0.67
2	−0.50	0.57	0.51
3	−0.28	0.35	0.18
4	0.33	−0.26	−0.35
5	0.65	−0.56	−0.34
6	0.64	−0.55	−0.60

Table 12.2 The correlations between the parameters of the individual response functions and the responses for the evaluation of experiences

Stimulus	Correlations between the responses for different stimuli and parameters from the individual response functions for		
	magnitude estimation		*category scaling*
	β	α	β
1	−0.85	0.87	0.72
2	−0.62	0.65	0.64
3	−0.45	0.48	0.54
4	0.31	−0.26	−0.31
5	0.56	−0.52	−0.29
6	0.65	−0.60	−0.35
7	0.69	−0.65	−0.53

tions are even higher though that may also be due to the fact that the opinions of the respondents may vary in this case. It can also be observed that the correlation with the extreme stimuli is the highest and that the correlation gets lower as we move towards the middle of the scale. This is clear if we consider that the regression coefficient according to Equation (1) should be the score for the specific opinion or the logarithm of this score (in case of magnitude estimation) except for standardisation. It is clear that the correlation coefficients indicate the same order as the order of the stimuli with one minor exception. It can also be seen that the correlations are just as high for the categorical data as for the magnitude estimation data. This means that this phenomenon is independent of the measurement procedure.

Table 12.3 The correlations between the evaluations of six sizes of squares using magnitude estimation

stimulus	1	2	3	4	5	6
1	1.00					
2	0.29	1.00				
3	0.16	0.23	1.00			
4	0.00	−0.10	0.04	1.00		
5	−0.12	−0.07	0.06	0.29	1.00	
6	−0.03	−0.05	0.00	0.26	0.55	1.00

Table 12.4 The correlations between the evaluations of the sizes of squares using category scaling

stimulus	1	2	3	4	5	6
1	1.00					
2	0.45	1.00				
3	0.16	0.21	1.00			
4	0.02	0.04	−0.08	1.00		
5	−0.19	−0.18	−0.17	0.02	1.00	
6	−0.24	−0.21	−0.16	−0.10	0.36	1.00

The second kind of prediction which has been derived on the basis of the assumption of individual variation in response function concerns the structure of the covariance matrices if the variables have been ordered according to the size of the stimuli. In Tables 12.3 to 12.6 the results are presented for the evaluation of sizes of squares using magnitude estimation and using category scaling and, for the evaluation of experience, also using magnitude estimation and category scales.

Tables 12.1–12.6 show the structure which was predicted on the basis of the assumption of variation in individual response functions. The pattern is even clearer for the evaluation of experience than for the evaluation of squares. A reason for this result may be that in the evaluation of experience some difference in opinion is involved, while this is unlikely for the sizes of squares. Another possible reason is that people are more aware of the differences between the sizes of squares and therefore restrict their response behaviour more in that situation than in the other. Whatever the reason may be for this difference, it is clear from these data that for both topics and for both

Table 12.5 The correlations between the evaluations of experience using magnitude estimation

stimulus	1	2	3	4	5	6	7
1	1.00						
2	0.57	1.00					
3	0.52	0.47	1.00				
4	−0.03	0.15	0.19	1.00			
5	−0.19	0.00	0.11	0.64	1.00		
6	−0.27	−0.11	0.04	0.60	0.79	1.00	
7	−0.29	−0.16	0.02	0.54	0.79	0.84	1.00

Table 12.6 The correlations between the evaluations of experience using category scaling

stimulus	1	2	3	4	5	6	7
1	1.00						
2	0.62	1.00					
3	0.54	0.61	1.00				
4	−0.07	−0.07	−0.04	1.00			
5	−0.14	−0.08	−0.04	0.50	1.00		
6	−0.28	−0.18	−0.12	0.45	0.68	1.00	
7	−0.29	−0.19	−0.15	0.38	0.66	0.76	1.00

measurement procedures the phenomena occur which we had expected.

12.5 DISCUSSION

Without doubt the presented results show the predicted correlations between the parameters of the individual response functions and the judgements as well as the predicted pattern in the correlation matrix for the different response variables. These results have been found for different topics and using different measurement procedures. In fact we have found the same phenomena for many different topics besides the two mentioned, but these two have been selected as topics on which it is most likely that people do not differ in opinion too much.

One could argue that no distinction can be made between differences in opinions and differences in response function. This is indeed true, but we have tried, in our choice of topics, to minimise this problem. Especially with respect to sizes of squares it is very unlikely that the respondents have different opinions. Now that we have found the predicted results for these topics, we dare to conclude that variation in response functions is also plausible for other topics.

Other explanations for the obtained results have also been considered. In the literature there seem to be two theoretical candidates. The first possibility is that the simplex model, introduced by Guttman (1954), can be applied to these data sets. In that case the stimuli should be ordered according to the complexity of the task and all correlations should be positive. However, neither of these conditions is met and therefore we do not think that the simplex model can be applied on these data.

A second possibility is the Metric Unidimensional Unfolding model developed by Davison (1977), which allows for negative correlations between the judgement variables. This model is based on the assumption that the respondents have a preferred point on the scale. But for the two data sets discussed here the respondents cannot have a preferred point on the scale. A different explanation of this phenomenon must therefore be given.

As we cannot find an alternative explanation for the results presented in this chapter, we are inclined to accept the hypothesis that these results are due to variation in the individual response functions. There is also evidence in the psychophysics which suggests that these results are not isolated results. An overview of this literature can be found in Rule and Curtis (1982).

If this conclusion is correct, a lot of the variation in the responses which is now seen as random measurement error may be explained by individual response behaviour. This factor may explain up to 64 per cent of the measurement error variance for some of the stimuli, as we have shown, and must therefore be considered one of the more important disturbing factors in social science research. How this disturbing factor can be detected and how such errors can be avoided or corrected for will be discussed in another publication (Saris, 1987).

REFERENCES

ANDERSON, N. H., 'Cognitive Algebra and Social Psychophysics', in WEGENER, B. (ed.) *Social Attitudes and Psychophysical Measurement* (Hillsdale: Earlbaum, 1982) 123–47.

DAVIDSON, M. L., 'On a Metric Unidimensional Unfolding Model for Attitudinal and Developmental Data', *Psychometrika*, **42** (1977) 523–48.

GUTTMAN, L., 'A New Approach to Factor Analysis: The Radex', in LAZERSFELD, P. F. (ed.) *Mathematical Thinking in the Social Sciences* (Chicago: Free Press, 1954).

HAMBLIN, R. L., 'Social Attitudes: Magnitude Measurement and Theory', in BLALOCK, H. M. (ed.) *Measurement in the Social Sciences* (Chicago: Aldine, 1974).

LODGE, M., *Magnitude scaling: Quantitative Measurement of Opinions* (Beverly Hills: Sage, 1981).

RULE, S. J. and CURTIS, D. W., 'Levels of Sensory and Judgemental Processing: Strategies for the Evaluation of a Model', in WEGENER, B. (ed.) *Social Attitudes and Psychophysical Measurement* (Hillsdale: Earlbaum, 1982) 107–23.

SARIS, W. E., *Variation in Response Behaviour: A Source of measurement Error in Survey Research* (Amsterdam: Sociometric Research Foundation, 1987).

____ BRUINSMA, C., SCHOOTS, W. and VERMEULEN, C., 'The Use of Magnitude Estimation in Large-scale Survey Research', *Mens en Maatschappij* (1977) 369–95.

____ NEIJENS, P. and VAN DOORN, L., 'Scaling Social Science Variables by Cross Modality Matching', *MDN*, **5** (1980) 3–22.

SEIP, H., MAAS, K. and SARIS, W. E., Auto correlation in judgements, (forthcoming).

STEVENS, S. S., *Psychophysics: Introduction to its Perceptual, Neural and Social Prospects* (New York: Wiley & Son, 1975).

WAGENAAR, W. A., 'Misperception of Exponential Growth and the Psychological Magnitude of Numbers', in WEGENER, B. (ed.) *Social Attitudes and Psychophysical Measurement* (Hillsdale: Earlbaum, 1982) 183–300.

WEGENER, B., *Social Attitudes and Psychophysical Measurement* (Hillsdale: Earlbaum, 1982).

13 Why Biased Answers on Evaluations of Own Job Qualities in Survey-interviews Arise

C. Bruinsma and W. E. Saris

13.1 INTRODUCTION

Interviewing as a method of inquiry is universal in the social sciences, Hyman (1975) argues. Therefore, he writes, it is clear that fundamental inquiry into the problem of interviewing may have wide ramifications and general value far beyond the specific context of survey research within which the study was initiated.

Many possible factors which would affect a response are mentioned by Hyman; perception of opinion of significant others; characteristics of the interviewer; characteristics of the respondent; characteristics of the survey question, and so on. For an overview of studies on these effects see Boyd and Westfall, 1965, 1970; Cannell and Kahn, 1968; Dijkstra and van der Zouwen, 1977, 1982; Dijkstra, 1983; Hyman, 1975; Schuman and Presser, 1981; Sudman and Bradburn, 1974; van der Zouwen and Dijkstra, 1982; van der Zouwen et al., 1984; Weiss, 1975. The results of these studies, however, do not lead to a theory in which the factors are specified and the empirical processes that produce the effects on the responses are not indicated.

Bruinsma, Saris and Gallhofer (1980) studied the reasons why respondents gave different answers to questions with respect to hypothetical persons and to themselves. Respondents were asked to evaluate job performances of workers with a large variety of qualities. They evaluated the qualities of a hypothetical worker and also their own qualities. One of the qualities of the hypothetical worker was equal to that quality of the respondent himself. In this way the respondent evaluated a hypothetical worker with the same quality (General Job Evaluation) and he explicitly evaluated his own qualities (Own Job Evaluation) for the aspects Experience, Education and Leadership.

As a first hypothesis it was expected that evaluations of the same characteristics would lead to the same scores except for random measurement error. This hypothesis was falsified. The 'General Job Evaluations' and the 'Own Job Evaluations' have correlations of 0.765, 0.581 and 0.616 for the three aspects, which is rather low if we consider that the stimuli were the same and that corrections for attenuation have been made.

In order to explain the differences between the two evaluations it was hypothesised that the perception of the evaluation by significant others (the management) could affect this Own Job Evaluation. The evaluation by the management was available to the respondent because he knew his Function Classification. The perception effect has been tested for three kinds of qualities: years of experience, education and leadership. The analysis of this study shows that the effect of the perception of evaluation by the management on the answers of the respondents is not significant.

We conclude that in this case the differences were not affected by the perception of the most significant other: the opinion of the management. Given the hypothesised process, the effects of the respondents' perceptions of the characteristics of the interviewer on the answers were also not very likely to influence our results.

In another study (Bruinsma and Saris, 1984) two other effects were tested: (i) effects of situational factors and (ii) effects of variation in response functions. The analysis led to the conclusion that the error variance of the General Job Evaluation can be reduced much more by correcting the scores for the individual variation in the response functions than by the situational factors. The error variance of the Own Job Evaluation, however, is not so much reduced by the transformation process as the General Job Evaluation.

In this study we try to find an explanation why these errors occur.

13.2 THE DATA

The data were collected from a sample of 505 respondents out of a population of workers at a Dutch steel factory.

An important topic in this study is work classification. The research on the classification of workers is in general based on sixteen different dimensions (Hazewinkel, 1967). In this study we analysed only those dimensions which in earlier projects had been found to be the most important for the workers themselves. The three most important dimensions were: years of experience, formal education and number of subordinates (i.e. leadership). For each aspect of the work classification, the respondent was asked to compare one of eight levels of the quality for a single worker to a standard stimulus. The interviewers were trained to put the card with the standard stimulus in front of the respondent. They then shuffled the other cards on which the stimuli were presented and displayed the top one next to the standard.

The judgements were measured by magnitude estimation as developed by Stevens (1975) and on a category scale. These judgements were written down by the respondent. The interviewer then took away the first stimulus and presented the next stimulus for comparison with the standard. The other stimuli were judged in the same way. For each aspect the evaluation of the eight judgements was measured on a category scale and by magnitude estimation.

Experience is measured, for example, by asking the respondents how qualified workers are if they have experience in the factory of 1, 2, 3, 4, 6, 10, 15 or 20 years. The standard for this aspect is four years The standard for Education is technical school and two courses organised by the company. For the aspect Leadership the standard is having five subordinates.

A full description of the measurement procedure has been given in Saris et al. (1977).

For each of the aspects Experience, Education and Leadership, the respondents evaluated eight stimuli, comparing them to a standard. When one of these eight stimuli is equal to the characteristic of the respondent for an aspect, we can compare the score on that stimulus (the General Job Evaluation) with the score the respondent has given for his own quality, which was also explicitly asked (the Own Job Evaluation). The personal characteristic was identical to one of the General Job characteristics presented for each aspect to different groups of respondents out of the sample.

In earlier research it was found that the General Job Evaluation score is not always identical to the Own Job Evaluation score. So far we have not been able to detect the reasons for these differences. In this study we have constructed a variable which indicates whether the respondent overestimates or underestimates his own qualities or not.

The difference between the scores of the Own Job Evaluation and the General Job Evaluation can be expressed in magnitude estimation and on a category scale. To summarise the difference we constructed a composite variable of the magnitude estimation and the category variable. If either one of the two or both scores of the Own

Table 13.1 Classification of the different scores between Job Evaluation and the General Job Evaluation for the three aspects. Percentages of the row total are given in parentheses

Aspect	Underestimation	Equal	Overestimation	Total
	Evaluation of Own Job Qualities			
Experience	18 (15.6)	66 (57.4)	31 (27.0)	115
Education	42 (19.1)	63 (28.6)	115 (52.3)	220
Leadership	9 (18.4)	25 (51.0)	15 (30.6)	49

Job Evaluation are greater or less than the General Job Evaluation, the composite variable has a value which indicates over – or underestimation, respectively. If both scores for the two evaluations are equal, the composite variable has an equal value. This procedure leads to a variable of which the values express that the Own Job Evaluation is less, equal or greater than the General Job Evaluation. Respondents who give opposing answers for the two measurements are assigned a missing value code. For the aspect Education we obtained three missing cases and for the aspect Leadership one missing case. For the aspect Experience there were no missing cases. The results of the differences in scores between the Own and the General Job Evaluation are shown in Table 13.1.

This table indicates that 27 to 52 per cent of the respondents overestimate the Own Job Evaluation compared with the General Job Evaluation. Per aspect, about the same percentages of the respondents answer equally. About 15 to 19 per cent of the respondents underestimate on the Own Job Evaluation, but the percentages of the respondents who overestimate on the Own Evaluation are always higher.

For the first two aspects we will test a hypothesis that attempts to explain why respondents answer differently. The number of people for the aspect Leadership is 49. This is too few to analyse for separate categories. Therefore we will give the results for the first two aspects only.

13.3 A POSSIBLE EXPLANATION

A possible explanation for the overestimation effect is that people with a low quality for a particular aspect tend to overestimate their own quality for this aspect in order to present themselves somewhat better than they actually are. They anticipate an evaluation of their own qualities in the future and a more positive self-evaluation might lead to a better job classification. Especially those respondents with low qualities for any aspect will present themselves as being somewhat better. This process can be described by the theory of self-evaluation in social psychology developed by Festinger (1954). This theory of social comparison processes has often been summarised (e.g. Suls and Miller, 1977; Rijsman and Wilke, 1980). We will mention only those aspects of the theory that are relevant for this study.

Festinger began with the study of the effects of social communication on opinion change in social groups (Festinger, 1950). The theory was extended to the appraisal of abilities as well as the evaluation of opinions (Festinger, 1954). He hypothesised that in the human organism there is a drive to evaluate one's opinions and abilities. When people do not succeed in evaluating their opinions or abilities through objective nonsocial means, they evaluate themselves by comparison with the opinions or abilities of others. The drive to evaluate opinions and abilities should produce a state in which an acceptable evaluation can be made.

There is an important difference between attitudes and abilities. There is a unidimensional drive upward in the case of abilities which is largely absent in opinions. This upward drive indicates a preference for a good performance, which indicates high ability. Festinger concluded from the literature on levels of aspiration that an individual's level of aspiration is above his performance. When he is told the average performance of others like himself, his level of aspiration is set above this reported group average (Festinger, 1954, 127). It is called the 'self-enhancement motive' by Thornton and Arrowood (1966). This notion has generated subsequent studies on social comparison processes (e.g. Suls and Miller, 1977 and also von Grumbkow, 1980).

A reformulation of social comparison theory, combining Kelly's (1955) personal construct theory and interactionist psychology (Endler and Magnusson, 1976), with the emphasis lying on the salience of dimensions instead of stimuli, has been given by Kuyper (1980). In his view, social comparison is inherent to the evaluation of social stimuli or dimensions. The question is 'Along what dimension(s) does a person prefer to compare himself?' He rephrased this question as: 'Given a situation, what dimension(s) is (are) salient to a person?'

One of the most important sources for self-enhancement for the aspect experience that might produce the difference between the Own Job Evaluation and the General Job Evaluation could be the years of experience of the respondent himself. It is expected that respondents with relatively few years of experience will overestimate their own qualities for this aspect with respect to the general judgements they give. The relationship between years of experience and the differences in scores between the Own and the General Job Evaluation is shown in Table 13.2.

In this table there is a significant relationship between the two variables. When the number of years of experience is less than four, respondents tend to overestimate the own quality. When their experience is greater than or equal to four years, the tendency is for them to answer both questions in the same way.

Table 13.2 Relationship of differences between the Own Job score and the General Job score to years of experience. Percentages of the row total are given in parentheses

Years of experience	Evaluation of Own Job Qualities			
	Underestimate	Equal	Overestimate	Total
Less than 4	3 (8.8)	14 (41.2)	17 (50.0)	34
Greater/equal 4	15 (18.5)	52 (64.2)	14 (17.3)	81
Total	18 (15.6)	66 (57.4)	31 (27.0)	115

Chi-square = 13.158, $df = 2$, prob. = 0.001.

For the aspect Education the same argumentation can be given for the judgement of the own qualities compared with the general judgement.

When respondent's level of education is low compared to other respondents, it might be a reason for him to overestimate his own educational qualifications. Most of the workers in this sample have an educational attainment of primary school *(PS)* and technical school *(TS)*, both with one or more additional company-organised courses.

It is hypothesised that the respondent will overstate his own educational qualifications when his level of education is low, compared to his colleagues, and when his level of education is higher this effect will disappear.

For this aspect it is assumed that respondents with an educational level of primary school and technical school are less educated than respondents with the same education but who attended additional courses organised by the company. In Table 13.3 the results are shown.

Table 13.3 Relationship of differences between Own Job score and General Job score with Educational attainment.
PS: primary school.
TS: technical school.
Percentages of the row total are given in parentheses

Education	Evaluation of Own Job Qualities			Total
	Underestimation	Equal	Overestimation	
PS and TS	20 (15.6)	30 (23.4)	78 (60.9)	128
with courses	22 (23.9)	33 (35.9)	37 (40.2)	92
Total	42 (19.1)	63 (28.6)	115 (52.3)	220

Chi-square = 9.211, df = 2, prob. = 0.01.

This table shows that 60.9 per cent of the workers with a primary-school and technical-school education overestimate their own qualities. With the additional education of company-organised courses, 40.2 per cent of the workers overestimate their own job qualities. When workers have a relatively low educational attainment we see a tendency for them to overestimate their own qualities, compared to the same quality they would estimate for a hypothesised worker. The evaluations of their own qualities might be enhanced by the social comparison processes.

In Section 13.3 we try to find theoretical reasons for the evaluation process.

13.3 MODELS FOR THE EVALUATION PROCESS

When rewards are allocated to actors on the basis of various types of task and status criteria, they will come to anticipate particular levels of reward allocation; i.e. in such situations actors will develop reward expectations (Berger *et al.*, 1983). They assume that reward expectations arise from the task and the status characteristics possessed by actors. An actor can possess a state of a characteristic that is relevant for his reward expectations. How the states of certain characteristics that individuals possess are associated with differences in reward levels is given by the concept of a referential structure (Berger et al., 1972). Referential structures describe distribution principles. Workers expect, for example, that rewards are distributed on the basis of task abilities. Referential structures can serve as generalised standards on the basis of which workers in specific situations come to develop reward expectations. In general, task ability levels are related to reward ranks. When a characteristic is salient for a worker he will form reward expectations for the referential structure of that characteristic; i.e. a referential structure will be activated. This will produce new expectancy bounds between the high and low states of the characteristic possessed by the actor and the high and low states of reward ranks. If there is a referential structure that associates different educational levels with different states of the reward rank, the level of education will be salient for a worker because it is relevant to the state of reward rank. In that case workers with different levels of educational attainment will come to expect different rewards. A worker can possess a characteristic that is salient for him but which is not connected to the task component for the reward rank or connected only very indirectly. It is the 'burden-of-proof process' in which these characteristics may become relevant to the task component. The workers may act as if the characteristics are relevant (Berger et al., 1983, p. 139). In general the total evaluation will be based on the dimensions of the information that are most salient to workers. This process is presented in Figure 13.1.

Figure 13.1 The judgement process (model 1)

evaluation of one dimension ⟶ total evaluation

A problem with respect to this judgement process has been stipulated by Bronner and de Hoog (1980). They studied the problem on which aspects a party-choice is based. Do we choose a party because it is reliable or do we think a party to be reliable because we prefer the party?

Bronner and de Hoog caution researchers to beware of what they call 'proxy-measures', which are variables affected by the party-choice. For our problem their study is relevant because the evaluation of one dimension can be affected by the total evaluation. The effect of the total evaluation is presented in Figure 13.2.

Figure 13.2 The judgement process for the effect of the total evaluation (model 2)

```
evaluation of    ◄──────────   total
one dimension                  evaluation
```

Combining these two processes we would get the model presented in Figure 13.3, as suggested by de Jong (1984).

Figure 13.3 The judgement process with reversal effects

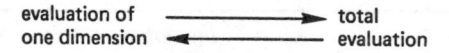

```
evaluation of    ──────────►   total
one dimension    ◄──────────   evaluation
```

We suggest that an evaluation of a quality will affect the total evaluation if the respondent has a high score on that quality (Figure 13.1), but otherwise not. In addition, we suggest an effect due to the total evaluation on the evaluation of one quality when the score on that quality is low (Figure 13.2). The argument for these two rules is as follows:

When a respondent's quality for a job aspect is high he can gain a lot when this quality is taken into account for his total evaluation. It will raise his reward expectations.

When a respondent's quality is low for a job aspect, it will not be a salient dimension for his total evaluation. This will be based on other dimensions.

13.4 TEST OF THE MODEL

What are the effects of these evaluations? Educational level and the number of subordinates are the basis of the work classification system (Scholten, 1979). Therefore we can expect that people with a high classified job have a high score on the aspects education and number of subordinates.

In this study respondents evaluated four aspects of their experience, education and leadership qualities as well as their work circumstances.

They also evaluated a combination of these four aspects, the total evaluation. The whole sample was divided into two classes of the work classification: low-level jobs (2–7) and high-level jobs (8–14). For the four aspects, workers can be qualified differently in the low- and the high-level jobs. The respondent's educational level and his number of subordinates are the basis for the work classification system; years of experience and work circumstances are not included (Scholten, 1979). Therefore we can expect that people with a high-level job have a high score on the aspects education and number of subordinates. We expect people with a low-level job to be especially high on the other two aspects. We thus expect the differences presented in Table 13.4.

Table 13.4 Qualifications for the four aspects for the low and high jobs

Aspect	low jobs	high jobs
Education	low	high
Leadership	low	high
Work circumstances	high	low
Experience	high	low

As we have mentioned, we expect that when a worker's quality is high for one aspect, the evaluation of this salient aspect will affect the total evaluation. On the other hand, the evaluation of one aspect will be affected by the total evaluation when the quality is low for this aspect. The total evaluation will be salient in that case.

For the analysis of the data we used the model shown in Figure 13.4.

Figure 13.4 Effects between evaluation of one aspect and total evaluation

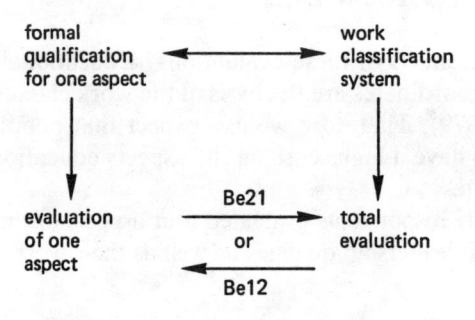

```
formal                              work
qualification    ◄──────►           classification
for one aspect                      system

      │                                   │
      ▼            Be21                   ▼
evaluation     ──────────►            total
of one             or                 evaluation
aspect         ◄──────────
                   Be12
```

Given this theory, we predict that, for the respondents holding low-level jobs, the evaluation of the aspects work circumstances and experience will affect the total evaluation, while we expect an effect of the total evaluation on the evaluation of the aspects education and leadership. For the same reasons we predict that for respondents holding high-level jobs, the evaluation of the aspects education and leadership will affect the total evaluation and that the total evaluation will affect the evaluations of the aspects work circumstances and experience.

Model 1 and 2 can be analysed using the program LISREL-V (Jöreskog and Sörbom, 1981) with the evaluations as unmeasured variables but with two indicators (Bruinsma and Saris, 1984). The fit of the models for the four aspects is presented in Table 13.5.

Table 13.5 Fit of the models with the low- and high-level jobs for the four job aspects

Aspect	Work. Class.	Model	N	Chi-Square	df	prob.
Education	low	2	272	9.16	5*	0.103
Education	high	1	131	7.41	6	0.284
Leadership	low	2	59	7.93	6	0.243
Leadership	high	1	114	3.24	6	0.778
Work circumstances	low	1	317	10.91	6	0.091
Work circumstances	high	2	168	9.93	6	0.128
Experience	low	1	318	12.09	6	0.060
Experience	high	2	168	5.99	6	0.425

* An extra effect from Work Classification on evaluation of own education was necessary.

These models fit the data well. The judgement effects for the low-level jobs are as presented in Table 13.6.

These results are in agreement with our hypotheses. Upon testing, the model for the high-level jobs conforms to our expectations and we get the results shown in Table 13.7.

In Table 13.7 we see that the effects are also in agreement with the patterns we expected. Only the effect from the leadership dimension is not significant, but it is the expected direction.

We should mention that the power of the test of the models for the low-level jobs is high for the aspects education and experience. For

Table 13.6 Effects of evaluation of one aspect on total evaluation and vice versa for the low-level jobs

Aspect	N	Standard. Be21 coef.	t-value Be21	Standard. Be12 coef.	t-value Be12
Education	272	0	–	0.125	1.993*
Leadership	59	0	–	0.288	2.962*
Work circumstances	317	0.446	7.331*	0	–
Experience	318	0.267	4.323*	0	–

* Significant at the 5 per cent level.

Table 13.7 Effects of evaluation of one aspect on total evaluation or vice versa for the high-level jobs

	No. of Cases	Standard. Be21 coef.	t-value Be21	Standard. Be12 coef.	t-value Be12
Education	131	0.190	2.374*	0	–
Leadership	114	0.261	1.563	0	–
Work circumstances	168	0	–	0.297	3.512*
Experience	168	0	–	0.330	3.199*

* Significant at the 5 per cent level.

the high-level jobs the power of the test is not high for the four aspects. Therefore, although the models fit the data, there is no very strong argument to prefer model 1 over model 2 or vice versa (Saris and Stronkhorst, 1984).

13.5 CONCLUSIONS AND DISCUSSION

Respondents may evaluate their own characteristics differently from the same characteristics in general. When their own quality for the characteristic is low, an overestimation effect can be detected.

An explanation for the enhancement of their own qualities can be given by the theory of social comparison processes developed by Festinger. When workers enhance some qualities, they do this on the basis of reward expectations. The distribution principles for the reward expectations are described in referential structures. When there is a referential structure that associates different levels of qualities with different states of the reward rank, the high qualities will be salient in the judgement of other aspects on which the worker is less qualified. Salient aspects will affect the judgement process. In other words, we find an explanation for the differences in scores of the same stimulus. When respondents are asked to evaluate their own quality (e.g. education or leadership) and their level on that quality is low, they will overestimate their own qualities. The evaluation of these aspects shows an effect due to their total evaluations on the evaluations of a single aspect.

When the qualification is high for certain aspects (e.g. experience for the low-level jobs) it will result in an effect from the evaluation of this single aspect on the total evaluation.

This systematic pattern can be detected for respondents with relatively low-level jobs. For respondents with high-level jobs the overestimation effect was not found. For the judgement process, however, the same systematic pattern could be detected for the low- and high-level jobs.

NOTES

1. The power of the test for the fixed-effect parameter $Be21$ or $Be12$ in the models assuming an error of 0.2 and an alpha level of 0.05, while $df = 1$.

Aspect	For low-level jobs		For high-level jobs	
Education	0.81	(N=272)	0.05	(N=131)
Leadership	0.08	(N= 59)	0.13	(N=114)
Work circumstances	0.22	(N=317)	0.15	(N=168)
Experience	0.65	(N=318)	0.19	(N=168)

For the computation of the power test the program 'Powert', developed by J. den Ronden (1984), was used.

REFERENCES

BERGER, J., ZELDITCH, M., ANDERSON, B. and COHEN, B. P., in BERGER, J., ZELDITCH, M. and ANDERSON, B. (eds) *Sociological Theories in Progress*, vol. 2 (Boston: Houghton Mifflin, 1972).

___ HAMIT FISEK, M., NORMAN, R. Z. and WAGNER, D. G., 'The Formation of Reward Expectations in Status Situations', in MESSICK, D. M. and COOK, K. S. (eds) *Equity Theory, Psychological and Sociological Perspectives* (New York: Praeger, 1983) 127–68.

BOYD, H. W. and WESTFALL, R., 'Interviewer Bias Revisited', *Journal of Marketing Research*, 2 (1965) 58–63.

___ and WESTFALL, R., 'Interviewer Bias Once More Revisited', *Journal of Marketing Research*, 7 (1970) 249–53.

BRONNER, F. and HOOG, R. de, 'Partijdigheid van partijbeelden', *Acta Politica*, xv (1980) 227–46.

BRUINSMA, C., EEDEN, P. van den, ROOS, J., SARIS, W. E. and SCHOOTS, W., *Verslag van het onderzoek gehouden onder de leden van de vakbond NKV werkzaam by Hoogovens*, Intern Rapport, Vakgroep Methoden en Technieken, Vrije Universiteit (1976).

___ and SARIS, W. E., 'Effects of Response Functions in Survey Interviews on Evaluation of Job Qualifications', *Kwantitatieve Methoden* 15 (1984) 87–109.

___ SARIS, W. E. and GALLHOFER, I. N., 'A Study of Systematic Errors in Survey Research: The Effect of Other People's Opinions', in MIDDENDORP, C. P., NIEMOLLER, B. and SARIS, W. E. (eds) *Proceedings of the Dutch Sociometric Society Congress* (Amsterdam, 1980) 117–35.

CANNELL, C. F. and KAHN, R. L., 'Interviewing', in LINDZEY, G. and ARONSON, E. (eds) *The Handbook of Social Psychology* vol. II (2nd ed.) (Chicago: Addison-Wesley, 1968) 526–95.

DIJKSTRA, W., *Beinvloeding van Antwoorden in Survey-Interviews* (Utrecht: Elinkwijk, 1983).

___ and ZOUWEN, J. van der, 'Testing Auxiliary Hypotheses behind the Interview', *Annals of System Research*, 6 (1977) 49–63.

___ and ___ 'Introduction', in DIJKSTRA, W. and ZOUWEN, J. van der (eds) *Response Behaviour in the Survey-Interview* (London: Academic Press, 1982) 1–12.

ENDLER, N. S. and MAGNUSSON, D. (eds) *'Interactional Psychology and Personality'* (New York: Wiley & Son, 1976).

FESTINGER, L., 'Informal Social Communication', *Psychological Review* 57 (1950) 271–82.

___ 'A Theory of Social Comparison Processes', *Human Relations*, 7 (1954) 117–40.

GRUMBKOW, J. von, *Sociale Vergelijking van Salarissen* (Tilburg: Bureau van Spaendonck, 1980).

HAZENWINKEL, A., *Werkclassificatie, een Wetenschappelijk Instrument?* (Amsterdam: Free University Press, 1967).

HYMAN, H. H., *Interviewing in Social Research* (Chicago: University of Chicago Press, 1975).

JONG, PH. de, 'On the Problem of Endogenous Measurement Error', Leiden University, Center for Research in Public Economics, report 84.20, October 1984, Paper presented at the International Conference on Methodological Research, I.S.A. and Dutch Sociometric Society (Amsterdam, 1984).

JÖRESKOG, K. G. and SÖRBOM, D., *LISREL V. A General Computer Program for Estimation of Linear Structural Equation Systems by Maximum Likelihood Methods* (Chicago: International Education Service, 1981).
KELLY, G. A., *The Psychology of Personal Constructs* (New York: Norton, 1955).
KUYPER, H., *About the Saliency of Social Comparison Dimensions* (Meppel: Krips Repro, 1980).
ORTH, B., 'A Theoretical and Empirical Study of Scale Properties of Magnitude-estimation and Category-rating Scales', in WEGENER, B. (ed.) *Social Attitudes and Psychological Measurement* (Hillsdale: Lawrence Erlbaum Ass., 1982) 351–77.
RONDEN, J. den, *Powert Instruction Manual* (Vakgroep Methoden en Technieken, Vrije Universiteit, 1984).
RIJSMAN, J. and WILKE, H. (eds) *Sociale Vergelijking: Theorie en Onderzoek* (Deventer: Van Loghum Slaterus, 1980).
SARIS, W. E., *Variation in Response Behaviour; A Source of Measurement Error in Survey Research* (Amsterdam: Sociometric Research Foundation, 1987).
SARIS, W. E., BRUINSMA, C., SCHOOTS, W. and VERMEULEN, C., 'The Use of Magnitude Estimation in Large Scale Survey Research', *Mens en Maatschappij*, **52** (1977) 369–95.
SARIS, W. E. and STRONKHORST, L. H., *Causal Modelling in Nonexperimental Research: An Introduction to the LISREL Approach* (Amsterdam: Sociometric Research Foundation, 1984).
SCHOLTEN, G., *Funktiewaardering met mate: een analyse van funktiewaardering in de Nederlandse arbeidsverhoudingen* (Alphen aan den Rijn: Samson, 1979).
SCHUMAN, H. and PRESSER, S., *Questions and Answers in Attitude Surveys* (New York: Academic Press, 1981).
STEVENS, S. S., *Psychophysics: Introduction into its Perceptual, Neural and Social Prospects* (New York: Wiley & Son, 1975).
SUDMAN, S. and BRADBURN, N. M., *Response Effects in Surveys* (Chicago: Aldine, 1974).
SULS, J. M. and MILLER, R. L., (eds) *Social Comparison Processes* (New York: Wiley & Son, 1977).
THORNTON, D. A. and ARROWOOD, A. J., 'Self-evaluation and the Locus of Social Comparison', *Journal of Experimental Social Psychology* (1966) suppl. 1, 40–8.
WAHLKE, J. C., 'Pre-behavioralism in Political Science', in *The American Political Science Review*, **73** (1979) 9–31.
WEISS, C. H., 'Interviewing in Evaluation Research', in STRUENING, E. L. and GUTTENTAG, W. (eds) *Handbook of Evaluation Research* (Beverly Hills: Sage, 1975) 355–95.
ZOUWEN, J. van der and DIJKSTRA, W., 'Conclusions', in ZOUWEN, J. van der and DIJKSTRA, W. (eds) *Response Behaviour in the Survey-Interview* (London: Academic Press, 1982).
ZOUWEN, J. van der, DIJKSTRA, W. and BOVENKAMP, J. van de, 'Inadequate Interacties en Informatievertekening in Interviews', *Kwantitatieve Methoden* **16** (1984) 73–95.

14 The Measurement of Income Satisfaction

L. van Doorn and B. M. S. van Praag*

14.1 INTRODUCTION

One of the basic problems of an orderly quantitative study of any phenomenon is the development of a measurement system. The problem mostly is not recognised in everyday life as such. The measurement of *time* on a scale of 24 hours a day is pretty well ingrained in our life; however, this system has not always been used. Primitive people and little children do not have such a system and indicate times of the day by vague expressions such as 'early in the morning' or 'late in the afternoon'. The choice of our system is actually an arbitrary one. This holds as much for the daily periodicity, as for division of a day into 24 hours, but even more basically for the choice of the hour as a fixed unit. Much could be said in favour of a variable hour length, thus allowing the period of daylight to be broken down into the same number of hours over all seasons. Our accepted system of time measurement cannot be advocated as being *the* natural time system. Its choice is one of convenience as it is easier to construct mechanical clocks with a fixed hour length than with a variable length. Also as hours are frequently the basis on which people are paid for the product of their labour, it stands to reason that an hour should be a fixed time interval, in order that the wage per hour can be fixed on economic grounds. The gist of the argument is that the choice of the method for measuring time is made for reasons of utility, and not because it is dictated by Nature.

The same holds for the measurement and definition of temperature. The development of two systems, Celsius and Fahrenheit, indicates already the underlying arbitrariness. There is no natural system. An especially interesting case is the measurement of *sound*, i.e. high and low notes. For scientific purposes we indicate the level of a note on the piano by its oscillation frequency: the standard, A, is

* We thank Emiel Bon for computational assistance.

defined as 440 oscillations per minute. This suggests that fixed differences between notes correspond with fixed differences in oscillation frequencies. Actually a logarithmic scale is used.

All those examples show that the choice of a system to measure a phenomenon is always to some extent arbitrary, but that one system may be much easier to work with than another.

Just as we have low and high temperatures, low and high notes, so we may speak of low and high levels of income.

The measurement of income in terms of a monetary amount per year, say $20 000 or $30 000, is simple, but the emotional connotation of whether it is a high- or low-income level is more difficult to determine. We call the feeling of satisfaction derived from an income y the *welfare*, *utility* or *satisfaction* (we shall use these three terms indiscriminately) derived from that income. The central question of this paper is how income satisfaction should be measured and what the relationship is between an income level y and the welfare level U derived from it. This relationship has been called [van Praag (1968)] the individual welfare function of income (*WFI*), $U = U(y)$, or income satisfaction function (Rainwater, 1971).

In Section 14.2 we discuss the debate in the economic literature and in Section 14.3 we outline the measurement method developed by van Praag (1971). In Section 14.4 we discuss other related measurement techniques and we describe the empirical data set to be analysed. In Section 14.5 we present and discuss the results. In Section 14.6 we give our conclusions.

14.2 THE UTILITY FUNCTION OF INCOME

It is a widely held belief that people derive decreasing marginal satisfaction from additional income increases, the higher their income is already.

Let the satisfaction from income y be described by $U = U(y)$; it is generally accepted that U increases with an increase in income, that is $U'(y) > 0$, but also that $U''(y) < 0$. The function $U(y)$ is called a *utility function* and $U'(y)$ is called the *marginal utility*.

The first author who formalised the notion of falling marginal utility was Gossen (1854), and the idea is now known as the (First) Law of Gossen. The idea was based purely on introspection.

The interesting feature is that a difference is drawn between income and utility and, moreover, that utility is a non-linear function of income. A similar distinction was made by Bernoulli (1738) who considered lotteries where one could win an amount of 2^n with a chance of 2^{-n} with $n = 1, \ldots, \infty$. Although the expected return of such a lottery was $\sum_{n=1}^{\infty} 2^{-n} \cdot 2^n = \infty$, Bernoulli observed that people were not willing to pay an infinite price for a ticket.

He concluded that individuals used a utility function $U(y)$ such that the ticket price was set equal to $P = \sum_{n=1}^{\infty} 2^{-n} U(2^n)$ where the infinite sum converges to a finite P. Bernoulli proposed that $U(y) = \log y$.

In the domain of taxation theory the requirement frequently posed for the notion of a fair tax is that it inflicts the same pain upon rich and poor people alike. When the 'pain' of taxing by Δy is described by $U'(y)\Delta y$ a constant pain implies an increasing Δy if $U'(y)$ decreases. As $U'(y)$ decreases if y increases it follows that people with higher incomes should pay more taxes. This is the principle of *progressive taxation*.

All these examples may be seen as evidence that money is *translated* by individuals on a utility/welfare/satisfaction scale and that that translation is a non-linear one. Beyond that point there is no unanimity in economic nor in psychological literature.

The majority of economists believe that there is no way to measure utility, U, in a direct way. Such a measurement method being unknown, any increasing U with $U'(y) > 0$ and $U''(y) < 0$ may claim the status of a utility function. However, in practice, gambling behaviour or feelings about 'just' taxation indicate that some functional specification of U will conform to that behaviour or those feelings, while another U with $U' > 0$, $U'' < 0$ will not. In economics two parties have been formed. The first is that of the ordinalists who cling to perfect agnosticism with respect to $U(y)$, although for practical purposes they propose a function U on which to base their analysis. In the literature on taxation the analysis often begins as in a fairy-tale: 'Let us suppose that individuals have a cardinal utility function of income $U(y)$, and that $U(y)$ may be specified as follows . . .'

Obviously, all authors are aware of the fact that the function $U(y)$ is chosen on the basis of introspection only, but facing the fact that analysis becomes impossible otherwise, they have to choose for this way out.

The second party is that of the cardinalists. They accept the possibility that utility is measurable.

14.3 THE DIRECT ESTIMATION METHOD

The problem of estimating a utility function $U(y)$ may be approached in an indirect way by breaking it down into two separate steps. The first is a mapping F_1 from income space into a space of verbal labels like 'good', 'bad', 'sufficient', etc. The second step is a mapping F_2 from the verbal labels into the real line, where we take for convenience the [0,1] interval.

Figure 14.1 Breaking utility measurement down into two steps

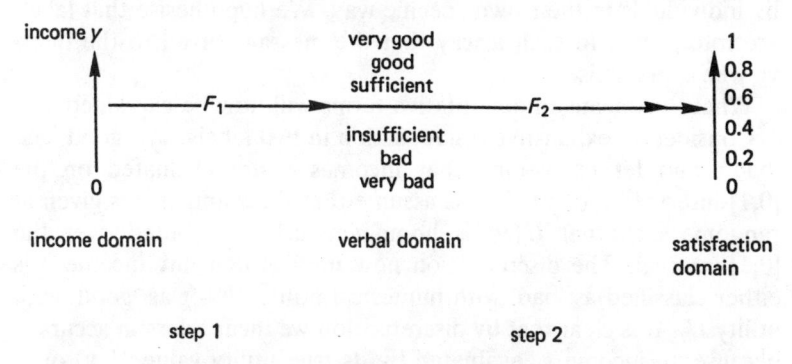

```
income y                  very good                    1
    ▲                       good                       ▲ 0.8
    │                     sufficient                   │ 0.6
    │──────F₁──────▶                   ──F₂──▶         │ 0.4
    │                    insufficient                  │
    │                        bad                       │ 0.2
    0                     very bad                     0

income domain            verbal domain            satisfaction
                                                    domain

   step 1                                           step 2
```

The choice of this intermediate step is suggested by the fact that people are not in the habit of evaluating income levels numerically in terms of utility or degrees of satisfaction, but that it is very usual to evaluate income levels in terms of verbal labels. The composite mapping is $F_2 F_1 (y) = U(y)$.

The first mapping can be assessed by simply asking people what amount of income they consider to be good, bad, etc., for their particular circumstances.

This can be done by using, for instance, the so-called Income Evaluation Question (IEQ):

> Please try to indicate what you consider to be an appropriate amount for each of the following cases? Under my (our) conditions I would call a net income per week/month/year of:
>
> about _____ very bad
> about _____ bad
> about _____ insufficient
> about _____ sufficient

about _____ good
about _____ very good

Please enter an answer on each line, and underline the period you refer to.

Let the response be denoted by $y_1, \ldots, y_6$ respectively; this response is then mapped on a set of labels 'very bad' to 'very good', that is denoted by $i = 1, \ldots, 6$. The question is then how the labels $i = 1, \ldots, 6$ are to be translated on to the $[0,1]$-axis. As there is no fixed emotional meaning attached to the labels, they are interpreted by individuals in their own specific way. We hypothesise that labels are interpreted in such a way that the message given to the interviewer is maximised.

What this means in quantitative terms will now be explained.

Consider an exhaustive discretisation in two labels, say 'good' and 'bad', and let us assume that incomes y are evaluated on the $[0,1]$-interval by $U(y)$. Let us assume that the stimulus y is given at random, such that $U(y)$ is homogeneously distributed over the $[0,1]$-interval. The discretisation now implies that any income y is either classified as 'bad' with numerical utility U_1, or as 'good' with utility U_2. It is clear that by discretisation we incur a loss in accuracy because an income y, evaluated by its true utility value $U(y)$ on a continuous scale, is discretely evaluated either by U_1 or U_2.

A measure for the average inaccuracy is

$$\int_{y \,\varepsilon\, bad} (u - U_1)^2 du + \int_{y \,\varepsilon\, good} (u - U_2)^2 \, du.$$

Clearly it will be minimised by setting the border between 'good' and 'bad' at the midpoint 0.5 and $U_1 = 0.25$ and $U_2 = 0.75$. It can also be shown that with other appealing generalisations of the inaccuracy measure we find the same result (see Kapteyn, 1977). In a similar way we infer that, with six adjacent labels, 'very good' will correspond with the interval $[5/6, 1]$, 'good' with $[4/6, 5/6]$, etc., and the average u-values with 11/12, 9/12, etc.

We notice explicitly that the argument depends on the assumption that the stimulus distribution is homogeneous. However, it may be that the stimulus in a certain experiment is non-homogeneous; for instance only incomes with a utility above 0.3 are offered. In that case the suggested mapping is not the most informative as the interpretation will gradually be adapted to the change of the distribution, such that the interval [0.3, 1] will be subdivided into six equal intervals of length $1/6 \times 0.7$ each.

The second mapping, F_2, is the *cardinalisation* process proper. The first mapping does not involve any cardinalisation. Combining F_1 and F_2, we find points of an individual's $U(y)$, say $\{(y_i, U_i)\}_{i=1}^{6}$, and these may be used to fit a curve in (y, U)-space. The lognormal distribution function was chosen for theoretical reasons and empirical evidence as the curve to be fitted (see Kapteyn, van Herwaarden and van Praag (1977), Buyze (1982)).

That function is specified by $U(y) = \Lambda(y; \mu_t, \sigma_t^2) = N(\ln y; \mu_t, \sigma_t^2)$, where $N(.; \mu, \sigma^2)$ is the normal distribution function with expectation μ and variance σ^2 and where (μ_t, σ_t^2) varies with individual t. We shall try to find additional empirical evidence for this type of cardinalisation, using recently developed instruments.

14.4 INSTRUMENTS FOR CARDINALISATION

In the spring of 1984 a small experiment (involving twenty-eight subjects) was done by Saris and van Doorn on computer-assisted interviewing. In this survey the IEQ was posed in combination with two other questions. The first question asked the respondent to identify the expressions, 'very good', 'good', 'sufficient', 'non-sufficient', 'bad' and 'very bad' income with numbers between zero and hundred. More precisely, the question was worded: 'Suppose that an income level, that you would call *excellent*, is evaluated by you as 100, and an income of 0, as 0, which number would you then associate with a "very good" income"?' Similar questions were asked for the other five levels, while the six levels were offered in a randomly varying order to the individual subjects. Let the responses be denoted $v_1, \ldots, v_6$; if they are divided by 100 they are scaled on [0,1] just like U(.).

Second we asked for evaluations in terms of varying line lengths. In this case the verbal evaluations were not judged in terms of a 0–100 scale, but in terms of the ratio to a standard line. At first this standard line was supplied, representing an income between 'sufficient' and 'insufficient'. Then the instruction said 'this implies that an income level that you evaluate three times as high will be represented by a line three times as long and similarly that an income evaluated three times as low will be represented by a line three times as short'.

After this introduction the respondents were asked to represent the verbal labels 'a sufficient income', 'an insufficient income', etc., in terms of line segments of varying length. The six levels were supplied in a randomly varying order to the respondents.
All in all this survey yielded:

(a) Income amounts for six levels: for each respondent t, say, $y_{1t}, \ldots, y_{6t}$.
(b) Six numerical evaluations between 0 and 100, say, $v_{1t}, \ldots, v_{6t}$.
(c) Six evaluations in line segments, say, $\omega_{1t}, \ldots, \omega_{6t}$.
(d) A repetition of (a) in fixed increasing order.

We hypothesise *a priori* that the evaluations should be expressed on a bounded interval, where 0 stands for an evaluation of zero income and 100 for the evaluation of an infinitely high income, and where the six levels are equally interspersed between zero and 100, that is 'very bad' corresponds to $1/12 \times 100$ and 'bad' to $3/12 \times 100$, and so on. We call this the 'equal-jump' assumption.

14.5. EMPIRICAL RESULTS

Although the sample is small it allowed us to investigate the question whether people are able and willing to evaluate incomes by means of cardinal scales.

The first thing to consider are the evaluations $v_{1t}, \ldots, v_{6t}$. Their means roughly correspond to the equal-jump assumption, but there is a considerable dispersion about the means.

Empirical mean	Standard deviation	Theoretical prediction
$\bar{v}_1 = 22$	(13.7)	$1/12 \times 100 = 8.5$
$\bar{v}_2 = 31$	(13.8)	$3/12 \times 100 = 25.5$
$\bar{v}_3 = 38$	(14.7)	$5/12 \times 100 = 42.5$
$\bar{v}_4 = 58$	(12.3)	$7/12 \times 100 = 59.5$
$\bar{v}_5 = 70$	(12.3)	$9/12 \times 100 = 76.5$
$\bar{v}_6 = 86$	(9.3)	$11/12 \times 100 = 93.5$

We see that none of the empirical means lies more than a standard deviation from the theoretically predicted value. Given the fact that there is a variety of respondents, each with their own interpretations of the wording of the questions, that the respondents are inexperienced in this type of questioning and the fact that the wording itself might be replaced by other terminology, we do not believe this to be a bad result.

Let us now try to compare the income amounts with the line-segment responses ω_{it} and the number responses v_{it}, which are both expressions on the value domain.

Consider the income norms $y_{1t}, \ldots, y_{6t}$ of an individual t. As various people have different norms we suppose that an income norm depends on two components. First there are some objective circumstances such as current income y_c, indicating the average position of $(y_{1t}, \ldots, y_{6t})$ on the income axis. We take for the average position the average log-norm $\mu_t = 1/6 \sum_{i=1}^{6} \ln y_{it}$. Earlier research [van Praag (1971), van Praag and Kapteyn (1973)] demonstrated that it was strongly dependent on current income. The second component is the relative proportion of norms to the average, e.g. measured as $(\ln y_{it} - \mu_t)$. We surmise that it does not depend on t, but only on the level i. The most simple hypothesis is then the following relationship:

$$\ln y_{it} = \hat{\alpha}\mu_t + \hat{\beta}\omega_{it} + \hat{\gamma} + \hat{\varepsilon}_{it} \tag{1}$$

where ideally $\hat{\alpha}$ equals one. Similarly we may test

$$\ln y_{it} = \alpha\mu_t + \beta v_{it} + \gamma + \varepsilon_{it} \tag{2}$$

where again ideally α equals one.

The two equations have been estimated from the complete data set of six (levels) × twenty-eight (individuals), with four missing observations, yielding 164 observations. Estimation is performed by means of OLS without making any adjustment for the presumably positive correlation between the error terms ε_{it}, $\hat{\varepsilon}_{it}$ and $\{\varepsilon_{it}\}_{i=1}^{6}$, $\{\hat{\varepsilon}_{it}\}_{i=1}^{6}$, which might be expected. It is well known that this will not bias the estimates. It is obvious that μ_t is correlated with the variable to be explained, causing a bias, but this correlation will also be ignored. As an alternative we might have regressed

$$(\ln y_{it} - \mu_t) = \beta\omega_{it} + \gamma + c_{it} \tag{3}$$

which is tantamount to setting $\alpha = 1$ *a priori*. We used the first specification to see whether the optimal α is near one or not.

We found the following estimation results:

$$\ln y_{it} = \underset{(0.05)}{0.95} \mu_t + \underset{(0.07)}{0.57} \ln \omega_{it} - \underset{(0.3)}{1.6} \quad R^2 = 0.83 \tag{4}$$

$$\ln y_{it} = 0.89 \;\mu_t + 0.57 \ln v_t - 1.4 \quad R^2 = 0.83 \quad (5)$$
$$(0.04) \quad\quad (0.05) \quad\quad (0.30) \quad N = 164$$

These results are quite remarkable. Indeed, it can be seen that α is nearly equal to one, the difference being attributed to measurement errors.

$$(\ln y_{it} - \mu_\tau) \approx 0.57 \ln \omega_{it} + \gamma \approx 0.57 \ln v_{it} + \gamma . \quad (6)$$

An even more remarkable point is that $\ln \omega_{it}$ and $\ln v_{it}$ have identical coefficients, viz., 0.57. It follows that the two responses, the lines ω_{it} and responses v_{it} on a [0–100]-scale seem to measure an identical phenomenon, viz. the satisfaction *value* assigned to income labels like 'good', 'bad', etc. Also, in terms of standard deviations and R^2s, there is virtually no difference.

An interesting opportunity is provided by the fact that we have repeated measurement for the IEQ questions and that, on the basis of the results above, the line and number responses can be used as repeated measurements of the same variable. This latter point is also in accordance with previous findings (Saris, 1982).

With repeated measurement for the variables studied it is possible to correct for measurement error. An efficient method to correct for random measurement error in structural equation models is provided by the LISREL approach developed by Jöreskog (1973), Jöreskog and Sörbom, 1977, 1983). In this approach the structural relationships are formulated for variables corrected for measurement error. These variables are normally unobserved but relationships are specified between these theoretical variables and the observed variables in a set of measurement equations. In this specific case the two observed variables measuring the logarithm of the income norms are denoted by $\ln y_1$ and $\ln y_2$ and the theoretical income norm, corrected for measurement error, is denoted by η_1. The two observed cardinal welfare judgements, so far denoted by v and ω are now denoted by x_1 and x_2 and the theoretical welfare variable corrected for measurement error is denoted by ξ_2. As we expect a much lower measurement error for the mean income levels, we have ignored the measurement error for this variable. In the LISREL notation this variable is denoted by ξ_1. The observed variable is assumed to be identical to this theoretical variable and is denoted by x_3. The measurement error variables are denoted by ε_1 to ε_4. Assuming linear relationships between these variables as we have done so far we can formulate model 1 in the following set of LISREL equations:

$$\eta_1 = \gamma_{11}\xi_1 + \gamma_{12}\xi_2 + \zeta_1 \qquad (7)$$
$$y_1 = \lambda_{y_{11}}\eta_1 + \varepsilon_1 \qquad (8)$$
$$y_2 = \lambda_{y_{21}}\eta_1 + \varepsilon_2 \qquad (9)$$
$$x_1 = \lambda_{x_{21}}\xi_2 + \varepsilon_3 \qquad (10)$$
$$x_2 = \lambda_{x_{22}}\xi_2 + \varepsilon_4 \qquad (11)$$
$$x_3 = \xi_1 \qquad (12)$$

The disturbance term in the structural equation is denoted by ζ_1. The effect of the exogenous variable ξ_j on the endogenous variable η_i is denoted by γ_{ij}. And the loading of the theoretical variable (η_i or ξ_i) on the observed variable ($\ln y_j$ respectively $\ln x_j$) is λ_{yij}, respectively λ_{xij}. The variances and covariances of the exogenous variables are represented by φ_{ij}. With respect to the disturbance and error terms it is assumed that they are independent of each other and of the independent variables in the different equations, except for ζ_1 which will be related to η_1.

The hypotheses formulated in Equations (7)–(12) can also be represented by the model of Figure 14.2. The parameters of this model can be estimated with the LISREL program and the model can be tested using the likelihood ratio test and the χ^2 distribution (Jöreskog, 1973).

Figure 14.2 provides the estimated values of the unstandardised parameters. The variances and covariances are presented between brackets.

The results are also presented below in Equations (13) to (17):

$$\eta_1 = 0.94\,\xi_1 + 0.69\,\xi_2 + \zeta_1 \qquad R^2 = 0.94 \qquad (13)$$
$$\ln y_1 = 1.0\,\eta_1 + \varepsilon_1 \qquad (14)$$
$$\ln y_2 = 0.98\,\eta_1 + \varepsilon_2 \qquad (15)$$
$$\zeta_1 = 1.0\,\xi_1 + \varepsilon_3 \qquad (16)$$
$$\zeta_2 = 1.04\,\xi_2 + \varepsilon_4 \qquad (17)$$

The goodness-of-fit index for this model is 9.77 for three degrees of freedom. Although this fit is only mediocre we decided to accept this model as a reasonable description of the data, for the following reasons. Inspection showed that the largest residuals were found for the line responses. This would indicate that corrections of the model

Figure 14.2 The model formulated in the equations (7)–(12) presented in a path diagram

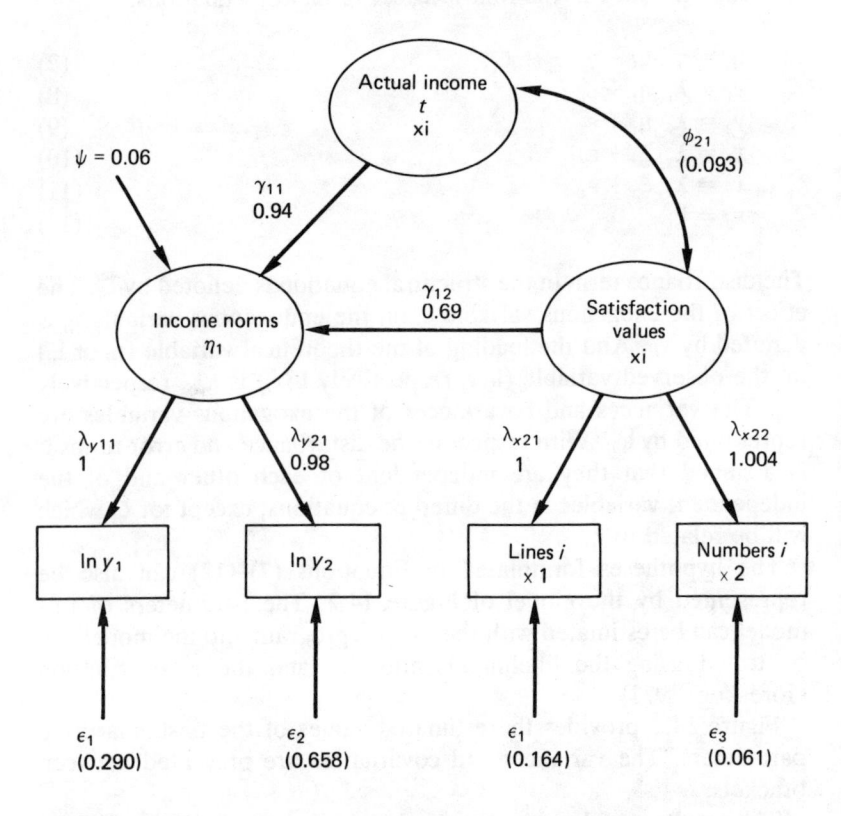

Figure description: Path diagram with three latent variables: "Actual income t ξ_i", "Income norms η_1", and "Satisfaction values ξ_i". Parameters shown: $\psi = 0.06$; $\gamma_{11} = 0.94$ (Actual income → Income norms); $\gamma_{12} = 0.69$ (Satisfaction values → Income norms); $\phi_{21} = 0.093$ (covariance between Actual income and Satisfaction values). Loadings: $\lambda_{y11} = 1$ on $\ln y_1$; $\lambda_{y21} = 0.98$ on $\ln y_2$; $\lambda_{x21} = 1$ on Lines $i \times 1$; $\lambda_{x22} = 1.004$ on Numbers $i \times 2$. Error variances: $\varepsilon_1 = 0.290$, $\varepsilon_2 = 0.658$, $\varepsilon_1 = 0.164$, $\varepsilon_3 = 0.061$.

should be introduced for relations where this variable is involved.

However, on the basis of what has been found for this type of measurement in previous research (van Doorn *et al.*, 1982; Saris, 1982) it is unlikely that the line and number responses are *not* measuring the same variable.

Another possible correction of the model, the introduction of correlated errors, was also rejected. These errors may occur because of sequential effects in the responses (van Doorn *et al.*, 1983). In this case this was also an unattractive solution because the questions were presented in random order.

A more likely explanation for the residuals is, in our opinion, individual variation in the way responses, both as lines and numbers, are given. This possibility will be studied in depth in a future research project. As the residuals were not very large we decided to accept the model in this form for the moment.

The explained variance of the Income Evaluation, when corrected for measurement error, is 0.94 and this is the most remarkable difference with the regressions of the Equations (4) and (5).

We therefore conclude that a large proportion of the unexplained variance in those equations is not caused by variables that were not taken into account in the model, but because the subjects made random errors when they allocate scores in response to interview-questions like the IEQ. Correcting for this error improves the already good results even further.

The next topic is the test of the lognormality-hypothesis.

In Section 14.3 we conjectured that income levels y are evaluated on a zero-one scale by a function $U(y)$, which is a distribution function on [0,1], i.e. monotonically increasing from zero to one on $[0,\infty]$.

Moreover, we hypothesised that $U(.)$ is a *lognormal* distribution function, i.e.

$$U(y) = \Lambda(y; \mu, \sigma) = N\left(\frac{\ln y - \mu}{\sigma_t}; 0, 1\right)$$ with N a normal distribution function.

If that is true, and if v_{it} is the evaluation on a [0–100] scale of y_{it}, it follows that

$$N\left(\frac{\ln y_{it} - \mu_t}{\sigma_t}\right) \approx v_{it}/100$$

or

$$\ln y_{it} = \mu_t + \sigma_t N^{-1}(v_{it}/100) \tag{18}$$

where N^{-1} is the inverse function of $N(\cdot)$.

To make things tractable we pose, as before, $\mu_t = 1/6 \sum_{i=1}^{6} \ln y_{it}$ and we set $\sigma_t = \sigma$, i.e., constant over t.

When we use this explanatory variable, $N^{-1}(v_{it}/100)$, in a model instead of the satisfaction value, we obtain the result represented in Figure 14.3.

The R^2 of the Income Norms is 0.930. The χ^2 value is 0.08 for 1 degree of freedom.

Thus $y_{it} = \mu_t + \sigma N^{-1}(v_{it}/100)$ appears to be a very good approximation of reality. The coefficient 0.944 is statistically not very different

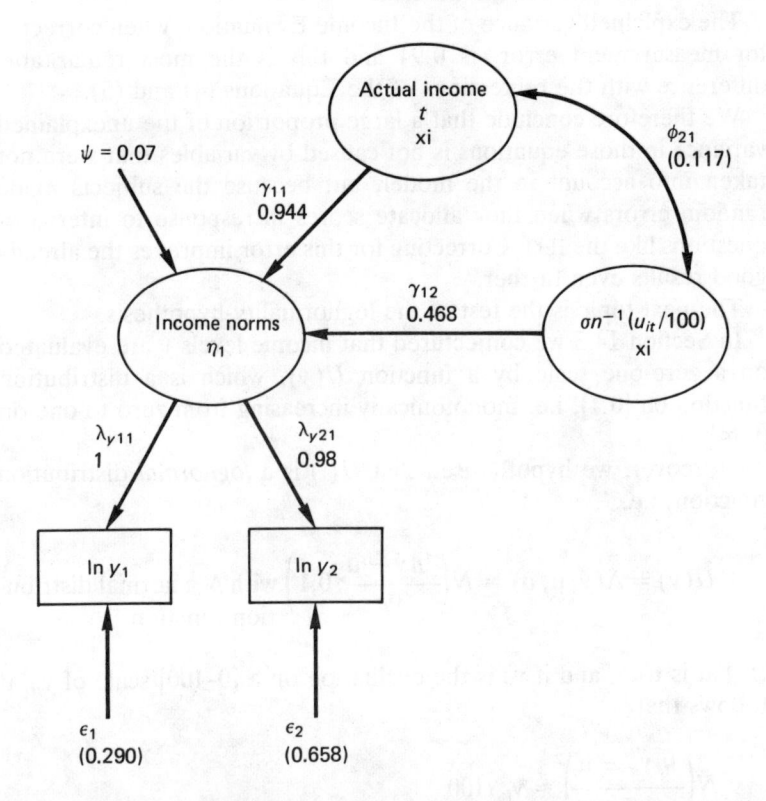

Figure 14.3 The model and the results of the test of the lognormality hypothesis

```
                      Actual income
                            t
                           xi
    ψ = 0.07                                    φ₂₁
                     γ₁₁                       (0.117)
                    0.944

                                  γ₁₂
       Income norms              0.468        σn⁻¹(uᵢₜ/100)
            η₁                                      xi

      λy₁₁            λy₂₁
        1             0.98

      ln y₁          ln y₂

       ε₁             ε₂
     (0.290)        (0.658)
```

from one. Moreover R^2, which may be compared to the result of the model in Figure 14.2, is nearly as high.

Finally, let us introduce in addition the *equal-quantile assumption* where $v_{it}/100$ is replaced by $(2i - 1)/12$ in the above model.

The χ^2 is in this case 0.12, with 1 degree of freedom. This model gives an even better explanation in R^2 (0.973) than the previous ones and also the coefficient of μ_t is nearly one (0.998).

It follows that we infer that the individual evaluation of level i by v_i (as in the model of Figure 14.3) is actually a statement with an error component and that there is every reason to say that y is lognormally evaluated and that the best explanation of the income evaluation is provided by the model in Figure 14.4, with actual income and a variable representing the *equal–quantile assumption* as explanatory variables.

Figure 14.4 The model and the results of the test of the equal-quantile assumption

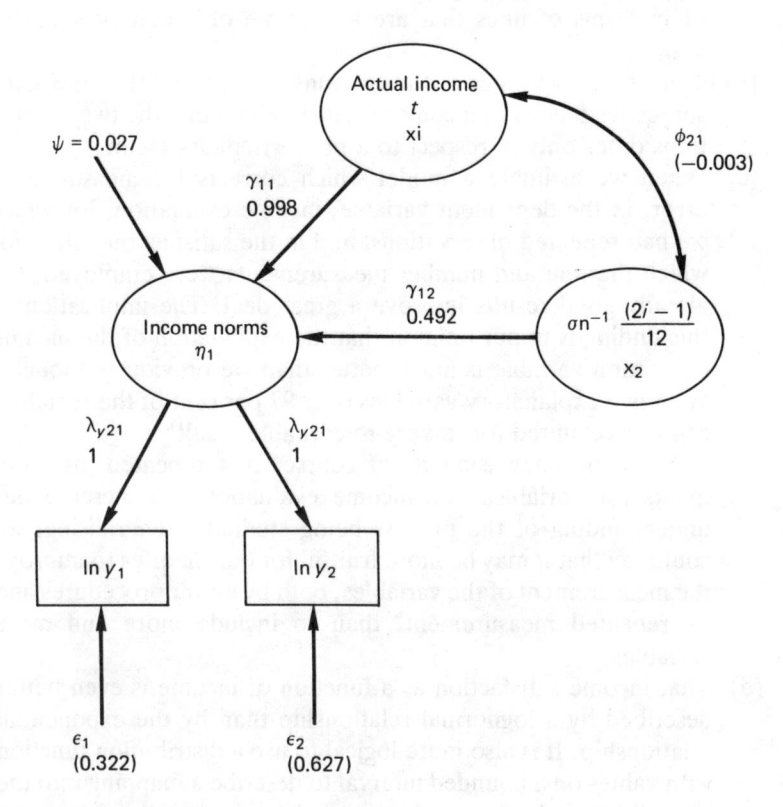

[Figure: Path diagram showing "Actual income t ξ_i" connected to "Income norms η_1" via $\gamma_{11} = 0.998$, with $\psi = 0.027$; "$\sigma n^{-1} \frac{(2i-1)}{12}$ x_2" connected to Income norms via $\gamma_{12} = 0.492$; ϕ_{21} (-0.003) between Actual income and x_2; Income norms connects to $\ln y_1$ and $\ln y_2$ via $\lambda_{y21} = 1$; with ϵ_1 (0.322) and ϵ_2 (0.627).]

14.6 CONCLUDING REMARKS

In this chapter we have tried to make *explicit* the *implicit* income norms corresponding to specific, verbally described satisfaction levels and the associated satisfaction values on a satisfaction scale. We did this by defining welfare in terms of verbal labels (1, . . . 6). In one direction we tried to measure the income levels ($y_{it}, \ldots y_{6t}$) associated by an individual t with the levels (1, . . ., 6) by means of the IEQ question. In the other direction we elicited explicit *value* statements corresponding to i in terms of linelengths λ_i, compared to a standard, and in terms of numbers v_j on a [0,100] scale.

We succeeded in confirming several conjectures:

(a) First we found that evaluations of income in terms of verbal levels *can* be translated in terms of numbers between 0 and 100 or in terms of lines that are a multiple of a unit of standard length.
(b) That these two types of 'translations' seem to refer to the same subjective feeling of income satisfaction and that the two translations differ only in respect to a proportionality factor.
(c) When we estimate a model which corrects for measurement error, in the dependent variable, income evaluation, for which we had repeated observations, and in the satisfaction value, for which the line and number measurements were employed, the already good results improve a great deal. The implication of this finding is in our opinion that the explanation of the income evaluation variable is much better than we previously thought. With two explanatory variables over 97 per cent of the variation can be accounted for: a very remarkable result!

A second conclusion is, of course, that repeated measurements for variables like income evaluation can increase our understanding of the process being studied. Generalising, we could say that it may be more fruitful for our theories to improve the measurement of the variables, both by better procedures and by repeated measurement, than to include more and more variables.
(d) That income satisfaction as a function of income is even better described by a lognormal relationship than by the exponential relationship. It is also more logical to use a distribution function with values on a bounded interval to describe a mapping into the [0–100]-interval, than an exponential function that increases beyond all bounds.
(e) That the conjecture, introduced by van Praag (1968), van Praag (1975), Kapteyn (1977) and studied by Buyze (1981), that the verbal labels are interpreted by respondents as *equally interspaced levels* on a bounded interval is confirmed by the results, both directly by considering the level responses v and indirectly by the fact that the assumption of equally interspaced levels has more explanatory value than the individual responses v_{it}.

The data set used here is small and was not obtained with the specific objective of the study in mind. Hence we believe that replication and extension of these experiments is needed for corroboration.

However, with the above caveat, it seems safe to state that income satisfaction is measurable by more than one method and that the results are stable and regular across the different methods used. Although it is beyond the scope of this chapter, not much fantasy is needed to evaluate the significance of this finding for social sciences and social policy.

REFERENCES

BERNOUILLI, D., 'Specimen theoriae novae de mensura sortis', translated by SOMMER, L., *Econometrica*, **22** (1959).
BUYZE, J., 'Holiday Expenditure and Preference Formation', *Report 81.05* (Leiden University: Center for Research in Public Economics, 1981).
——, 'The Estimation of Welfare Levels of a Cardinal Utility Function', *European Economic Review*, **17** (1982) 325–32.
DOORN L. J. van, SARIS, W. E. and LODGE, M., 'The Measurement of Issue-variables. Positions of Respondents, Candidates and Parties', *Proceedings of Sociometric Research* (1982).
—— SARIS, W. E. and LODGE, M., 'Discrete or Continuous Measurement: What Difference Does It Make?', *Kwantitatieve Methoden*, **10** (1983) 104–120.
GOSSEN, H. H., *Entwicklung der Gesetze des menschlichen Verkehres und der daraus fließenden Regeln für menschliches Handeln* (Braunschweig, 1854).
JÖRESKOG, K. G., 'A General Method for Estimating a Linear Structural Equation System', in GOLDBERGER, A. S. and DUNCAN (eds) *Structural Equation Models in the Social Sciences* (New York: Seminar Press, 1973) 85–112.
——, 'Analyzing Psychological Data by Structural Analysis of Covariance Matrices', in KRANTZ, D. H. et al. (eds) *Contemporary Developments in Mathematical Psychology*, vol. 2 (San Francisco: Freeman, 1974).
—— and SÖRBOM, D., 'Statistical Models and Methods for the Analysis of Longitudinal Data', in AIGNER, D. J. and GOLDBERGER, A. S. (eds) *Latent Variables in Socio-economic Models* (Amsterdam: North-Holland, 1977) 285–326.
—— and ——, LISREL *VI Users' Guide* (Uppsala: Department of Statistics, Uppsala University).
KAPTEYN, A., 'A Theory of Preference Formation', PhD thesis, Leiden University, 1977.
PRAAG, B. M. S. van, *Individual Welfare Functions and Consumer Behavior* (Amsterdam: North-Holland 1968).
——, 'The Welfare Function of Income in Belgium: An Empirical Investigation', *European Economic Review*, **2** (1971) 337–69.
——, and KAPTEYN, A., 'Further Evidence on the Individual Welfare Function of Income: An Empirical Investigation in The Netherlands', *European Economic Review*, **4** (1973) 33–62.

___ 'Utility, Welfare and Probability: An Unorthodox Economist's View', in WENT, D. and VLEK, C. (eds), *Utility, Probability and Human Decision Making* (Dordrecht: D. Reidel Publishing Co., 1975) 279–95.

RAINWATER, L., *What money buys: Inequality and the social meaning of income* (New York: Basic Books, 1971)

SARIS, W. E., 'Different Questions, 'Different Variables?', in *Fornel; A Second Generation of Multivariate Analysis*, vol. 2, 78–96 (New York: Praeger, 1982).

Bookkeeper®

Deacidification for Libraries and Archives

October 2011